I CAN FLY

Teaching Narratives and Reading Comprehension to African American and other Ethnic Minority Students

Angela Marshall Rickford

University Press of America,® Inc.
Lanham • New York • Oxford

Copyright © 1999
University Press of America,® Inc.
4720 Boston Way
Lanham, Maryland 20706

12 Hid's Copse Rd.
Cumnor Hill, Oxford OX2 9JJ

All rights reserved
Printed in the United States of America
British Library Cataloging in Publication Information Available

Library of Congress Cataloging-in-Publication Data

Rickford, Angela Marshall.
I can fly : teaching narratives and reading comprehension to African American and other ethnic minority students / Angela Marshall Rickford.
p. cm.
Includes bibliographical references and index.
1. Afro-American students—Education (Middle school)—Case studies. 2. Reading—Study and teaching (Middle school)—United States—Case studies. 3. Afro-American students—Books and reading—Case studies. 4. Minority students—United States—Books and reading—Case studies. 5. Reading comprehension—Study and teaching (Middle school)—United States—Case studies. 6. Ethnic groups in literature. I. Title.
LC2778.R4.R53   1998   428.4'0712—dc21   98-40770 CIP

ISBN 0-7618-1279-2 (cloth: alk. ppr.)
ISBN 0-7618-1280-6 (pbk:alk.ppr.)

∞™ The paper used in this publication meets the minimum requirements of American National Standard for Information Sciences—Permanence of Paper for Printed Library Materials, ANSI Z39.48—1984

To my parents Sydney and Stella Marshall,
and my sisters Sheila, Paulette and Lynsyd

and

to my husband John,
and my children Shiyama, Russell, Anakela, and Luke

with thanks for giving me wings to fly!

Students from the study with their teacher and the author

CONTENTS

Foreword	vii
Preface	xi
Acknowledgments	xix

PART 1: INTRODUCTION, FRAMEWORK, AND BACKGROUND

1	Introduction	3
2	Conceptual Framework and Literature Review	14
3	The Research Site: Community, Classroom, Students	31
4	Culture-Based Classroom Discipline and Organization	40

PART II: NARRATIVE STRUCTURAL ANALYSIS, RESEARCH DESIGN AND METHODS

5	Structural Analysis of the Six Study Narratives	65
6	Research Design and Methods	96

PART III: DATA ANALYSES AND INTERPRETATION

7	Quantitative Results: An Overview	119
8	Narrative Genre and Literal Meaning Questions	130
9	Interpretive Reading and Critical Evaluation Questions	150
10	Effect of Story Length in Higher Order Questions	174
11	Creative Reading Questions, and Effect of Ethnicity and Gender	183

PART IV: IMPLICATIONS OF STUDY

12	Summary, Implications, and Conclusions	209
	Appendix A: Stories and Comprehension Questions	230
	Appendix B: Teacher Interview Protocol	274
	Notes	277
	References	280
	Index	289
	About the Author	303

FOREWORD

> This, books can do -- nor this alone: they give
> New views to life, and teach us how to live;
> They soothe the grieved, the stubborn they chastise....
> They fly not sullen from the suppliant crowd....
> But show to subjects, what they show to kings.
> [George Crabbe, The Library, 1, 41]

This extract from an obscure English poet aims to serve three purposes. First, it celebrates the richness of the English language, as seen in the varied meanings of a simple word like fly. Second, it connects with Dr. Rickford's emphasis on the importance of the book, of that marvelous invention that allows spoken language to be captured (much like a butterfly in a net) and portrayed - but unlike the hapless insect, the best of books ensnare not simply an empty shell but the rich vitality of life and thought. Third, it points out the universality and equitability of literacy. Many - most notably Paolo Friere - have emphasized in thought and action the revolutionary potential of the printed word, if only the correlation between social class and the acquisition of literacy could be broken.

This work begins with the assumption that schooling can make a difference - a big difference! The initial hypotheses were straightforward, and the design well suited to assessing the predictions - adolescents will comprehend more fully texts that connect with their ethnicity. The results are serendipitous. Ethos turns out to be more important than ethnos; socio-cultural identification is more significant than prescribed social group. Practically speaking, adolescents are more tuned in to gender relations than to race. Another serendipity is the critical role of the researcher in establishing a context that demonstrates what adolescents can do rather than what they can't do. Rickford's book downplays her personal investment in connecting with her "subjects," but this investment is an essential lesson of this study. Comparisons are always problematic, but I am reminded of Shirley Brice Heath's Ways with words, an investigation grounded in years that Heath spent with families in North Carolina's Piedmont regions. Rickford's palette is not quite as extensive, but the style seems similar. By the way, I recommend to readers an exploration of the origins of serendipity, which brings attention back to my first point - the magnificence and mystery of the English language - and blessings to the Princes of Serendip.

Now to a few substantive points. The first point is my pride in the association with Dr. Rickford. This work is quite solid, and equally provocative. To have been privy to the birthing of these ideas and findings was a genuine honor.

The second point is a reiteration of Scott Paris' emphasis of the interplay of "skill and will." The current movement in the "reading wars" is back toward the basics, a swing that ignores a century of findings both practical and empirical. We are frustrated with student achievement - how can the nation survive when half of our students are below average! The problem, to be sure, is that those falling in this category are not random, but are disproportionately impoverished, from families for whom English is a second language, and from underrepresented minorities. The question - is the below-par performance of these students due to a lack of skill or a dearth of volition? Rickford's work suggests that motivation matters.

The third point is an effort to capture a couple of cross-cutting themes from this monograph. Theme one -- "Me Matters." Adolescents are self-centered in present-day society, for better or worse. They are disconnected from their parents, and their friendship patterns are grounded in relations that center around individual rewards. Middle schools, as it turns out, focus on subject matter more than the subjective. Just when young people need opportunities to think about themselves and their peer relations, schooling emphasizes grammar and algebra. Many states now mandate standards-based assessments for eighth graders-"Like, who cares?" Rickford's monograph centers around motivation, more particularly contemporary adolescent concerns. As noted above, these concerns center around sex roles more than ethnic identities.

Theme two -- context matters, even in research design. Would an investigator learn much about the character of snowflakes by studying snowflakes in an oven? Probably not. Yet student achievement is often examined in a metaphorically desiccated setting. Rickford established a context - she built relations with the students, she reflected on how to design attractive (but well controlled) materials and tasks to explore the students' capacities to express their understandings of complex texts - expressions in the form of written texts! Anyone familiar with adolescent compositions will appreciate this challenge. The length, quality, and readability of the texts produced in this study are truly remarkable. They illustrate what is possible - and that's perhaps the most important lesson from this research.

And so, what is possible? Rickford mentions the Ebonics debate, a hot topic in 1996, but the times keep a'changing. As I draft this note, the San Francisco School Board has wrestled with the question of appropriate diversity in "required readings." What should high school students read? The debate centered around not this question, but rather a numerical matter - what proportion of required readings should reflect the contributions of under-represented groups. Four of ten required texts, three of twelve?

Silliness. What does it mean to "read a text?" To "comprehend a narrative?" To "engage with a book?" Should we demand that African-American youngsters study Tale of two cities? That Hispanics struggle with Don Quixote? Should all students wrestle with The people could fly? Rickford's monograph transcends the "reading list" question in fundamental ways. The text matters, but often in non-stereotypical fashion. Thematic issues transcend surface matters - counting African/African-American (or male-female) texts on the reading lists will miss the point. Many - perhaps most - of those students whom we characterize as "at risk" are capable of success if we can connect them to matters of consequence. Effective teachers manage this connection far more often than is recognized. Angela Rickford has accomplished this task within the more demanding and more public province of a research study - demonstrating what can be...

Stanford, California
August 1998

Robert C. Calfee

PREFACE

I believe I can fly
I believe I can touch the sky
Think about it every night and day
Spread my wings and fly away.[1]
(R. Kelly)

    Learning to read--to extract meaning from writing or print--is one of the most fundamental requirements for success in school, and for rewarding employment and effective functioning in today's society. Teaching students to read--and read well--is one of the most fundamental responsibilities of schools, but American schools fail at this fundamental task far too often with African American students and other ethnic minorities. What's more, while American schools do progressively *better* with White students the longer they stay in school, they do progressively *worse* with African American students (cf. Steele 1992:68).
    Take two neighboring school districts in northern California where I live and work. In predominantly White Palo Alto, third graders in 1990 scored at the 96th percentile statewide on standardized tests of reading; but sixth graders did even better, scoring at the 99th percentile, and establishing themselves as the very best readers at that level in the state. By contrast, third graders in predominantly African American and Latino East Palo Alto (the Ravenswood School District), scored at only

the 16th percentile on the same reading test that year; but sixth graders did even worse, scoring at the 3rd percentile, revealing that they were among the very worst in the state at that level.[2]

National data point in the same direction. In the 1994 National Assessment of Educational Progress (NAEP), African American 9-year olds were, on average, 29 points *behind* their White counterparts on a 500-point measure of reading; but African American 13-year olds were further behind (31 points), and African American 17-year olds even further behind (37 points). On reading achievement tests administered in 1992-93 in fifty of the largest urban school districts nationwide, nearly 61% of White students at the elementary level and 65% at the high school level scored above the norm. The expectation, if students are reading on target, is that 50% of students will score above the norm, so these students were obviously doing well, and improving steadily with age and grade level. By contrast, only 31% of African American and 32% of Latino students at the elementary level scored above the norm; and by high school, those percentages had dropped to 26.6% and 24% respectively.[3]

The consequences of these increasing failures in reading are enormous. African American and other ethnic minority populations do more poorly than their White counterparts in school more generally, and they drop out at higher rates. They also show significantly higher rates of unemployment and underemployment, and they tend to be significantly over-represented in the prison population. These are devastating consequences, not only for the individuals and ethnic groups behind the depressing statistics, but for American society as a whole.

This book proposes two essential means for helping schools succeed in the teaching of reading to African American and other minority populations. The first is the increased use of culturally congruent literature, that is, the inclusion of more texts in which students can see characters like themselves portrayed, an experience which author Maxine Hong Kingston described recently as nourishing and affirming.[4] The second proposal is that schools modify their teaching and testing of reading comprehension (the basic measure of reading achievement) to make it more engaging and challenging, replacing the stultifying focus on literal recall with questions which push students to make inferences, evaluate actions and motives, and display expressive appreciation and creativity.

On a deeper level, this book is about adults setting things up so that children succeed more often than they fail. It is about teachers helping students do the difficult tasks that they must accomplish in school by providing a curriculum that is familiar and engaging and responsive to their needs. It is about teachers giving students a chance to show what they know well and are good at doing, and then using what they do know as a foundation to carry them forward to what they don't know but need to learn. These are practices that have been proven through psychological research to yield positive results in educating children. This book is about teachers who work in public elementary schools in low income, predominantly ethnic minority communities expecting high levels of achievement from their students, and then teaching in pedagogically and conceptually sound ways designed to tap performance and achievement and help students live up to these demands and to their potential. It is about treating students who are backward in reading, (some of whom even have reading disabilities) with the kind of dignity and respect, care and compassion usually reserved for mainstream students from the White majority in the wealthy suburbia of America. Finally, It is about teaching African American and other ethnic minority kids that they can fly, showing them how to, supporting them as they try their wings, and then letting them soar.

In the context of reading, the book is a case study of approaches, techniques and strategies for teaching reading comprehension of narrative text in a multi-ethnic inner-city type middle school classroom of twenty-five students. Its primary foci involve issues of culture-based narrative text selections, strategic comprehension questioning techniques, and innovative and effective discipline practices. The book is both conceptual and practical in its orientation. For example, Chapter 5 discusses a conceptual approach to the analysis of narrative, one of the most significant genres in the teaching and enjoyment of reading, and it outlines a technique for analyzing narratives from a structural perspective. It describes a mechanism for generating a graphic portrayal of narrative features that includes not only the fundamental elements of character, theme, plot, and setting, but also the important elements of character involvement and interaction, and an index of the emotional intensity that often drives a good story. In fact, the conceptual foundation of the book hinges on this central idea of story structure.

But the book also contains practical approaches to teaching reading comprehension, an orientation that I hope is discernible throughout. For example, beyond the foundational chapters, the book discusses techniques for motivating students and maintaining control when behavioral difficulties and issues of discipline threaten to impede teaching and learning. The middle chapters give teachers practical suggestions for constructing a wide range of narrative comprehension questions for elementary and middle school students. They examine the outcomes of wise text selection and strategic questions from the point-of-view of the strength of the answers that students gave. The book is charged with their verbatim responses, as a testimony to the possibilities for engagement that purposeful questioning generates. Finally, the late and final chapters discuss the implications of the study for teachers and teacher-educators.

Amidst the many issues the book addresses, it makes three main contributions. The first is its evidence that ethnic minority adolescents want to read literature that centers around people like themselves, because such self-validation is important to their self-esteem generally, and especially during the critical teenage and pre-teen years. The second contribution is its demonstration that even though some students are poor readers (qua decoders), it does not follow that they are poor thinkers. These students, I argue, ought to be given more opportunities in reading classes to think and analyze, to explore and investigate, to problem-solve and create--in short, to engage with levels of questions that are interpretive and critical-evaluative rather than literal and basic, although these too have their place. The third contribution that the book makes is its introduction of the Narrative Map, an heuristic device that is useful for revealing (and teaching) the anatomy and structure of narratives. Teachers can profitably use the process of narrative analysis involved in the creation of Narrative Maps to construct more challenging comprehension questions and to teach narrative composition. The book is therefore a package for teaching ethnically diverse student populations how to "fly" where Reading and Language Arts are concerned. My hope is that it will prove useful, not only for these students, and not only to their teachers and parents, but to all who work with students at risk for academic failure, including curriculum planners, textbook writers, policy makers and administrative personnel.
In what follows, I describe the organization of the book into parts and summarize the content of individual chapters.

The book is divided into four **parts**. **Part I** (chapters 1-4) discusses the main issues with which my research is concerned and lays out the framework and background of the study. **Part II** (chapters 5-6) deals extensively with the structural analysis of the study narratives, the research design and methods. **Part III** (chapters 7-11) is devoted to an analysis and interpretation of the data from both a quantitative and a qualitative perspective. The final section, **Part IV** (chapter 12), discusses the implications and conclusions of the study. Although these four parts of the book are naturally interrelated, the fact that many Chapters begin with an Overview of the material to be presented, and end with a Chapter Summary, will hopefully help the reader situate the each chapter within the larger framework and context of the book.

In part I, **Chapter 1** provides the introduction to the study. There are segments on the background of the study, a personal prologue, and a statement of the problem. **Chapter 2** gives the study's conceptual framework and literature review. There are segments on the popularity of the narrative genre, the appeal of African American folktales and contemporary Black narratives, and the difference between the two genres, the cultural connection between African American literature and ethnic minority groups in the classroom, and the technique of questioning as it applies to the study of narrative comprehension. **Chapter 3** contextualizes the study, filling in general information and background profiles on the community, school, classroom, and students. **Chapter 4** focuses on discipline. The Chapter explores the variety of tactics that the teacher in this case-study used to maintain order in a group of difficult-to-manage youths, focusing on his teaching philosophy, and the culturally congruent teaching techniques that he utilized. There are segments on classroom organization, church-based discipline and seating procedures, on ways in which the teacher nurtured students' self esteem, instilled a sense of inquiry and involvement in them, on how he professed love and trust, balanced praise with punishment, and on how he enabled his students to live up to the high expectations he held for them.

In part II, **Chapter 5** is devoted entirely to a structural analysis of the Study Narratives. The Chapter takes the reader on a step-by-step journey through the four phases of the process. The first phase outlines the factors that were involved in the selection of the narratives. The second phase involves an exposition of the components of the narratives, with an emphasis on the contrastive features of the folk tale and non-folk tale genres. The third phase provides a segmentation of each of the narratives by episode, together with a summary of individual episodes. The fourth phase presents an explication of the distinctive features of The Narrative Map-- the final outcome of this four-part process, and the conceptual tool which is used to construct comprehension questions for the study. **Chapter 6** is reserved for an explanation of the research design upon which the study is built, and the research methods applied in executing that design. The chapter articulates the interconnection between the research questions, the study materials, and the research design. It identifies the four categories of questions which encompass the eleven comprehension questions for each story: General Questions, Literal Meaning Questions, Interpretive Reading and Critical Evaluation Questions, and Creative Reading

Questions. It also provides a thorough description of the characteristics, purpose, and distinguishing features of each of the eleven questions across stories, using specific examples for clarification. Details of scoring procedures and inter-rater reliability are also provided. In addition, chapter 6 describes how the study was conducted, and supplies information on the Student and Teacher Interviews that formed an essential part of the study.

In part III, **Chapter 7** gives an overview of the *quantitative* results and outcomes of the entire Comprehension and Cognition study. It is as an omnibus chapter in which the main effects of the quantitative analyses are delineated, and all other research results are recorded within its quantitative frame. **Chapter 8** initiates the string of four sequential chapters that provide *qualitative* analyses of the study's outcomes, to complement the quantitative results provided in chapter 7. Chapter 8 discusses the Effect of Genre using the Category of General Questions, and the Effect of Question Type using the Category of Literal Meaning Questions. The Chapter investigates the reasons why students scored relatively poorly on so-called "lower-order" thinking questions of the recall- and memory-type. **Chapter 9** continues the examination of the Effect of Question Category, using the Interpretive Reading and Critical Evaluation Category of questions to demonstrate this outcome. The chapter investigates the reasons why students achieved high scores on so-called "higher-order" thinking questions of inference, morality, interpretation, critical evaluation, reasoning, and argumentation. **Chapter 10** explores the Effect of Story Length, this time relying on both the Interpretive Reading and Critical Evaluation questions and the Creative Reading questions to demonstrate that student scores were often higher on the longer, more complex stories, than on the shorter, simpler stories. **Chapter 11** analyzes positive factors such as the group work dynamic, that an analysis of responses to Creative Reading questions revealed. The chapter also analyzes the effects of the Ethnicity and Gender variables in the study, and examines the sources of those effects.

In part IV, **Chapter 12** provides a general summary of the study's findings, and draws out the implications and conclusions of the work. It outlines six issues that are at the heart of teaching Reading and the Language Arts in ethnically diverse student populations. They are 1) The efficacy of ethnic-based literature materials; 2) The significance of culture-based teaching pedagogy; 3) The efficacy of challenging reading selections; 4) The need for strategic narrative comprehension questioning techniques; 5) The advantages of building a strong classroom environment, in which healthy teacher-student and student-

student relationships are facilitated; and 6) The cross-ethnic identity of multi-ethnic youth. Each of these issues is discussed in turn.

Appendix A provides a record of the stories and comprehension questions used in the Study, while **Appendix B** provides a record of the Teacher Interview Protocol.

ACKNOWLEDGMENTS

Many people contributed in some way to the writing and completion of this book. First I thank my parents Sydney and Stella Marshall for teaching me in the early years that a good education is an invaluable commodity. I thank Mr. Vivian Simon, my elementary school principal and the teachers who prepared me for the Guyana Common Entrance Exam for instilling in me good study habits. Next I thank the women who were my teachers and models at the Bishops' High School for Girls in Georgetown, Guyana during my adolescence. They gave us students an excellent foundation in education, and a unique preparation for life in teaching us all that we were capable of much and that much was therefore expected of us. Besides Shakespeare, Latin and Math, they taught us dignity, poise, steadfastness, and the pursuit of personal and professional excellence. Special thanks to Miss Viola Harper (Mrs. L.F.S. Burnham), Miss Lucille Campbell, Mrs. Carmen Jarvis, Miss Esther Burrowes, Miss Mavis Pollard, Miss Lilian Dewar, and Miss Edith Peters. They lived our school motto and passed on the baton for us to do the same: Labor omnia vincit.

The last several years have been both exhausting and exhilarating. I would not have made it through without the help of many. To my primary dissertation advisor, my mentor and friend, Professor Robert Calfee, I extend my heartfelt thanks. Thank you for teaching me so much about the field of education, the subject of reading, how to teach our children well, and for your continued guidance and support. Thanks also to my secondary advisors Professors Shirley Heath, Ewart Thomas, and John Baugh for the time and effort they gave to make my research a finer product. I am deeply grateful. Thanks too to Professor Claude Steele for his contribution.

I must also thank my family. In particular, thank you to my husband John for his devotion, dedication and unwavering support. Thank you for reminding me of my dream to return to academics, and for supporting me steadfastly throughout that journey. You are indeed the wind beneath my wings, and the one most responsible for helping me fly. Thanks to my children Shiyama, Russell, Anakela and Luke for your constant encouragement, declarations of support, and votes of confidence. Thanks too for your occasional but invaluable help with typing and tables, and for keeping me sane and normal throughout with your ongoing requests for counsel, financial assistance, conversation, attention, and care packages. Above all, thanks to my husband and children for your love. That it is that most inspires and propels me onward. Thank you too to my three sisters--Sheila, Paulette and Lynsyd--for their unwavering confidence in me and their interest in my work.

Thanks to all the colleagues, students and friends who supported and helped me in one way or another throughout the various stages of research from which this book mushroomed. Professors Robert Calfee, John Rickford, Kennell Jackson, Elizabeth Traugott, George Brown, graduate students Kristy Dunlap, Sugie Goen, Henry Hinds, Stuart Yeh, Norma Francisco, Verley O'Neal and several undergraduates helped select and rate the study narratives, divide them into episodes, review answers to comprehension questions, or grade student scripts. Jay Thorp was a constant source of support and encouragement. She helped with tables and figures, and was kind, gentle, willing, and understanding. Thank you all. Yuwen Kong and Luke Rickford also helped with the preparation of figures, and I am grateful to them both.

Thanks to Stanford University School of Education, and to San Jose State University for underwriting some of the expenses in relation to the research and publication of the material presented in this book. Last but not least, thanks to the various people at the school in which I conducted this study, without whose cooperation this book would not have been possible: Mrs. Hargrove, the principal, Mr. Daniels and Mrs. Bader, classroom teachers, and the talented, multi-ethnic students in Mr. Daniels' classroom. May they all fly and touch the sky.

Those who helped in the production of this study are in no way responsible for any of its shortcomings. That is entirely mea culpa.

PART I

INTRODUCTION, FRAMEWORK, AND BACKGROUND

CHAPTER 1

INTRODUCTION

It is only the story... that saves our progeny from blundering like blind beggars into the spikes of the cactus fence. The story is our escort; without it, we are blind. Does the blind man own his escort? No, neither do we the story; rather, it is the story that owns us.

Chinua Achebe, Anthills of the Savannah

In January 1997, Michael Casserly in testimony to the U.S. Senate Subcommittee on Education, Health, and Housing, gave some startling statistics about the condition of Reading Achievement for students from fifty urban school districts throughout the nation. The body that collected and published this information, the Council of the Great City Schools, calculated students' achievement in Reading by race and ethnicity based on their performance during the years 1992 and 1993. Given the standard expectation that at least 50% of students in any given sample would score above the norm, and taking the 50th percentile as the line of demarcation of that norm, ethnic minority students fared miserably in this survey. Among African American students for example, only approximately 27% scored above the 50th percentile at the middle school level, while among Latino students, only 30% scored above the 50th percentile at the middle school level. By contrast, for mainstream Anglo students, approximately 63%, or more than twice the number of students than those from either the African American or Latino groups, scored above the norm in Reading. As educators, we must ask ourselves what can we do to change this picture? How can we help reverse the shocking levels of reading failure in these and all other populations of ethnic minority students?

This book addresses these issues and poses partial solutions to problems of reading and literacy among ethnic minority middle school students. The text focuses on Reading in adolescent populations with a history of academic problems. I am particularly interested in the reading achievement of African-American students within this larger target group, but my work also encompasses a diverse range of students who are Latino, Tongan, Samoan and Fijian, in addition to the African-American group. Within the domain of Reading, my focus is on narrative comprehension. My thesis is that adolescent students who are at-risk for academic failure in reading and the language arts, tend to become involved in literary works that connect with their cultural-ethnic identity, and that this engagement enhances interest and comprehension. I claim that making this kind of connection has the potential to improve knowledge, critical thinking skills, and motivation. The result is opportunities for the disadvantaged--high-level cognition and comprehension that transcend a basic skills approach to narrative comprehension, and include instead meaningful critical analysis and literary appreciation of narrative texts.

My second point is that for a variety of reasons, some of which are culture-based, ethnic minority students are prone to do better at higher-order comprehension questions involving interpretive reading and critical evaluation, than lower-order questions involving literal meaning and memory. Because of this, and because psychological principles of learning suggest that we should teach to pupils' strengths, teachers need to encourage these higher-order questions in their classrooms, instead of focusing heavily on lower-order ones. Such an approach would promote interest, purpose, and motivation in the exercise of reading comprehension, and could also be used as a bridge for teaching students the skills they need to improve their expertise in text-based recall questions.

The third idea that emerges from my research is the conceptual and practical value of a narrative map--a graphic portrayal of the structural features of a story. The narrative map is a technique for analyzing short stories from the point-of-view of their underlying structural components of character, theme, plot, and setting. Building on previous work on story grammar, it uses the episode as the unit of analysis in the graphic, and in addition to the portrayal of narrative structure, the map also reflects the dramatic and emotional high points of the story, elements that are crucial to understanding its structure. The narrative map is therefore an heuristic. Potentially it can be useful in teacher education programs for training teachers in the rudiments of narrative comprehension and composition. Because it leads to a deep understanding of narrative structure, teachers can then make their own adaptations from it for teaching narrative comprehension and composition in their own classrooms. It can help give teachers the tools they need to improve students' cognition and metacognition of narrative text materials. It can also be used by anyone interested in the principles and processes of narrative construction. In addition, a skilled teacher can hone the procedures used in creating the narrative map, for teaching narrative analysis and appreciation.

My hope is that this innovation will advance our understanding of how stories are composed, and help ease some of the difficulty that teachers have in teaching narrative comprehension and composition, and that students have in understanding and creating narratives. I also hope that the other facets of the book will help improve standards of teaching reading and language arts in classrooms in general, and particularly in classrooms accommodating diversity.

Background and Personal Prologue

The work that I report on in this book, is a case study in a single classroom of twenty-five adolescents--twelve- and thirteen- year old students. My research is based on two years of work with these students (1993-1995), first while they were in a combined fifth and sixth grade classroom, and then in a combined sixth and seventh grade classroom at Lantana School in East Tall Tree, part of the Blendwood school district (all pseudonyms) of Northern California.

Public perception of the city that houses the school, primarily shaped by the news media, is that of a troubled place. It is a low-income, ethnic minority community of predominantly African Americans and Latinos, plagued by the ravages of gang warfare, drugs, alcoholism, and the other problems sadly typical of inner city communities (demographic and other details of this community are given in Chapter 2). But when I entered the community as a teacher volunteer during my first year in their classroom, I encountered a dynamic group of adolescents. They seemed ready to learn but stymied both by the approach to the teaching of reading and narrative comprehension that prevailed in their classroom, and by the discipline problems there.

The gravity of the situation struck me when I noticed that many children could not read well enough to sustain their own interest in a story, a reality that was reflected in their low reading scores, which mirrored the frighteningly low scores of the Great City Schools quoted above, except that in some cases these were even lower. On the most recent Comprehensive Test of Basic Skills administered several months before my study began in the Fall of 1995, (CTBS; Spring 1994), sixteen of the students in the class scored below the fiftieth percentile, including seven who were below the tenth percentile. Of the remaining nine students, there were only six who scored over the fiftieth percentile, three of them just scoring in the range of the cut-off point, while only two students scored at or above the seventieth percentile. Scores were unavailable for three students who were transfers from other schools, but my sense was that their reading was not very good either. Undoubtedly many of these students would have qualified for special education classes, a fact that their teacher subsequently mentioned in passing. But in a district where there was sometimes both under- and over- diagnosis of special needs cases, many of these students remained in their regular classrooms. These scores were by no means an anomaly--the low reading scores of the students in the Blendwood School District reported in Table 1 below, were recorded at the turn of the decade. They demonstrate the fact that low scores are the norm.

DISTRICT	SUBJECT: GRADE: 3	READING 6	READING 8	WRITING 6
Blendwood	89-90 237 State rank 16 (Percentile)	215 3	186 2	231 3
Mainstream Town	89-90 337 State rank 96	339 99	361 98	335 99

Table 1. California Assessment Program Scores (1989-90), Blendwood City versus Mainstream Town Scores.

Note for example, that even using a different instrument, in this case the California Assessment Program, scores in Reading and Writing for Blendwood City students (of which East Tall Tree is a significant part), are still considerably low. According to these results, Blendwood City students at approximately middle school level scored between the second and third percentile in Reading and Writing, compared with their mainstream town counterparts who scored between the ninety-eighth and ninety-ninth percentile.

While a volunteer teacher aide in the classroom in East Tall Tree, I noticed also, that even among those students who could read well, there was little interest in the class texts, which were usually either a standard textbook such as the basal reader, or trade books that the teacher selected. Generally these texts were traditional in their orientation, and neutral to cultures outside the dominant mainstream. These youths did not have many opportunities to read literature that connected in any way with their cultural or ethnic identity. Although otherwise alert and animated, students reacted to narrative reading with disinterest, and seemed particularly unmotivated to participate in the comprehension questions that their teacher set for them to do. By contrast however, they appeared involved in other literacy activities such as reading *Sports Illustrated* and *Young Sisters and Brothers* (YSB) magazines under cover of their desks, and in writing rap songs--the latter magazine, produced and published in Washington, DC, is aimed specifically for a young black readership, and is very popular among members of this group. So it became clear that their lack of interest in reading (and writing) was not the result of total incompetence in these areas, but of gross indifference. On one occasion while reading the assigned text, a student remarked dismissively "I hate this book," a comment that reflected the lack of enthusiasm that they all shared.

The teacher's efforts had obviously plateaued at a point at which very little constructive teaching and learning were taking place, although she was obviously trying very hard. During the early weeks of my visit, the children were reading the book *The Egypt Game* by Zilpha Snyder round-robin style, and in a mechanical fashion. The story progressed from paragraph to paragraph, chapter to chapter, student to student. But the students never seemed to make a connection with text or theme. At the end of each language arts period, the teacher would typically assign a set of questions which she wrote on the blackboard, and which the students either copied for homework or answered in class. Most of the questions were of the basic skills or recall type. Either they asked students to "pick out" isolated words that described particular characters that the teacher identified, to "look up" new vocabulary words in the dictionary, or to "Write one paragraph of at least six sentences that describe Character X or Y." The teacher explained to me that on occasions when students read from their assigned Basal Reader, *The Open Court,* Headway Program Series, she would assign the comprehension questions (also mostly at the literal level) which she took from that text.

Based on my experience visiting a variety of public elementary and middle schools, I would venture that this teacher was not atypical by any means. A cooperative, well-meaning individual, she had come to rely on the kinds of questioning techniques that reading texts and basal readers generally encourage. After several visits of the same kind, I racked my brain to come up with an alternative text to read to the students that might grab them, and an alternative approach to questioning that might break the syndrome of apathy that engulfed them. Clearly problems existed in areas of both content and method in the teaching of narrative appreciation and comprehension in this classroom. Determined to find texts that would appeal to the group, I administered a short and informal investigative questionnaire on their reading preferences. I wrote the following questions on the blackboard and asked them to respond in writing:

1. What kind of stories do you like to read?
2. Write the name of the most exciting story or novel you have ever read.

Although few students responded to Question 2, more than half of the students (thirteen out of twenty-five) responded that they liked to read fairy tales. Answers to Question 1 included, "fairy tail, fair tale, fairy tale, Fairy tails, and fairy tale," while six students wrote that they enjoyed "true stories" or "good stories." Four students expressed a liking for "scary or ghost stories," "witch or haunted house stories," or "animal stories." One boy wrote that he liked stories about gangs; another that he liked to read about karate and winning fights. The message that I gleaned from their comments was that the students enjoyed a complex blend of fantasy and reality. The vote was strongly in favor of fairy tales with a preference for real-life themes and motifs.

Rationale of the Study and Statement of the Problem

The Texts

I used the results of this questionnaire, combined with the affirmation of one African American teenage student (incidentally one of the town students) that the knowledge of her cultural heritage held great significance for her, and my own intuitions, to determine that I would use ethnic folk tales in investigating narrative reading and comprehension in this classroom. The student was responding to a question that the guidance counselor had asked her ninth grade class. It read: "If you could spend a day doing whatever you wanted, whatever the cost, what would you do? Her response was: "I would choose to travel back in time, and spending an hour with each person, I would want to meet, one at a time, my dead relatives and ancestors" (A. C.).

As a repository of culture, ethnic folktales seemed to combine the essential ingredients that the students had identified--fantasy, fiction, and real world themes and issues--with the appeal of a genre that provided a link with the unique past of a disfranchised people. I decided to explore the appeal of folk tales in addition to contemporary texts as ethnocultural narratives, with the aim of reviving an interest in narrative reading in these students. Having made the decision to examine Black folk tales, I realized that this classroom provided an ideal context for investigating their appeal in a cross-cultural setting. These ideas formed the cornerstone of my study, encouraged by current thought in this area.

There are scholars who believe that ethnic literature can appeal to members of the particular ethnicity that the literature represents, and also (more generally) to members of other ethnic groups. For example one anthropologist believes that Black folktales "celebrate black creativity" and "draw upon some of the most profound dimensions of African style" (Abrahams 1985, p.4). Again, a storyteller-in-residence (at the University of South Carolina) expresses similar sentiments:

> Here was a contribution to their (black girls and boys) racial pride--to know that their black forefathers had first told these stories and, in so doing, had added to the body of American folklore (Augusta Baker, 1985 in Lester, 1987, Introduction).

Here the potential for the appeal of Black folklore to Black children is implied, although that is not to say necessarily that the last two mentioned scholars are suggesting that their appeal is limited only to that group of students. In fact some researchers argue that such material can both enhance self-concept, and also inspire readers, presumably of any ethnic background, who resonate with the multiplicity of attitudes, beliefs, artifacts, traditions, mores, actions, and cultural knowledge of a particular group (Sims, 1982). And others (Harris 1995) go even further, and propose that African American literature is fundamental to the edification of *all* students, and is not just for students of the corresponding racial background. I believe that this universal appeal of literature applies to the "good" works that emerge from the complex tapestry of the lives of all ethnic minority peoples. Most notably, Banks (1993) proclaims the general appeal and potential importance of a multicultural curriculum in education in order to meet the needs of the country's changing demographics.

Upholding my belief in these philosophies, I too felt that it would be desirable and edifying for schools to incorporate ethnic literature in the curriculum from all the racial groups represented in the classroom. For present purposes, however, I decided to restrict my study to African American literature mainly because the majority of the students were African American, and because I wanted to control the proliferation of variables in the design. In addition, I envisioned a more than perfunctory approach to diversity and multicultural education which a one-day-in-January dedication to the celebration of Martin Luther King's life, or a recognition of the Cinco de Mayo festivities would represent. I hoped to involve all the ethnic groups in the study in the literature of one of its member-groups. My thinking was that if teaching is done well and with sensitivity, students from all ethnic backgrounds in any given classroom, could be guided to a full, deep, and wonderful appreciation and acknowledgment of any other culture represented in that classroom. Furthermore, such an excursion into another's culture would undoubtedly serve to heighten appreciation of one's own cultural background. After all, for years and years and years, ethnic minority students were all expected to appreciate and enjoy literature drawn predominantly from mainstream cultures. It should not be difficult, I reflected, to conceive of all students including ethnic minority students, being successfully guided through literature, in the exploration and appreciation of each other's cultures, and enjoying every moment of it.

The Questions

Having decided the kinds of text I would use, I then turned my attention to the issue of comprehension questions. With the knowledge that the way in which a story is comprehended is heavily influenced by the teacher's questioning strategies (Kirby, 1996), I wanted to stimulate interest in comprehension questions that were purposeful and strategic, and of the kind that were not preempted by the basic skills approach of the students' current routine. Research has shown that low-income ethnic minority students are not only fully capable of responding to high-level kinds of questioning, but also tend to be indifferent to more traditional, old-style questions (Heath, 1982). Yet, critics have observed that these students have unjustly been denied access to the kinds of questions that stimulate the intellect and raise students' levels of cognition. They contend that:

> tests, textbooks and curricula have increasingly focused on minimal skills (e.g., literal comprehension, routine computation, and factual recall), rather than the skills that may lead to a higher level of thinking by African American and minority students, for example inferential and critical problem-solving, comprehension, representation, elaboration, inductive inquiry, synthesis and evaluation. (Darling-Hammond, 1985)

In my investigation therefore, I planned to give students the opportunity to free themselves from the lockstep routine of the Basal Reader questions, and to explore their intuitions and reactions to the substantive thematic issues that they would encounter in reading specially selected narratives. In the spirit of Bakhtin's concept of heteroglossia (1981), I wanted to encourage students to voice their own unique perspectives in interpreting the literature they read, based on their insights and life experiences. My intention was to design the kind of comprehension questions that would "help provoke students' thought and not merely force them to recall data" (Calfee & Patrick, 1995: p.150). In short, the aim of my study was to combine interest, motivation and purpose in narrative reading for pleasure, deep discussion and critical appreciation.

For purposes of analysis, I identified four categories of questions in my study: general questions, literal meaning questions, interpretive reading-critical evaluation questions, and creative reading questions. In the general questions category, I planned to ask for general information and reactions to the selected stories. In the literal meaning category, I planned to ask basic recall questions that conformed to their title in form and function. These lower-order questions would have a definite correct answer, and would require students to retrieve basic information and points of detail from the given text. They would be multiple-choice questions typical of many standardized tests including the CTBS, the assigned instrument of evaluation in reading comprehension for these and most other elementary school students.

In the final two categories, the interpretive reading-critical evaluation and creative reading questions would signify the higher-order questions. They were to be open-ended and life-based, and as described above, the force of the students' individual voice, argumentation, and discussion would determine the correctness of the answer. These questions would be of the short-answer or mini essay variety in order to accommodate this orientation (further details and examples of lower-order and higher-order questions are given in Chapter 2).

On my next visit to the classroom, I piloted my idea about ethnic literature by reading an African American folk tale entitled *Mufaro's Beautiful Daughters* by John Steptoe. As I read the story aloud to the class purely for their enjoyment and entertainment, they responded with animated, spontaneous dialogue about the characteristics and behaviors of the two daughters in the tale. "She black!" one shy girl, from whom I'd rarely heard in the classroom before, volunteered proudly. "I have that book at home. I like it," she further reported, and promised to bring her copy to class next time I came. The experience was gratifying, and I took note. The memory of the verbal and emotional expressions of enjoyment that came from the students, impressed and stayed with me.

On a subsequent visit, I read an African folk tale entitled *Olode the Hunter* by Harold Courlander (with Ezekiel Eshugbayi) about a poor, homeless individual, who inherited a fortune because of his goodness, but who lost it all again because of curiosity and disobedience. In a corner of the room, a small group of students erupted in active discussion about the story, citing examples from their own life experiences of people they knew in their community who shared characteristics and experiences similar to that of Olode, the protagonist. Although the students who were grouped together represented four different racial backgrounds (African American, mixed Anglo and African American, Tongan and Fijian, an ethnic microcosm of the entire classroom), I noticed that they intermingled well and seemed to have common experiences in their background, partly as a result of living in the same community. They focused on one individual, whose name everyone seemed to recognize, a well-known riches to rags community character and folk figure about whom one student remarked: "I know a man like that. He's a hobo. An' he wear dirty clothes all the time. But he useta be rich."

The attraction that these two stories held for the students seemed to reinforce some of the ideas discussed above pertaining to the vitality of socio-cultural traditions in reading texts. The students' engagement stemmed from three factors. First of all, the genre was the short story, so they knew there was a built-in limit to the length of time they would need to stay engaged, making it easier for them to pay attention. Secondly, as intimated in the preceding discussion, they seemed to identify with the central characters in both stories-- in the first story, the Black daughters; in the second, the poor, struggling hunter embroiled in battles of the conscience--and with the real-life issues of kindness, betrayal, temptation, power, excess, disappointment and poverty portrayed in the tales. Thirdly, they seemed to relish the increased mental activity that the narrative engendered, as their discussion amounted to a virtual critique of the folk tale. The teacher observed the children's transformation, and gave me the green light to continue "doing whatever it is you're doing with them". My research study was born.

Chapter Summary

In summary, my study investigated 1) the efficacy of using ethno-cultural texts, namely African and African American folklore as regenerative historical narrative, as well as contemporary Black short stories, in teaching language arts to a group of low-achieving ethnic minority youth; 2) the benefits of encouraging these students to engage in high-level thinking of the sort that higher-order questions afford in narrative comprehension in addition to the more traditional kind of lower-order questions; 3) the outcome of the other story and student variables in the research design such as preference for narrative genre, the question of narrative length, and issues of student ethnicity and gender.

CHAPTER 2

CONCEPTUAL FRAMEWORK AND LITERATURE REVIEW

These tales grew up in the soil of our nation. They came from the soul of a people. They endure [as] lasting elements in the cultural heritage of our nation.

Joel Chandler Harris, 1955

Conceptual Framework

Two of the basic building blocks of my conceptual framework were discussed in some detail in Chapter 1: ethno-cultural narratives and strategic questioning techniques. The third component of the framework is an equally important one, the salience of narrative structure. This factor plays an integral role in my research design. The technique of structural analysis of the narratives selected for the study serves to interconnect the stories with the questions in a dynamic way (see Chapters 5 and 6 for further details). Further, the structure of stories is fundamentally interwoven with the process of narrative comprehension. In order for young children and adolescents to have the ability and desire to comprehend a story, they need to be cognizant of the parts that make up a story--character, theme, plot, setting. If students are also able to relate to the socio-cultural aspects of the story, the likelihood that they will become engaged readers increases. These ideas are the cornerstone of my conceptual framework. The factors that drive these criteria, and connect them to my research population include: 1) the popular appeal of the narrative genre, 2) the particular appeal of African and African-American folk tales and the contemporary narratives that represent the stimulus materials, and 3) the cultural connection between the study narratives and the ethnic minority students present in the classroom. I elaborate on each of these elements in turn, then discuss the issues pertaining to narrative structure and techniques of questioning.

Popularity of the Narrative Genre

People of all ages--young children, adolescents, and adults--are naturally drawn to stories. I was reminded of this attraction a few years ago when, immersed in my data gathering, I read on the front page caption of the *San Francisco Chronicle Newspaper* (February 20, 1994), that the art of storytelling was finding a revived role in the San Francisco Bay Area and other places. The clip announced that a Bay Area storyteller had quit her job of seventeen years to take up storytelling full-time. She reported that "friends thought I was crazy", but being a third generation storyteller, she was persuaded by the importance of the tradition. A few months later, another Bay Area newspaper, the *San Jose Mercury News,* (May 8, 1994), announced that a 64-year old female Appalachian storyteller had learned to read and write so she could record the folk tales of her people as a living record of Appalachia before she passed on. Like the teenager's yearning for affirmation about her people's past mentioned in Chapter 1 (admittedly more a historical kind of narrative), and the zealousness of the Lantana school students to listen to stories, this elderly woman's dream to bequeath a record of her people's oral culture to her community is evidence of the paramountcy of the story.

Psychologists and literary analysts have also alluded to the importance of stories. Freud pointed out the significance of tales for the psyche of our children (in Bettelheim, 1984), and a critic of children's literature reminds us that stories are both psychologically and emotionally fulfilling: "children read to explore the world, to escape the confining present, to discover themselves, to become someone else" (Lukens 1976, Preface). I would argue further that stories are especially relevant to children such as the ones who are the subjects of this study, whose difficult circumstances in life make occasional psychological and emotional escape therapeutic.

Within stories, folk tales are a sub-genre. In fact they are an important aspect of any culture because they act as a permanent repository of the group's values and mores. They are the result of humanity's experiment--texts that have undergone the most rigorous kind of experimentation, by being told and retold over time. They survive because they have a universal quality and are worthy to be valued and preserved within the culture. Thus they are an invaluable resource and are unifyingly, transcendentally human. Definitions and characterizations of folk tale reflect this fundamental appeal. Thompson (1984) defines a folk tale as an oral fictional tale which originated ultimately in preliterate cultures and which has now become "practically universal in both time and place" (p. 458), while Abrahams (1964) suggests that they represent "the functional unity which men in groups can create for themselves." (p.5).

Appeal of African American Folktales and Contemporary Black Narratives

African and African-American folk tales comprise a distinctive subset in terms of their origin, thematic base, character icons and language use. They originated from the same source, namely the Black people of Africa, although they were adapted to suit local conditions in terms of specifics such as characters and animals once the slaves who transported them reached the Caribbean, America, and Brazil. For example, the hare in trickster stories from West Africa became the spider in Anansi stories and Brer Rabbit in the South. Black folktales (I use the terms African American and Black interchangeably throughout the book) are more than just entertaining. They are also educational, uplifting, and didactic. Their themes covered a wide range of topics designed for multiple purposes, including the need to teach the younger generation ways to negotiate the complexities of life, and to convey to simple people the information they needed to carry on their lives properly.

Folk tales were also the repository of certain kinds of logic, understanding and reasoning. They demonstrated and proved puzzling things like riddles, and set them out in a way that made them persuasive. Blacks viewed tales as a dialogue between the listener and the speaker in which the listener was being challenged by what the speaker said. Tales became examples of intellectual conundra and puzzlements. According to one expert, Black historian Kennell Jackson (personal communication, Stanford University), Blacks were attracted to the Bible for the same reasons that they were interested in folk tales-- there were lots of problems to resolve, and lots of issues that were close to their lives. On the other hand, there were also issues and resolutions that were mysterious. In Jackson's opinion, folk tales bore the same kind of relationship to Blacks that Homer did to the Greeks. They carried meaning and teaching with which they could identify.

For example, the character of Spider became an icon that imbued the souls of an uprooted and displaced people with hope and comfort. Small and helpless, he always defeated his opponents, the larger animals, with his wit, humor and wisdom (Lester, 1989). Similarly, Brer Rabbit, the protagonist of one of the stories used in this study, came to symbolize the likable trickster's indomitable spirit in the Black folk tradition that produced the tales. It seemed that for the students in my study, the potential appeal of a folk tale that focused on such a character would be strong. Their marginalized status in the world of mainstream America, together with their own personal life circumstances in many ways paralleled Brer Rabbit's encounters with persons in positions of power and authority who tried to exploit him.

Apart from the unique history and underlying ethos of Black folk tales, I thought that students would also resonate with the dimensions of dialect and orality germane to the tales. The use of Black dialect in the speech culture of the Black community is well-established (Labov, 1970), and Black adolescents in particular use African American Vernacular English (AAVE, more recently termed Ebonics) as a mark of cultural identity and peer group solidarity. Recent research (Rickford & Rickford, 1995) shows that the incorporation of Black dialect into textual material may even improve reading comprehension in African-American youth. Furthermore, apart from the use of dialect, there were other discourse features that promised to be attractive. The language of Black folktales often reinforces the expressive and creative ability of AAVE found in the stylized forms of word play common to the Black community and practiced especially among adolescents--rapping, playing the dozens, signifying and toasts. Since most authentic folk tales were recorded or translated at least in part in the Black dialect that was the language of the people who told them, this reality promised to add another dimension of appeal to the materials. All in all, the words of a Black Folklorist crystallize the appeal of African American folk tales:

> Black folklore bring[s] us close to the hearts and minds of the people who first told them ...who formed them, expanded them, and passed them on to us. These tales were created out of sorrow, but... passed on full of love and hope. We must look on the tales as a celebration of the human spirit."
> (Hamilton, 1992: Introduction p.xii).

Apart from folk tales, which I thought would be one of the most attractive elements in the study, I also thought that contemporary narratives by Black authors or stories that portrayed a Black perspective, would be interesting to the students, and would draw them into the exercise of reading comprehension. Basic psychological principles of self-validation and self-esteem support this line of thought, and recollection of my own experiences in adolescence reinforced it. Raised in the Caribbean, I remember the lure of the novels and short stories of native authors like Wilson Harris and V.S. Naipaul which I read with the kind of excitement and anticipation born only of a deep, reflexive, cultural participation in the story. The appeal of contemporary narratives written by Black American authors such as Maya Angelou, Alice Walker, and James Baldwin fueled my desire to include "regular" non-folk tale stories in the study. The need to conform to the study variables (such as the selection of short stories of a particular length) limited my range of choice for contemporary narratives to less well-known authors, but the pieces nevertheless met the crucial criteria outlined above.

Difference between African American Folktales and Contemporary Black Narratives

The distinction between African American folktales and contemporary Black narratives is an important issue in its own right, but also because it is one that accounts for two of the variables in my research design. For this reason, I provide a thorough exposition of the differences between the two genres in Chapter 5 in conjunction with the structural analysis of each narrative selection. Generally the major distinctions center around 1) general characteristics that separate the spoken from the written word, or the difference between oral and literary modes, and 2) the divergence between the form and function of folktales and contemporary (Black) short stories.

In the tradition of oral literature, folk tales retain many of their usual characteristics such as repetitiveness and formulaic expressions. These are the devices that aid memory since folk tales were subject to survival in the minds of men (Encyclopedia Britannica 1984; Macropedia 7: 456). As mentioned before, they are also more interactive (as in Story #3: *Brer Rabbit falls in Love*), given to rhythm and rhyme, and to other literary flourishes. Folk tales are also anonymous. By contrast, contemporary short stories are generally not as repetitive, but tend to be more tightly drawn stylistically. They may or may not depend on literary flourishes according to the textual dynamics of the author. In addition, unlike traditional folk tales, they are authored productions with specific narrative personae (as in Story #6: *Ride the Red Cycle,* which is focused squarely on Jerome's struggles). His character is portrayed with precision, as are the others in the story (see Appendix A for all stories used in the Study).

In terms of function, folk tales are didactic and pedagogic. Despite their seemingly light nature, they have a very serious purpose. At large, they are designed to provide support for the behavior patterns of a culture, and to ensure its survival. African American folk tales are particularly designed to provide teaching, support and encouragement to its oppressed people. Themes exalt individuals who exemplify admirable virtues, but they also give the small, beleaguered character a winning role as an icon of triumph of good over evil. Story #1: *The Woman and the Tree Children*, exemplifies some of these features.

The element of the supernatural in folk tales stretches the imagination of the listener, and helps him or her conjure up a world where possibilities are limitless. As such folk tales also have an escapist quality. In addition they address such cosmic issues as the origin of the world and its inhabitants. For example Story #5: *Why Apes look like People*, tells why certain animals look the way they do. In this respect, folk tales are etiological in nature while contemporary narratives are less constrained in their purpose, and speak to themes that are more custom-made and shaped by the author for his or her particular audience. Story #4: *Remembering Last Summer* is clearly written for a young pre-adolescent audience. To the extent that they are didactic (as is the case with Story #2: The Runaway Cow), contemporary short stories might even run the risk of becoming dry if the didactic element is not incorporated skillfully.

Ultimately however, good stories are good stories, and overlap between folk tales and contemporary narratives is not unusual, and even common.

Cultural Connection between African American Literature and Ethnic Minority Groups in the Classroom

The best approach to understanding the cultural connection between the Black texts that I planned to select for this study, and the range of ethnic minority students (apart from the African American group where there is an obvious connection) in the class--Hispanic, Tongan, Samoan and Fijian, is perhaps through an understanding of the term "ethnic minority" as it is used in this book. I use the term to refer to all students of ethnically and racially diverse backgrounds who share corresponding membership characteristics. As members of non-mainstream races, they all have experienced the conditions and effects of second-class citizenship resulting from their ethnic status as members of the non-White groups living as they do on the periphery of the dominant society. In addition, as a result of growing up in the same predominantly ethnic low-income neighborhood, they share a strong sense of community with their physical surroundings. As members of the same marginalized and disenfranchised community, they face the same struggles with poverty and disempowerment, and share similar hopes, dreams, and aspirations for the future. Finally, as participant members of parallel, non-mainstream cultures, they all communicate via a language other than Standard American English, ranging from African American Vernacular English dialect (or Ebonics), to various dialects of Spanish, to Tongan and Samoan and Fijian dialects. In fact, the use of non-standard language was one of the chief sources of cross-cultural identity that I observed in the group. Whether socializing on the playground or working in groups in the classroom, many non-Black students (especially the boys) incorporated features of Black dialect in their speech both as a status marker, and as an indicator of "coolness" and strength. As a group therefore, they have homogeneous characteristics that transcend the usual biological factors of race. As a result, these students intermingled and interacted beyond the usual boundaries of ethnicity. Thus it seemed safe to think that the entire group would take a positive approach to the narrative text selections.

Literature Review

Research on the effects of story structure on narrative comprehension has evolved in terms of three constructs: a) story grammar; b) story schemata; c) reader-based intrusions.

Story Grammar

The concept of story grammar was inspired by the graphic representation model or tree diagram originally created by the linguist Noam Chomsky (1957) for depicting relationships between grammatical functions in a sentence. Story grammars similarly depict relationships between idea units or propositions in stories. The formula is to construct a set of rewrite rules that lay out the basic components of a story in hierarchical order. The hierarchy ranks essential story elements along the highest nodes, which in turn subsume the second set of elements in the tree, and so on until all of the elements and sub-elements in a story are accounted for completely. According to Bower's story grammar (Guthrie, 1985), the story setting, theme, plot and resolution are located along the highest nodes, and these elements subsume characters, location, events, and episodes. Story grammarians build two postulates around this construct or "macro structure"--first that information in the higher nodes should be more frequently recalled than information in the lower nodes because of its centrality to the story, and second that any violations in the integrity of story structure should decrease comprehension and recall (Pearson & Camperell, 1981).

Research on story structure has also bequeathed valuable insights into the complex processes involved in comprehension at the micro level. In addition to the main effects of story grammar theory, we also know for example, that within stories, goal hierarchies are correlated with causal connectives (Van den Broek & Trabasso, 1986), and that logical relationships connecting various story parts influence story comprehension (Stein and Glenn, 1978).

Though insightful, the problem with this line of research however, is that much of it has been undertaken from a psychological perspective by cognitive theorists, and more recently, by researchers in artificial intelligence. In line with the dictates of these disciplines, such research has involved fine-tuned procedures for inquiry into stripped down narratives often of no more than a few lines long, rather than techniques for capturing the different dimensions that might be involved in regular length narratives of the kind read in schools. For example, the summary of one story of the kind that bona fide cognitivists use for their experiments, condensed from a 250-word version of the familiar tale *The Boy and the Wolf,* reads: "A boy deceives villagers. The villagers ignore him. Boy doesn't get help when needed. The boy suffers." Not surprisingly, the ordering of story elements in hierarchy, a critical component of the story grammar model, might differ with real stories. For example, character elements might be more sensitive to placement in the hierarchy, and might have to compete with theme or resolution which get pride of place in the current psychological model.

An Innovation in Story Grammar

In this study, I build on the foundation of story grammar discussed above, and on the analysis of the constituent elements of the folk tale undertaken by a Russian linguist (Propp, 1977), in creating an innovation: the Narrative Map (see Chapter 5). The map is a concept suitable for portraying elements of narrative structure at the level of real-length short stories. The model divides the story into its consecutive episodes in a graphic portrayal that highlights character interaction and plot development, while it subsumes the components of theme and setting. Overall, the narrative map represents the systematic and comprehensive deconstruction of a story, and demonstrates the kind of skeleton framework or bare bones model that can be used to reconstruct a narrative in its entirety. It also uses symbols to display differential levels of emotion in narratives. Given the importance of knowledge structures in cognitive learning, the narrative map may be viewed as a device for representing knowledge about narrative structure at a conceptual level.

Story Schemata

While the concept of story structure is powered by the external forces of the text, story schemata are generally activated internally within the individual or culture. The mental structures or "schemata" that students bring to the task of reading have also been found to affect comprehension. Schema theory is thus a fundamental concept in the domain of cognition. It plays a prominent role in Piaget's account of cognitive development and has been incorporated into a theory of narrative comprehension (Bartlett, 1932). According to Piaget, schemata are the structures by which all individuals, including infants, intellectually adapt to and organize their environment (Athey, 1985). In terms of narrative comprehension, a "schema" refers to the mental codification of certain aspects of a person's experience. It is the material in our heads and hearts that has originated from our experience in the world. As we live, we interact with people and with the world and it is our reactions to these experiences, and our interpretations of them that are organized and stored, and become our schemata. These schemata then become the experiential base which guides our interactions with literature.

For example, the concept of "tea-time" in some cultures (as in England and in daughter countries that were former colonies), might connote a hot drink, accompanied with crackers, crumpets, and cheese or pastries and scones, served around 4 p.m., while in other cultures (as in the U.S. for example), it might mean simply a cup of hot tea with no regard to time of day or the presence of tasty snacks. Individuals in these two cultures would have different schemas about "tea-time."

I have actually had an experience that exemplifies this phenomenon. Soon after my arrival in the US from Georgetown, Guyana, a former British colony, I was invited to tea by an acquaintance who was quickly becoming a close friend. Conjuring up in my mind an image of delectable pies and-or pastries, and a wide range of teas of both the herbal and caffeined variety, I dressed rather nicely (no blue jeans and T-shirt) and showed up for the event. When I arrived, my friend was still getting dressed, but she shouted from inside that I should go on into the kitchen, and help myself to a cup of tea. When I entered the kitchen, there was a kettle on the boil, and a packet of Lipton tea sitting on the dresser. I made myself a cuppa, but deep down inside I was terribly disappointed, because I was denied the feast I had envisioned. My friend and I obviously had different schemas about "tea-time."

By the same token this "archive of past experience" (Applebee, 1979), is what shapes our expectations about what will come next. It is our real-life stories that guide our intuitions about the stories that we encounter in narrative text. These are some of the important postulates of schema theory. For example, the words of a text might be sensitive to a person's schema (Adams & Collins, 1979). Elaborated versions of schemata known as "scripts" (Schank & Abelson, 1975) and "frames" (Minsky, 1975) are also variations that have been suggested.

Schema theory therefore highlights the fact that there is often more than one possible interpretation of a text depending on specific cultural and other (related) factors that intrude from the reader's background (Anderson, 1985). Anderson also points out that cultural interference might be triggered either from the text itself--these are of the "bottom-up" or "data" driven variety, or from "top-down" sources driven by the specifics of a group's culture.

Reader-Based Intrusions

One argument against story grammar and schema theory is that they "subsume only the compelling meaning of a story" (Singer & Donlan, 1982); they do not include the less obvious yet potentially efficacious reader-based dimensions that might intrude in comprehension. This is the "other stuff" if you will, that is left over after theory accounts for story structure and mental structure in the process of reading comprehension. Some of these remaining factors include symbolic reconstructions, affective responses, and other reader-based elaborations to text-based material. It is this ancillary measure that Van Dijk and Kintsch (1985) refer to as "rationalizations of different sorts", as for example, in the emotional attitude of the subject with respect to the story and its content.

Despite all that research has taught us about comprehension and recall, there are still things we do not quite understand. The schema model is fraught with difficulties of abstractness and indefiniteness. Indeed we may not even now know all that we need to know or do not yet know, in order to understand the processes of comprehension. But there is enough knowledge available for us to help students improve their comprehension and feel more comfortable and confident in the company of literary text. We could give students a chance to discuss and negotiate texts the way they do in real life situations. We could encourage them to question and argue about differences of opinion and perspective, postures essential for success in the Academy that are easily accessible to children of privileged backgrounds, but denied to children who are not from cultures of power (Delpit, 1991) . Finally, we could give them opportunities to read and absorb narratives that enhance their self-esteem and draw them into the arena of literary appreciation.

Tierney & Pearson (1981) propose a framework for improving classroom practice. They include the recommendation that teachers offer a general program of schema development: field trips, films, library materials, and discussions with knowledgeable parents, that teachers in effect, move beyond mere comprehension skills, and begin helping students learn how to learn. These are very laudable intentions.

They reflect metacognitive approaches that would undoubtedly enhance reading comprehension as would enriching the funds of knowledge and experience that students bring to bear on the endeavor. But these measures would probably not solve the puzzle significantly. Mental and cultural orientations and approaches are fragile but powerful indices that might not respond to such an "additive" model treatment. The problem is more like Calculus, not Arithmetic. We therefore have to reach compromise, and rethink how we plan and structure comprehension activities for students, from curriculum materials to techniques of questioning, to systems of assessment, all elements of a paradigm that the present study investigates and for which Greene & Ackerman (1995) articulate the following position:

> We argue for pedagogical practices that a) are flexible enough to recognize the rich resources that students draw upon in constructing meaning, b) respect different constructions of text sense, and c) enable students to use language in different language communities... We also want to underscore the need to develop rhetorical and contextual research practices that are flexible enough to view anomalous data, divergent interpretations, or culturally and situationally idiosyncratic behavior as normal and necessary (p.410).

The Technique of Questioning

Aside from the influence of story grammar on comprehension, much of the research on this subject has devolved around models of reading rooted in an hierarchical structure of comprehension questions. Reading and listening are viewed as "thought-getting" processes, and the responsibility of the language arts teacher is to develop in his or her students a whole range of thinking skills (Clark, 1972). Various models for making constructs of comprehension questioning techniques, have adduced evidence for hierarchical structures ranging from literal skills on the lower end of the spectrum, to highly inferential, interpretive, and evaluative skills on the higher end. Categories of thinking skills reflect different nuances in the thinking levels identified as critical. These tend to vary depending on the particular paradigm that the author uses. For example, among the more inclusive constructs is a comprehensive program of comprehension instruction and active meaning construction that Ruddell proposed in a plenary session at the International Reading Association convention in Atlanta in May, 1997. It involves four levels of thinking--the factual level, the interpretive level, the applicative level, and the transactive level. Some of these levels are also embedded in the components of four interrelated levels of comprehension skills proposed by Rouch and Birr in 1984. They are the literal level, the interpretive level, the critical evaluation level, and the creative level. The model of comprehension questioning used in this book is configured by a combination of these two models both in terms of the language used to differentiate between categories of question, and the kind of ideas supporting the generation of such questions.

Unquestionably therefore, a vital route for improving Reading Comprehension is by improving the art of questioning in elementary school. At this level, the onerous dependency on lower-order thinking suffocates the cognitive processes of students at a time when they are calling out to be challenged and enhanced. Growing out of an out-dated "factory model" approach to education, the mode of questioning throughout the elementary school has tended to be rigid and uninspired. Although recent reading series and programs have been working toward a face-lift, and an understanding of a system of classroom questioning techniques such as Chuska (1995) offers can help reverse such trends, the source of this kind of questioning has been traditionally and still continues to be the basal reader, the assigned reading text in the large majority of elementary classrooms (Cochran-Smith, 1995).

As a case in point, I reproduce below the following two documents: 1) a sequence of six questions extracted recently from a story entitled "The Runaway Cow" in the basal reader assigned to the seventh-grade students who participated in my comprehension study. The questions are based on one of the narratives selected for my study (although I did not use the questions that came with the story); and 2) another sequence of six questions reproduced from a recently published Reading Series, touted as "questions that encourage careful reading as well as stimulate thinking" (*Kim Marshall Series in Reading,* 1996; Book 1, p.19). In both cases, the questions are weak and lack authenticity and purposefulness. Comprehension questions from "The Runaway Cow" provided in the Teacher's Guide to The Headway Program, Level H, (1985) *Burning Bright,* p.287, are basal reader examples of lower-order questions:

1. What were some of the good things about Annette's life?
2. Did Annette mind Julie riding on her?
3. What things did Louis wish he was doing instead of being in school?
4. What did Annette do when Pete got on her back?

5. What happened to Pete?
6. What mistake did Pete make?

These are all simple recall type questions that would probably be placed mostly on the lower or factual end of the questioning spectrum. They require essentially only memory work, little engagement or interaction with the text, and are often answerable in a single word or short phrase. The actual comprehension questions based on this story that were used in the study explored a much wider range of possibilities--see Appendix A. Similarly, comprehension questions from the Kim Marshall Series (p.62), are also examples of lower-order questions:

1. Where did Meriwether get the idea of running in track races?
2. What does it mean that he had no style?
3. What clothes did he wear to race in?
4. Why did he continue wearing these clothes?
5. How did he do in the race in Maryland?
6. What was his excuse for not winning?

Again, these questions provide little opportunity for authentic questioning or open-ended discussion. All of the answers are contained in the text in a rather straightforward manner. They provide no opportunity for the exercise of higher-order thinking skills such as inference and deduction, analysis, interpretation and synthesis. These are the kinds of questions that have engendered criticism of the following kind:

In the elementary classroom, simple narratives usually intended to be read for enjoyment are often sabotaged by an excessive use of poorly fitting questions (e.g. detail questions dealing with trivial information) under the guise of skill objectives (Tierney and Pearson 1981,:866).

By contrast, reading teachers have found parallel programs like the Chicago-based Great Books Reading and Discussion Program that promote open-ended discussion and interpretive questioning as necessary and useful.

My aim in undertaking this study was to avoid the effete questioning indicative of a minimal skills approach, and to incorporate instead a wider, more inquiring range of questions that would extend beyond basic recall. In addition to questions requiring recall information, the study questions would encourage critical thinking, literary analysis, and creative interpretation of narrative texts. I wanted to get the students to perceive the task of reading as connected to and not detached from their own experiences, to "alert them to the importance of their own ideas, perspective and purpose in communication" (Tierney & Pearson, 1985, p. 873). Distinctive types of comprehension questions therefore became a central variable in my conceptual framework (see Figure 2 below). Beyond this approach, I also developed a process of question construction that incorporated aspects of the structure of narratives as the springboard for creating these questions (see Chapter 6 for details).

The Conceptual Framework: Explication of Components

My conceptual framework focused on the students' cognition and comprehension of a set of six narrative texts--three Black folk tales and three contemporary narratives. I chose one African folk tale and two African American folk tales. The three contemporary narratives were all selections from the students' past and current basal reader series. In addition to genre, I varied two other text factors, length and readability level. There were three levels in the length variable--short, medium and long--in both narrative genres. The readability factor also had three levels. The first two stories had the "low" level of second-third grade; the two middle stories had the "middle" level of third-fourth grade; the last two stories had the "high" level of fifth grade. I calculated the readability level of the texts using two commonly used readability formulae--the Fry Readability Scale, a manual procedure and the Flesch-Kincaid Readability Statistics, a computer-based program (See Chapter 5, note, for details).

The comprehension questions in the study were derived from the structural components of the stories. They were divided into four categories--general questions, literal meaning questions, critical thinking questions and creative reading questions. The questions in the General Questions category (Q1 and 2) asked students to react to the elements of character, theme, plot, and setting in the narrative selections. The questions in the Literal Meaning category (Q3, 4, & 5) focused on surface issues of character and theme as represented in an early and late story episode. The questions in the Interpretive Reading and Critical Evaluation question category (Q6, 7, 8, & 9) investigated deep issues of character--character values, character actions, character qualities, and character feelings. Finally, the questions in the Creative Reading category (Q10 & 11) addressed issues pertaining to the development of plot, and were derived from the final episode or coda in each story.

The general questions therefore invited holistic reactions to the text, while the literal meaning questions category consisted of the traditional information-based memory questions. By contrast, the experience-based questions fell largely under the last two categories of critical thinking and creative reading questions. I labeled each question according to its unique thrust as follows:

General Question--Q1
General Question--Q2
Literal Meaning Question--Q3
Literal Meaning Question--Q4
Literal Meaning and Inference Question--Q5
Moral Judgment Question--Q6
Favorite Character Question--Q7
Character Feelings/Qualities Question--Q8
Deductive Reasoning Question --Q9
Problem Solving Question--Q10
Student-as-Author Question--Q11

Chapter Summary

In this chapter, I gave an overview of the conceptual framework of the study and a review of pertinent aspects of narrative literature. I discussed the popularity of the narrative genre in general, and the appeal of ethno-cultural narratives and folk tales in particular, the latter two items from the point-of-view of their relevance to the study participants. The literature review focused on issues of story structure including story grammar and story schemata, and on techniques of questioning. Finally, I discussed the various components of my conceptual framework. As indicated in Figure 2 below, they include text, question, and participant effects of the study.

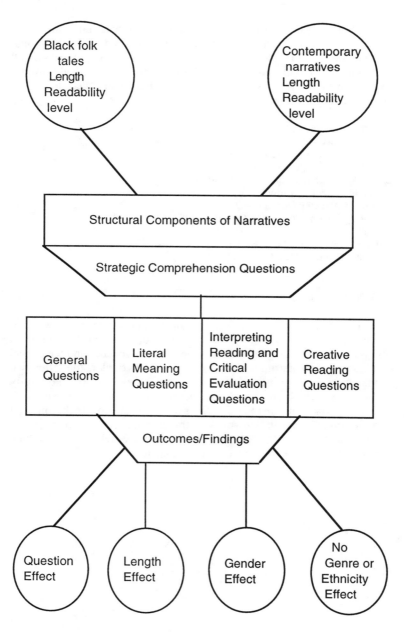

Figure 2. Narrative Cognition and Comprehension in Ethnic Middle School Students: A Conceptual Framework.

CHAPTER 3

THE RESEARCH SITE: COMMUNITY, CLASSROOM, STUDENTS

Society in the United States is comprised of a class structure that maintains and reproduces itself through social institutions and agencies...Although there are increasing numbers of ethnic minorities who attain middle- and upper -class income levels, the percentage remaining in poverty is still disproportionately high when compared to Euro-Americans.

Etta R. Hollins, 1996

Overview

    This chapter sets the contextual stage for the study. It portrays the students' community setting, school context, and particular classroom, sites that combine social and cultural factors which are directly linked to an investigation of the effect of cultural dynamics on narrative comprehension. In describing the classroom environment where their learning is constructed, I also include profiles of individual students in order to introduce the reader to an authentic cast of characters.

The Community

Historically, East Tall Tree (ETT), the city that houses Lantana School--the school in which my study took place--was one of the first Black communities on the San Francisco Peninsula, and until about the 1950s, was rather proud of its status. Many of the adults worked in shipyards, had regular jobs and lived in a stable community. Homes were modest, but some residents maintained manicured lawns and small gardens. With decades of increasing poverty however, circumstances changed and high crime rates accompanied a burgeoning drug trade. Conditions worsened rapidly, and in 1992 the community held the dubious distinction of being the city with the highest per capita homicide rate in the nation. More recently, community members have made bona fide efforts to improve the city's reputation, by involving the youth in sports activities and in tutor-tutee partnerships with students from the neighboring ivy league university. Neighborhood-based organizations such as "Families in Transition", and other projects, established to alleviate the familial stresses of divorce, separation and abuse, are also confronting the challenges of a distraught community.

Within the past decade, the immigration of other cultures to ETT--particularly Latino families and South Pacific Islanders, has added another layer of complexity to the pre-existing tensions in the community. As a result, the strongly entrenched African-American culture has had to sensitize itself to the demands of equally needy cultural groups for community and schools that incorporate the new cultural diversity.

ETT therefore fits the description of a small "urban" multicultural community whose members are of lower socioeconomic status, and whose challenges and vicissitudes typically include low employment rates, teenage pregnancy, alcoholism, drug infestation, and gang warfare. However, the urban label should be attenuated by the demographic realities of ETT and not aggravated by the presumption of vastness that the term connotes. According to the most recent census, (1990), the population of the city included approximately 23,500 people of whom a large segment or 42% were African-American, a slightly smaller percentage were Latino, (36%), and the remainder represented other ethnicities, as follows: 12% Anglo-American, 6% Pacific Islander, 3% Asian, and 1% other.

The School

Lantana is one of eight elementary schools in the Blendwood School district. It is a neighborhood school, and most of the 500 students live in the immediate community. The school spans grades K to 8, as do all the other elementary schools in the district. The school itself, a low set, ranch type cream complex of several rooms, has an inauspicious entrance bordered by large flat areas of enclosed dry land, a side street, and low-income houses. It is located on the outskirts of the main town center, near the San Francisco Bay on the Baylands, about five minutes from the bridge to the East Bay. The bridge is a main thoroughfare, traversed primarily not by ETT residents, but by the predominantly White mainstream population who live in the East Bay and work in the wealthy computer industry in "Silicon Valley" and in other places in and around Tall Tree. Traffic in and out of the main street near the school is therefore heavy, belying the lack of genuine business activity and entrepreneurship to be found in the community itself.

The composition of the teaching staff at Lantana School reflects the formerly dominant African American element in the school and surrounding community, while the composition of the current student body marks the shifting demographic trend. Seventeen of the twenty teachers at Lantana are African American, one is Latino, and two are Anglo American, while 40% of the students are Latino, and 30% are African American. But the teaching and administrative staff are in constant flux, although at least three of the current teachers have taught at Lantana for many years.

The school has had a troubled history within recent years. Extremely low test scores and the influx of new and diverse ethnic populations have increased the challenge for teachers amidst dwindling economic resources. The abysmally low 1990 CTBS scores for the Blendwood School District (of which East Tall Tree is a significant part) cited in Chapter 1, has shown little improvement over time. The now defunct state achievement test, the California Learning Assessment System (CLAS), which the school administered almost four years later, showed similarly poor results (Note 1). What appears to be improved scores for the Blendwood school district, proves otherwise on close examination. According to the reported 1993-94 scores (San Jose Mercury News March 9, 1994; p.12 A), fifty-eight percent of the Ravenswood fourth graders who earned some of the better scores, scored a 3 or higher in reading, and seventy-eight percent scored at the same level in writing. But a score of 3 on the six-point CLAS evaluation scale is not a very demanding measure of achievement. The grading criteria for a CLAS score of 3 in Reading stipulates: "Makes superficial connections. . . unwilling to take risks, with little toleration for difficulties in a text" while the criteria for writing include the following description: "The writing may contain some insights but also demonstrates confused, superficial or illogical thinking. . . noticeable errors." Schools have now reverted to the former California Test of Basic Skills as their standardized measure, and the challenges of teaching the basic literacy skills of reading and writing remain real for teachers at Lantana school, and also for students who attend school in the Blendwood School District and nearby locations.

The Classroom: Year 1 (1993-4) versus Year 2 (1994-5)

Currently, as one enters Room 22, the immediate impression is of a neat and tidy classroom. There are heterogeneous groups of students; five groups of five--mostly three boys and two girls. The groups are spread out over the main floor space in the room. Books are neatly arranged on the shelves that line one side of the room, including a complete volume of World Book encyclopedias that add to the intellectual atmosphere of the room. Posters and signs on the walls encourage mannerliness, good class citizenship and exalt learning. The upholstered furniture that lines the other side of the room enclosing the students in the center, is relatively new and clean; in fact it is still covered in protective plastic which everyone sits on comfortably, and no one thinks to remove. I learn later from their teacher, Mr. Peters, that he has deliberately left it on for the proper care and maintenance of the chairs. He says he wants his students to learn to value their surroundings and to keep them clean. A big waste basket sits in the middle of the room. Students seem lured to the bin many times during class to dispose of waste paper and other material. But at work time they are busy and engaged, and even when they visit the dust bin in the center, they do so quietly and purposefully. This is a picture of the new classroom that I observed in the second year of my work with these students from 1994 to 1995.

I am rather surprised by this picture of orderliness and control. These are the very students who a year ago in their previous class, created enormous discipline problems for their teacher. They were boisterous and difficult to manage. At that time the classroom atmosphere was characterized by almost total anarchy. The then teacher tried valiantly to control her students and maintain some semblance of order and direction in the classroom, but to no avail. These same students were loud, disrespectful and unmanageable. The picture of their combined fifth and sixth grade classroom remains quite vivid in my mind. The following excerpt taken from the journal that I kept that year during the time when I volunteered in their class as teacher's aide (1993-1994), is typical of their behavior, and symptomatic of the general malaise that engulfed the classroom all year round:

> About 11.10 am. 10-18-93: Suddenly a student gets up, stomps around the room, drags her desk in a circular fashion, shouts out to another student, "stop following me around" and sits down loudly. Other students traipse repeatedly over to the pencil sharpener mounted on the wall in one corner of the room, to sharpen their pencils whether or not they already have sharp points. During all this commotion, another student is trying to read a paragraph out loud. [The teacher's expressed plan is to alternate her own reading of paragraphs with the students' reading]. She keeps raising her voice higher and higher in an effort to drown out the noises of the disruptive students. Eventually her voice is overcome by theirs, and by the added din of pieces of chalk and pages of paper being crushed (paper balls) and thrown, in some instances, clear across the room. Finally, the teacher shows her anger and intervenes: "My God! You guys are impossible." Then turning to me: "That's why I don't do anything different or creative with them. As soon as you start to try something new, they go wild. This is just awful." And then to the students: Be quiet! Now. All of you." And wild they were indeed.

So with this image in my mind, I was visibly impressed when I first visited the "new" version of the classroom, and observed their teacher Mr. Peters closely to find out why he seemed to be succeeding in maintaining order and control in this classroom with the same students who were so unruly the previous year. I soon determined that Mr. Peters succeeded by using multiple techniques to curb, control, motivate and challenge his adolescent students. Some of the techniques were rooted in the cultural background of his students and therefore matched the conceptual approach of my narrative cognition and comprehension research study. In fact, his success in the area of discipline facilitated my work in his classroom; it would have been virtually impossible to conduct any systematic inquiry under the classroom conditions of the previous year. Although the teacher worked hard (see Notes), the behavior of the students remained severely wanting. But the culture-based techniques that Mr. Peters used generated a lot of positive and creative energy that were directed towards class control and discipline, and his methods seemed to be working.

The Students: Individual Profiles

In this section, I offer some student portrayals in order to give a more rounded and complete portrait of their daily lives than purely academic statistics could provide. The data were gathered during individual and small-group interviews recorded at the time of my study. They show the enormous challenges and responsibilities that these adolescents face in their personal lives.

R.S. is a twelve year old African American girl. She lives in East Tall Tree with her sister, brother and father. They have lived there for twelve years. Her mother is White and her father is Black. She has seen her mother only a few times since birth because she has been in a mental institution for many years, originally committed there following several drug-induced "attacks". R.S.' father works full time and is often gone late into the night. She has the responsibility of helping to raise her younger sister and brother. But she is a good student and is well behaved and on task in class. She is very shy and likes to read *Ebony* magazine and "Sweet Valley Twins".

W.E. III is a thirteen year old African American boy. Both his parents are Black. He lives with his mother, father, sister and brother. His father is the breadwinner of the family; his mother is a homemaker. They have lived in E.T.T. for eleven years. Reflecting on W.E.'s future, his teacher said: "I see him as being someone who will probably get frustrated, but if they can find his needs, and tell him "here" I can see how he would make it in some area that would probably be geared to his area of strength." During the previous academic year (1993-4) he was both the class clown and the class bully. He was very disruptive in class and rude to the teacher. He did very little work. This year, his behavior has improved significantly, but he still has occasional angry outbursts. W.E. sometimes still does very little work in class. He seems to have potential for achieving academically, but most of his energy is diverted to other things. On the other hand, he is sometimes very helpful to others and willing to show another side of his personality. For example, he would always volunteer to help fetch materials for my study (papers, tape recorders, pens and pencils, sodas and snacks, etc.,) from my car and take them to Room 22 for me. He likes to read the newspapers and *Sports Illustrated* magazines.

T.R. is Samoan; his parents migrated to this country thirteen years ago, when he was just a few months old. They still speak Samoan to him at home. His family has lived in E.T.T. for fourteen years. Home is a small apartment that he shares with his mother, father, brother and twelve other family members, including grandparents, aunts, uncles and cousins. He did not respond when I asked during a brief interview, what work his parents did. His oral English is very good, but his writing is poor and like many of his classmates, he needs remedial work. Although he follows instructions and stays out of trouble, T.R. usually seems distant and disengaged in class. He performs very poorly on tests. When I asked him what books, novels or magazines he liked to read, he replied decisively: "I do not read books."

D.P. is thirteen and a half years old, an Indian teenager who hails from the Fiji Islands. She lives at home with her parents, two siblings and grandmother. Her father works full time. Her best friend L.L., is also Indian and of Fijian descent, but was born in the US. She also lives with her parents and two siblings, and her father is also the family breadwinner. They have both lived in E.T.T. for approximately ten years. In sixth grade, they sat next to each other in the center back of the classroom and disassociated themselves from the rest of the class. They always behaved well and soon became known as "Teacher's pets". The teacher would often ask them to share out papers, collect homework and do other class chores. This situation earned them the kudos of the teacher and the distrust and annoyance of the other students in the class, especially the girls. Unlike the other students for whom English is not the first or only language, D.P. and L.L. often speak to each other using their native language, effectively excluding any of their peers from their conversation. However, since they have been in Mr. Peters' class, they no longer sit together and have become more fully integrated with the separate groups of which they are members. Mr. Peters acknowledged that D.P. is much brighter than L.L. who sometimes looks to her best friend for help with school work. In her own words, D.P. likes to read "scary book that have a lot of action in it", while in addition to scary books, L.L. also reads mystery books.

Finally, D.J. is a Latino male who is thirteen and a half years old. His parents were both born in Mexico, but D.J. is a first-generation American citizen. He is bilingual, and speaks mostly Spanish at home and mostly English at school. He is fairly new to the area. His family has lived in E.T.T. two years, and this is D.J.'s first year at Lantana School. He lives in a small apartment with his parents, two brothers and three sisters. At school D.J. identifies with the Black boys. His close friends are all African-American guys in the class, and he jokes and interacts with the same group of guys outside of class. When socializing with his peer group, his language even has features of African American Vernacular English. D.J. is an average student whose attention to work has improved this year, and who would probably do much better if he were more motivated. When I asked what kind of books he liked, he responded, "I do not read books."

The individuals profiled above were selected to convey to the reader the multi-ethnic character of this classroom. Classrooms of this kind are becoming more commonplace than ever before in California, a state that is rapidly increasing the numbers of its ethnic minority peoples, a state that is predicted to hold an ethnic minority population of more than 50 % by the year 2020. What is unique about this classroom, however, is the strong sense of shared culture that emanates from it. Part of the reason for this is the element of unity that exists in difference as explained in the previous chapter. That is not to say that there is no conflict among the various groups in East Tall Tree. As suggested earlier in this chapter, this is my no means the case. But what the range of diverse cultures in the classroom share is the common fact that they are all removed from the dominant mainstream culture. Displays of unity and cross-ethnic identification are particularly noticeable, for instance, among the Pacific Islander and the African American students, some of whom have formed tight friendships within genders. In addition, the fact that all the youth dress in a similar fashion wearing big, baggy pants and oversized T-shirts and sneakers, increased the sense of an in-group dynamic in the classroom.

Chapter Summary

In this chapter, I set the stage for the study by portraying aspects of the community that the students live in. I included a description of the school and the classroom, and a representative sample of student profiles. Finally, I drew a contrast between the students' behavior during the first and second year of my involvement in their classroom, citing the discipline strategies of the teacher during the second year as a significant part of the explanation for the dramatic change in their behavior. The upcoming Chapter 4 complements this one. There I will discuss the teacher's culturally relevant discipline and teaching techniques, and point to ways in which the classroom environment that he created and nurtured made it possible for his students to learn and for me to conduct my research study there.

CHAPTER 4

CULTURE-BASED CLASSROOM DISCIPLINE AND ORGANIZATION

It goes right back to that love, that deep concern. And you can't get that in a university. It's just something to that, to care for them or not, and these kids are so sensitive, they will know. Because if you show the least bit of not caring, or you know...distrust toward the kids, they pick it up. And instead of them working for you, they work against you.

Mr. Peters, Lantana Elementary School, 1995

Overview

In this chapter I discuss the culture-based discipline strategies and classroom organization techniques that Mr. Peters used to control his difficult-to-manage class. It is included primarily for contextual purposes, providing an example of the approaches that one teacher used in order to create the kind of positive behaviors and classroom environment needed for his students to learn. Issues of discipline and classroom control are ones that every teacher must face. Far too often, however, teachers, especially novices, find their attempts to teach sabotaged by an unruly and poorly-disciplined group of students. Mr. Peters inherited one such group, but he dedicated his energy and expertise to turning them around. Moreover, he succeeded. He worked out ways to educate other people's children by creating a near-perfect balance between power and pedagogy in his classroom and in his teaching (Delpit, 1995). In this chapter I analyze the elements of his success. I do so in some detail firstly in order to understand and record his modus operandi for the benefit of my readers and myself, and secondly, to honor this teacher publicly.

Teachers in low-income ethnic minority schools are often maligned, as though they alone (and not the larger socioeconomic and political factors that undermine such schools) are responsible for the children's failure. In Mr. Peters' case, the reverse was true in that he was one of the primary reasons the students in my study came to believe "they could fly." Here I acknowledge this, and discuss Mr. Peters' overall teaching philosophy and his attention to cultural congruence as the bedrock of his orientation.

Students like those in Mr. Peters' classroom who grow up in challenging circumstances, and are not doing well in school, are usually unwilling to do much reading and writing. The tendency is to avoid it, either because they are not motivated or because the task brings them little pleasure. For example, six of the twenty-five students in Mr. Peters' class who responded "I do not read books" or "nothing" or "I do not like to read" when asked in individual interviews what kinds of books or magazines they enjoyed, were probably reflecting the feelings of many of their peers. It is therefore remarkable that these students were motivated enough to fulfill the demands of a study that required a considerable amount of reading and writing. During each of the six experimental study sessions that spanned the scope of my study (plus several other meetings for interviews and questionnaires), I asked the students to answer questions and write about their ideas and opinions based on their understanding of the narrative texts. The work required pages of writing; each student answered eleven questions, including seven short essay questions (for each of six stories), a significant task by any standard, but one with which they readily complied. On two occasions when I presented my research recently, to an audience of educators at the University of Colorado, and to a group of over fifty teachers in San Jose, California, they asked how I managed "to get the students to do all this work". In this chapter I conceptualize some of the reasons for their willingness to invest the effort and energy that it took to stay with the study to the end, reporting as a participant observer.

Mr. Peters used several different strategies in motivating his students to buckle down to work. His techniques were all driven by a caring, nurturing, and supportive orientation towards the students, and by a keen consideration of the importance of cultural propensities in educating ethnic minority peoples. Both of these approaches--caring and attention to culture--have "oomph" in the process of education. These are the non-pedagogic aspects of curriculum and teaching that educators are striving to understand more and more, because we realize that they can have an even more vigorous impact on the process of education than any sound pedagogical approach that ignores them, especially among ethnic minority populations.

In terms of caring in education, Nel Noddings of Stanford University has advanced an appealing premise that turning out caring individuals should be fundamental to the intellectual enterprise (Noddings, 1995). Her point is that education devoid of humanity is sterile. Similarly Siddle-Walker of Emory University has articulated the importance of caring as part of the total package in educating African American children and in guiding them to stretch towards and attain their highest potential (Siddle-Walker, 1996). More recently, the success of a public alternative middle school in Chicago's West Side has demonstrated the potential of a caring environment (Pool & Hawk, 1997). It has reaped success for its disadvantaged inner-city children on several measures including improvement in reading, higher test scores, and greater retention, as a result of teacher demonstrations of love in the midst of desperation. Its founder and executive director, known fondly as "Momma Hawk", discusses the school's success in terms of caring writ large:

> Caring is most likely the greatest reason for the success of the academy, as well as what is most needed in public schools...This care is not only institutionalized in the form of hot meals at school, food, clothing, bank accounts, and laundry and kitchen facilities but is personalized to the extent of providing temporary places for children in crisis to live. (Pool & Hawk, 1997: 33)

In terms of culture, the Brazilian educator Paolo Freire has been at the vanguard in sensitizing the Western intellectual community to the importance of education as cultural action (Freire, 1970). His notion that as third world people, we learn to read the world long before we learn to read the word, is a powerful one (Freire & Macedo, 1987). To develop this metaphor, one might say that a reading of the word taken literally, that is, success in teaching students to read and write, is conditioned by a reading of the world as a caring, supportive place. On the contemporary scene, Ladson-Billings' investigations of culturally relevant pedagogy are less overtly political but upon examination, equally powerful (Ladson-Billings, 1995). She strives towards a theory of pedagogy that is at the intersection of culture and education, where culture is interpreted in a profoundly positive manner, and where ethnic minority children are successfully educated when the teaching curriculum builds on their cultural knowledge and strengths. For example, as instantiations of culturally relevant pedagogy, she cites teachers who select literature in which students can see themselves reflected positively, and teachers who use images and metaphors that debunk the myth of ethnic minority inferiority and instead project images of the beauty of diverse ethnicities to motivate and energize their pupils.

My own experience in teaching and counseling ethnic minority students has reinforced my sense of the importance of these perspectives in the practice of education. For two consecutive summers, I have been involved in teaching a college level linguistics course to pre-frosh ethnic minority student admittees at San Jose State University in Northern California. Prior to that, I held the position of Residence Dean and Resident Fellow for about two years and ten years respectively at Stanford University. These combined experiences exposed me to dealings with a wide range of ethnic minority students from diverse cultural backgrounds, and taught me that in order for these students to have a successful and happy experience, I needed two kinds of qualifications. When teaching, I needed to be a good teacher who knew her material well, but I also needed at all times, to be a caring individual who showed respect and concern for these students as individuals *and* as members of their particular non-mainstream cultural groups. The more that these two facets were embedded in my teaching contained evidence of these facets, the more empowered and competent the students felt, and the more successful was my teaching in terms of communicating vital content, information, and knowledge to them, and in motivating them to learn.

The work of several researchers underscores the significance of culture in education, and examines the educational needs of diverse students from slightly different perspectives. Irvine & York (1995) offer a comprehensive account of the learning styles of culturally diverse students using the framework of the literature review. They include cognitive, affective, and physiological perspectives as vital factors in surveying the domain of culturally congruent learning styles. Delpit (1991) examines the kind of mind-set necessary for educating and empowering other people's children (or children from ethnically diverse backgrounds) with the kind of culture-strong language and teaching in which Anglo students are bathed by virtue of their preponderant mainstream culture. Like King (1995), she focuses on African American students. King also analyzes the concept of culture-centered knowledge, and draws a distinction between cultural hegemony and cultural autonomy, arguing for the demarginalization and expansion of Black knowledge and culture in the curricular orientation of schools. Garcia (1995), reviews the theoretical and practical perspectives in the education of Mexican American students through a critical analysis of the concept of mainstream cultural superiority. He suggests that the prime institutional education objective of the "Americanization" of ethnically diverse children has been subtractive, unfair, and unsuccessful. Pang (1995) explores the complexity and diversity of Asian Pacific American students emphasizing the value of literary texts that reflect their culture and background. Representing multiple ethnicities, and giving voice to their various needs, these researchers all address issues pertaining to the intersection of culture and cognition in the process of educating ethnically diverse student populations.

Three factors in Mr. Peters' teaching style demonstrated consideration of some of the issues raised above, and created just the right kind of environment his students needed to develop feelings of competence, empowerment, and achievement: 1) his philosophy of teaching, which fitted well with the needs of his multicultural class; 2) his use of culture-based discipline techniques in the style of the Black Church, and 3) his "in loco parentis" brand of caring and tough love discipline.

Teaching Philosophy

High Expectations, Motivational Sayings, and Classroom Behavior

Ever since the landmark study on teacher expectations and pupil performance by Rosenthal & Jacobson, 1968 (see also Tauber, 1997), it is almost a truism in education that students will work as much or as little as they need to, in order to meet the standard that their teachers expect of them. This belief was an integral part of Mr. Peters' philosophy of teaching. He reiterated to his students that he was confident of their ability to succeed in school and that he had high expectations for them. Consequently, he held them to high standards of performance. The motivational sayings and admonitions contained on posters and plastered on the walls in his classroom reinforced this verbal sentiment. They contained affirmations, words of advice and formulae for success. Following are some of the verses that I recorded. They recreate the ambiance of the classroom:

I believe I can learn
I can learn and I will learn

No one is good at doing everything
But everyone is good at doing something.

Our work must always be: Correct, Neat
Comprehensive, Complete.

These dictums were an inherent part of the students' work day. Mr. Peters read them off several times each day as a constant reminder to the students that they were capable and competent individuals. Indeed his model for inspiring his class was characterized by his constant repetition and recitation of a variety of motivational sayings. One favorite saying which he invoked repeatedly, was derived from the first two lines of the Marva Collins Creed. He had the students stand and recite them first thing every morning as a self-esteem booster:

Society will draw a circle that shuts me out
But my superior thoughts will draw me in.

Next they repeated the "Pledge of allegiance to Me:"

I can be the best
By doing the best
In everything I do.
And taking pride
In who I am, my faith
Will see me through.

He also used language in a culturally familiar way to build a bridge for the students between the familiar of home and community on the one hand, and the unfamiliar of school and academia on the other. His language resembled the Black Artful Style (Foster, 1992), incorporating features that signaled an ethno-cultural mode of communication. It included the use of oral embellishments, variations in pitch, tone and tempo, and the use of poetic devices such as rhyme, rhythm, metaphor, alliteration, exaggeration, innuendo and more--features that grabbed the attention of the students, drew them in and contributed to their learning. He regularly used alliterative catch phrases such as "Wonderful Wednesday" and "Tremendous Thursday." His students responded well to this approach. For example, they seemed to know what work marked different days, and the phrases became a stimulus for preparation for different kinds of class work and activities.

Other rhymes and verses, some of which he rehearsed in the mode of a song which he would compose on the spot, were standard "texts" that framed students' behavior in the classroom. Classroom Rules, Arrival and Departure Procedures, Lifelong Guidelines and Life skills and Academic Prompts filled the walls in his classroom. Samples of these are displayed in Table 4.1 below.

Classroom Rules	Be in your assigned seat ready to work, when the tardy bell rings.
Arrival Procedure	Enter quietly, Greet teacher, Place homework in paper tray, Get a book and read for ten minutes.
Departure Procedure	Get homework assignment, Clean up. Wait for teacher to dismiss you.
Lifelong Guidelines and Life Skills	Truth, Trust, No put-downs, Active Listening, Personal Best. Integrity, Initiative, Flexibility, Perseverance, Organization, Sense of Humor, Effort, Responsibility, Cooperation, Caring.
Academic Prompts	A metaphor describes a thing or situation. A verb is an action word.

Table 4.1. Standard Texts Framing Classroom Behavior.

A considerable amount of wall space was thus devoted to advice and admonitions on conduct, and only one wall was given over to academic prompts. This apparent imbalance might puzzle the casual observer, but to an insider, one who had witnessed the disciplinary problems of the previous year, the emphasis was quite understandable. Mr. Peters' aim was to provide a vital framework within which his students were expected to operate. In an interview, he articulated the importance of order and structure in the school lives of his students whose home lives were often unpredictable. To this end, he set high standards and circumscribed their behavior closely and carefully, while trying not to stifle them.

Self-Esteem: Classroom Organization

In addition, Mr. Peters tried in the different ways he could to raise the self-esteem of his students. He was sensitive to the need to build structure, security and a sense of predictability into the lives of his students. One way in which he did this was to keep the environment organized. In addition to motivational sayings, he also used wall space to display the students' work. He took pains to display work that demonstrated high quality and commendable effort. Some of his comments on work displayed read: "Good Work!" "You did it!" "Nice try!" and "Good Job!" A "Student of the Week" poster detailed the name, birthplace, and favorite book(s) of that student, something that he or she did well, a person whom he or she admired, and what he or she liked most about school. The displaying of students' work might seem an obvious thing for teachers to do, and in many middle-class school classrooms it is done on a regular and rotating basis, but the practice occurs much less frequently in low-income areas where teachers' time and emotional energy are taken up with basic pursuits like getting enough books and other operating materials into the classroom, or maintaining discipline. In working-class school classrooms where the practice does occur, therefore, it deserves commendation.

Heath (1983) mentioned that the fluidity and lack of structure in the lives of a comparable population, the working class African American "Trackton" children in the Piedmont Carolinas meant symbolically, that those students were ill prepared for the structure and routine of the school environment. Mr. Peters strove to adopt compensatory measures in order to accommodate *his* student group, by overtly building in classroom routines and by continually striving to make his classroom a model of order and organization:

> I stress organization, a lot of good organization. That's very important to these children. If you come in my room right now, you'll see it's falling apart (laughter), but we try to be

organized. They have to organize to survive. That's so important, to be organized. . .Yeah, I'm adamant about that.

Self-Esteem: Multicultural Literature, the Vegetable Soup Technique, and Different Learning Styles

Mr. Peters was committed to the concept of multiculturalism and to nurturing a community of diverse learners in his classroom. To this end, he combined culture-based and tradition-based approaches in his teaching. His culture-based approach included the use of ethnic literature as content material in his reading-language arts curriculum. His hope was that his students would identify with the literature, because they would see themselves reflected in it and its effect would be to raise their self-esteem:

> I agree with the whole idea of giving them Black Literature because they read it better; they can relate to it better. . . they can identify with the feelings, the empathy. Even the choice of words that is in the flow, yes, I absolutely like it, doing Black Literature. . .I try pulling up Black stories, so we did James Baldwin, Caleb's Brother--that's just an excerpt from "Tell me how long the train's been gone". Stories about their culture they really enjoy. Even the Polynesian and the Indian kids enjoy stories about Blacks. And the kids enjoy stories about them. That's so.

Apart from Mr. Peters' commitment to multicultural literature, he encouraged acceptance of diversity among his students, and cooperation and mutual respect among the various ethnic groups represented in his classroom. He taught them to interact with each other and to learn from each other's cultures:

> I tell them that the first day of school--each one help one. I try to build support, so that everybody can work together in the classroom, and help each other. And I tell them, you know, that I am going to put down how much a person helps, because that's so important.

In this way, Mr. Peters fostered cross-cultural relationships within the classroom, discouraging individuals or groups of students from working together only according to ethnic similarity. When questioned on how he did this, he commented on this practice and his "vegetable soup technique" of ethnic intermixing:

I broke them up. Absolutely. Absolutely. The first day of school I would have them all to stand around a wall, and I would put everybody together, say we're just gonna have a nice vegetable soup. I want everybody mixing together in this classroom. Let me see, I want a carrot over here. You're a carrot. I say, I want some potatoes now. Potato, you go over to that group now. And I want a little broccoli here. And I break them up. I don't let them sit together, see. Break it up. Cause I say I don't want you to work against me now. I want you to work for me. So that's why I broke them up, and I let them know that the reason I did that is because you have recess and after school to socialize. When you're in class, you're going to work in groups. Right now I want you to work. And so that was my philosophy for breaking them up. No friends, no. Cause that will work against you.

In a forum in which I presented some of my research recently, one person felt that some pre-adolescents might object to this kind of deliberately contrived intermixing of ethnicities within the context of the classroom, and that they might resent being sorted by gender and ethnicity in so obvious a fashion. My response is that these objections might be raised under different circumstances, for example in classrooms where the teacher-pupil dynamic was much more "regular" and "ordinary", more "distant" and less "close" as it is in many places. However, as demonstrated in this chapter, the circumstances of this classroom were unique, and such circumstances encouraged and supported other unique situations. The teacher demonstrated a high degree of respect and caring for his students, and in return they trusted that he was always acting in their best interests. Throughout the many hours that I spent in the classroom during the year of my research there, I did not observe any hint of resentment on the part of the students. Because they saw that Mr. Peters never marginalized *any* ethnic minority group in his classroom, they interpreted his actions as he would theirs--in a positive, affirmative manner. The fact that he openly showed appreciation for each culture represented in his classroom helped them realize that this seating system in no way signified a melting-pot interpretation of multicultural education, and a dilution or amalgamation of their individual or collective cultural identities. What it did signify, however, was a bona fide attempt on the part of their teacher, to construct a community of learners operating in an each-one-help-one environment conducive to all learners from all cultures.

In fact, more than a year after my research was completed, I returned to Lantana school on a follow-up social visit to the students and Mr.

Peters. He happened to be on recess supervision duty out on the playground. While talking to him there, he mentioned that although the students from the previous year had graduated up to the next class, they still congregated around him whenever he was on yard duty, and especially when they had a problem that they needed to resolve with another student. The appeal of a good teacher lives on. Once trust is established, children depend on it and the bond strengthens.

Just as he valued ethnic and cultural diversity, Mr. Peters valued the wide range of individual ability represented in his classroom. He did not want his students to feel marginalized in his class because of their inability to achieve academically, or for any other reason. He therefore modeled respect for a diverse range of learning skills and styles among his students. During one of my experiments, he was pleased to see that one of the questions required the students to write a rhyming verse "because children learn in various modalities." Some were good at writing, he explained, and some were good at rhyming and rapping. By tapping into their unique abilities and strengths, Mr. Peters ventured to develop self-esteem and a sense of self-worth and value in all his students:

> We need to adjust to a lot of different learning skills, to the different learning styles of the children. I believe that everybody in my classroom can learn. And I believe that if we learn the different learning styles, we can address those so that we can meet the needs of all of our children.

> We have to learn the total child, and learn that they have other abilities beside, you know, the cognitive domain. Bertie had some learning deficiencies that weren't addressed at any early age when they should have been. But he, he, he's very sharp when it comes to psycho-motor skills; he really excels in that. Things that won't work, he'd fix it, you know. So he is brilliant in that area.

A Sense of Inquiry, A Sense of Involvement

Finally, Mr. Peters undertook to develop a keen sense of inquiry in his students and empowered them to take responsibility for their own learning and advancement. He encouraged them to become active learners, unafraid to question people in authority and challenge their ideas. He urged them to be confident in expressing their own opinions:

> Be curious about things, don't just accept everything that someone says to you. Go to the Library, ask your friends about it, ask your neighbor, ask your big brother, go and read, go to the computer, look for the references, check it out, you know, be curious about it. When we start a topic, be curious about it. Say, I'm gonna learn some more things. Write out the things that you think will be important for you to learn. I don't want you to be passive. I want you to challenge the teacher. Let them know that you are the best that there is. Say I don't understand. Will you please explain it? Exactly right. Teachers won't make a salary if you weren't there. See, I need to work for my salary, so ask me questions. So I want them to use the system.

This teacher therefore had a vision for his students that transcended the usual expectations for low-achieving students. He tried to prepare his class for continued success in school even after they graduated and moved on from his class. He taught them to explore any source of learning that they thought might be potentially rewarding--relative, friend, neighbor, books, computers--and to do so aggressively and unabashedly. In addition, he taught them to take control of their future and of their chances for success, secure in the knowledge that they deserved to have access to excellent teachers and powerful learning. He tried to give his students the invaluable gift of *entitlement*, a quality that most successful students in mainstream populations come to school with, but one that is scarcely found among, low socioeconomic, ethnic minority school populations. As Darling-Hammond affirms in her recent book, he taught them that each and every one of them had a right to learn (Darling-Hammond, 1997). He not only taught well, but prepared his students to demand good teaching after they left him by developing a strong sense of character and self-worth, and a hunger for learning and inquiry. He wanted to change their thinking about education and their experiences pertaining thereto, by changing the way they approached their own education.

Finally, Mr. Peters tried to involve his parents in the education of their children and in building collaborative school-family partnerships, documented as one characteristic of successful language-minority and ethnic minority schools (Lucas, Henze & Donato, 1990; Epstein, 1995). Mr. Peters invited his parents to visit the classroom at any time, to call or send him a note if there was a problem. He solicited the cooperation of his parents in motivating students, and urged them to keep him informed about changes in the family situation and living circumstances that might affect the performance of his students:

> I tell my parents that my classroom is always open. Please come in and see what I'm teaching. You need to know. Come in and sit around and ask the kids what they are learning. You know, be a participant in their child's education. Have a place at home where they can sit quietly and study. Ah, make sure that your kid, your child gets adequate rest, good nutritious food, well I don't go into food, but just plenty of rest and a place to study, so they won't be distracted by the radio. Have a time that you want your child to study, that's right, and you know, we talk, we talk, and it sounds as though they're cooperative, because as I say, I respect my parents.

Although I saw only three drop-in parent visits during my time in the classroom (apart from pre-arranged parent conferences), every parent with whom I spoke praised Mr. Peters' excellence as a teacher. Although his discipline techniques were firm and tough, his parents along with other faculty and staff, knew that he was a strong advocate for their children and that he loved and respected them. Parents seemed to appreciate the opportunities that their students had to benefit from the care, concern and dedication that they encountered in the classroom under Mr. Peters' direction. His earnestness and dedication earned him the affection and respect of his students, and his commitment to culture as the bedrock for learning and literacy, made his classroom an excellent place for my cognition-comprehension research study.

Church-Based Discipline

Mr. Peters incorporated the culture-based routines and rituals of the Black Church into the strategies that he used for classroom control. This is an area that has been explored by other researchers (Foster, 1995). His technique was to translate the church-appropriate behavior and comportment of that milieu rooted in the psyche and culture of so many Black children, into the situation of the classroom. In so doing, he reaped the benefits of good discipline by building on a tradition and background of experience that he shared with many of his students.

A slim African American man of about five feet eight inches, Mr. Peters describes himself as "a humble farm boy from the South". He is proud of the fact that he and his siblings had the opportunity to attend college and earn Bachelor's degrees. He was raised in the strong tradition of the Black Baptist Church, and is imbued with its rituals and traditions. He dresses formally for school--long sleeves, tie and vest--in the style of African Americans dressed for Sunday Church.

Like him, many of the students in his class are being raised in the church themselves. In East Tall Tree, there is an ironic juxtaposition of churches with liquor stores and bars. Churches are more numerous, however, and many of the adults in the community attend regularly on Sundays, taking their children and grandchildren along with them. During their pre-adolescent years, the youth tend to be staunch church-goers, singing in the church choir and participating in church activities with the encouragement and approval of the adult members. One cannot claim that all of the students in Mr. Peters' class are church-goers (I myself attended church in the community a few times during my research there, and noticed that there were many children and youth present), but it appears that enough of them are familiar with its routines and traditions to influence the entire group in following some of the church-based routines that Mr. Peters incorporated into his classroom.

Seating Procedures

One such routine was the seating procedure that he taught his students to follow when they entered or exited the classroom. They usually observed this routine at the beginning of each morning and afternoon session before class started, or at times during the day when the entire class had to leave the room either to go next door for their Math/ Science period or further down the hall to the Computer Lab. In the routine, the appointed Class Monitor for that day assumed the role comparable to that of Church Usher on Sundays. Taking her or his position of leadership at the head of the class, she or he directed the group to stand or sit in unison or to exit in single file. The students performed each action in response to their leader's direction. With arms outstretched, palms facing downward and slowly moving towards the floor and back to her sides, the monitor gave the signal to sit. Similarly, with arms outstretched, palms facing upward and slowly moving towards the ceiling, she gave the signal to stand. The signal to exit the classroom was given when the monitor put her left hand behind her back, and held it there while she pointed to the door with her right hand, palm up, fingers held together, and body slightly angled. Everyone responded (in silence) to each prompt by sitting, standing, or exiting the room row by row according to the monitor's instructions.

These classroom seating procedures represent direct borrowings from the Black Church where assigned ushers formally welcome members and visitors on Sunday morning, and escort them to their seats. The class monitor's hand signals and general body language also paralleled the directives of the Choir Leader, and as in Church, there is no speaking during these routines because the entire act is non-verbal. Further, the standing, sitting and exiting patterns described above are also reminiscent of the motions of the minister signaling his congregation to sit or stand according to the requirements of specific parts of the church service.

In effect therefore, Mr. Peters transported the familiar concept of church into the classroom, with all the connotations of respect, order, and reverence that the seating routine in that venue engendered, and from which he was able to reap similar benefits. Aside from using the routine for entrance and exit purposes, he also used it for pulling the class back under his jurisdiction, and reintroducing order when things got chaotic. At such times, he would beckon the appointed Class Monitor to assume her position in front of the class and initiate the routine. The students were trained to obey the instructions of the Class Monitor unconditionally. I once heard Mr. Peters remind the class that the monitor was carefully chosen because of that person's leadership potential, and therefore deserved their attention:

> I pick somebody who has leadership qualities to be the Class Monitor. And when he or she is standing here, you'd better obey him or her. See, like I told you, this is *your* seventh grade class. I had *my* seventh grade class years ago. This is yours, and you've got to run it right.

This comment had the dual effect of raising the level of respect for the role and person of the monitor, as well as improved discipline. Sometimes Mr. Peters even went on to extol the qualities of the individual(s) he chose as class monitor, such that in addition to increasing the self-esteem of that person, he set a goal of excellence for the other students to emulate. Since the position of Class Monitor was a rotating one, he was essentially reminding the class that they were all potential leaders; he was also urging self-respect, since their turn might come up soon. The element of psychology implicit here is that they would expect respect and cooperation when *they* serve as monitors, so they should give the same to others who have their turn now.

Clap and Click Routine

Another routine that Mr. Peters used to manage his class, one reminiscent of the call-and-response tradition of the Black church (Smitherman, 1986), is the "clap and click" routine, variations of which are also widely used in mainstream classes. The words describe the two actions involved in the routine that teachers use to gain the attention of their class at times during the day when they wish to communicate important information to them. If at a moment's notice Mr. Peters wanted to get his students' full attention, he would stand squarely in the center of the room and begin the clap and click routine. Beginning with both arms aligned straight down on either side, he would raise them both slowly with palms outstretched and clap them together in the air above his head. Then as he lowered them again, he would click with both hands simultaneously, using the thumb and middle finger of both hands, and repeat that routine for any length of time from a few seconds to about a minute, depending on how long it took for the entire class to respond with absolute quiet. In responding, the students answered the signal by repeating the claps and clicks that they heard in exact rhythm, the sound gradually growing as more students joined in, until it filled the room. Mr. Peters would vary the number of claps and clicks he made in a rhythmical pattern until everyone was responding by copying his pattern in unison and the class became attentive and eventually quiet. Then he would make an announcement and the class would act on it or return to their work.

This practice was very effective in getting the attention of the students because it prompted them to stop their current activity and focus their attention on the kinesthetics of the routine. They also needed to do this to remember the intricacies of the pattern, e.g. how many claps and how many clicks, in order to answer the teacher's call. One difference that I observed between Mr. Peters' clap and click routine, and that of other mainstream teachers that I've witnessed elsewhere, was the complexity of the rhythmic pattern that Mr. Peters demonstrated in his routine. It included a marked variation in time and tempo, and in the length and complexity of each "phrase". These characteristics made it unique and distinctive, and reminiscent of the complex ring shouts of South Carolina Sea Island churches (Carawan, 1989). The students also enjoyed the challenge of imitating it.

Tough love discipline: "In Loco Parentis"

In a doctoral dissertation based on the topic of creating success through family in an African American elementary public school in

Georgia, Willis reports that the conceptualization of schooling as a family affair led to significantly positive outcomes in the education of African American elementary school children in the South (Willis, 1995). Mr. Peters' demonstrated a similar approach, also with positive outcomes. He held high expectations for his students, and built up an atmosphere of support in the classroom that enabled them to perform and achieve. But when they misbehaved or fell short of his expectations, he behaved like an irate parent, walking back and forth in the front of the class preaching at the students, while expecting them to sit quietly and listen. The understanding at these times was that they had overstepped their boundaries, and that he was reining them back in with a tongue lashing. The tacit understanding was that he loved them like a parent would, and that he cared about them enough to be upset when they misbehaved. On one occasion when a student called "Damion", (a pseudonym), had behaved (in Mr. Peters' words) "out of line", he said:

> You'd better take that attitude and throw it in the waste basket. Damion is good; he helps set up the computer center, clean our blackboard, pass out the papers . . .he does a lot of good stuff. But he's got one problem, and we're working on it. He's got an attitude problem. If we could fix that, he'll be a good student. And I'll have to give him that trophy (pointing to a trophy placed up high on a ledge) by the end of the year. We're working on it.

Thus Mr. Peters remonstrates with the student, but does it in a way that allows him to save face, an example of the kind of balanced approach that he tends towards in these situations. Typically, he first recognizes the person's good qualities along with any areas in need of improvement. Then he addresses his speech to the offender indirectly, using the third person singular pronoun ("he...he...he") as if the person weren't actually there. While allowing Mr. Peters the opportunity to make his points, this strategy also helped the offender to hold on to his dignity by distancing him from the outburst. This technique allowed him to berate an individual student for his or her wrongdoing, while reminding the class that the teacher is still a benevolent person, as is the student in question.

Again, much like a parent, he was good at wringing a whole lecture out of a relatively small issue, or allowing one incident to piggy-back on another and to extend his outburst. These lectures became another demonstration of caring which the students did not fail to perceive.

During the Damion episode, for example, Patricia and Pamela started whispering to each other, and this action became the cue for a heightened onslaught:

> I'm talking, so you don't need to be talking right now; if somebody is talking to you, you'd better ignore that person, and I'll deal with them; I'll get *them* in trouble. Don't take up my time, because I'll take up your time. And every time I'll win, you see. So don't take up my time. Be quiet now. We have work to do. I'm here to educate you. That's why I'm here. So don't waste time, class. You see, time wasted is forever lost. Lost to me as a teacher and lost to you as a student.

Balancing Praise and Punishment

Mr. Peters did not spend all his time remonstrating with his class, however. When he was pleased with their work or behavior, he offered outbursts of praise that matched his outbursts of rebuke in their sincerity and intensity. Indeed he seemed to praise more frequently than he rebuked. One day when everything seemed to be going well with their work and behavior, he encouraged his students with the following spontaneous outburst:

> See, I like a big class, and I like the class when they are sitting up straight. Sit up straight please class. Your body language tells me a lot about the way you feel . . .your attitude. And I want that to be right. A big class gives me a sense of control. And I like that. . . Thank you Latisha, for sharing out the papers quickly and quietly. See, that makes my day when you behave and work this well. I think I'm going to have to let these children out early for recess today. If they keep behaving this well, there's nothing else to do but let them go early. See, if you behave like Latisha, I guarantee you'll have no problems when you do that. Because it means you are growing up. [You are] becoming mature, successful teenagers. And I like that. . You see, when you make me feel this good, I like it. Because when I feel good about myself, I feel good about other people too. See, that's how it works.

As the final two sentences of this excerpt show, the teacher uses language during his spontaneous praise monologue, to model some of the characteristics and behaviors, not merely of a good student, but of a successful person. He is therefore teaching more than mere school stuff, as exemplified by his wish that they would come to "feel good about [themselves] and other people too". Like a surrogate parent, he is interested in developing the whole child. Like a good parent, he is teaching not only by precept, but by example. True to his word that day, he rewarded them by letting the class out early for recess.

Professing Love and Trust

One of the ways Mr. Peters helped the students feel good about themselves and each other was by openly expressing his love for them and his trust in them. At the end of another good day, as he turned to write the homework assignment on the blackboard, I recorded his words:

> See, I trust you guys now, I could turn my back and write up the homework on the blackboard. I told you guys already-- when I first started teaching, I didn't trust those kids. I would never turn my back on those kids. I always stood and watched them straight in the eye, like this (turns around, folds his arms and puts on a straight, serious mien). But you see, I trust you guys. I could turn, and I know you guys would still behave yourselves.

Despite the focus on class control and discipline therefore, Mr. Peters created in his classroom the kind of caring community discussed above. The theme of trust and love kept recurring in our post-study interview sessions:

> It goes right back to that love, that deep concern. And you can't get that in a university, it's just something to that, to care for them or not, and these kids are so sensitive, they will know. They know the truth. I know. I know a lot of problems come up here today, and I know it. I indicated to the teachers that sometimes, you know, we have to stop and check ourselves, and see where we are coming from, because if you show the least bit of not caring, or you know . . . distrust toward the kids, they pick it up. And instead of them working for you, they work against you. They are very sensitive. They see that love.

He constantly let his students know that he cared about them:

I let them know that they're special, and I love them. I just love children. They are so nice. And I think you just got to. I respect them. I do so respect them. Then they give it back to me. And I think that's the main thing. And I tell them that constantly. To me [my] children are Number 1. They are our most important product, our children. These children will be our leaders of tomorrow, so that's why we must look after them today, and that goes for a lot of it, like socially and educationally. . . all of my children, they are so smart and so capable. So. . . the first thing I do is develop trust in them. And let them know I trust them and they have to trust me. And if you can develop that trust, then everything just falls into place, they develop respect, and everything, all the different life styles which we teach the children at school and which I believe in.

It became obvious early in the year that these feelings were reciprocal. One student seemed to speak on behalf of the whole class when he said to me : "Well, I like Mr. Peters because he like us too. And we know he like us, so. . . " Mr. Peters managed to create and nurture a strong bond with his students of the kind that a loving parent establishes with a child. He invested as much time and energy with his students as he needed to keep them on the right path. For example, Mr. Peters dealt with all his students' discipline problems himself in the classroom. This was unlike many teachers, including the previous one, who constantly sent misbehaving kids out to the office. There were definite benefits to this approach. By dealing with the problem himself, the misbehaving student was not robbed of valuable in-class time, and was spared the embarrassment and degradation of a conference with the principal. Furthermore, it reinforced the reality that the responsibility for good behavior and discipline rested squarely with Mr. Peters and his students within the boundaries of the classroom. Although they balked at Mr. Peters' "preaching", the students invariably straightened up their act after he chided them, because they seemed to understand that he genuinely wished to see them succeed.

Chapter Summary

Mr. Peters' techniques for motivating, inspiring, and managing his students therefore consisted of a confluence of traditional approaches and more imaginative culture-based strategies, communicated by way of both verbal and non-verbal discourse. On the one hand, he had high expectations of his students, and unlike other teachers, he did not succumb to the lack of discipline that they came to him with. Nor did he treat them like "throw-away kids," by merely marking time in the classroom instead of actively teaching. He was not afraid to set limits to their behavior and conduct in the classroom (and on the playground also, I came to observe, when his duties took him there). He created an environment that made it possible for them to live up to his high expectations, and counted on their help in doing so. He chided, lectured and rebuked them both publicly and privately when necessary, but he did this always from a position of parental-like love and caring. Because his students recognized this, and trusted in him (he often referred to them as "my children"), this gave him license to stretch them to achieve more than they normally would have done. On the other hand, he also praised them lavishly when they behaved well and worked hard, or when an individual or small group did something kind, thoughtful and deserving of acclaim. He continually held up the good example of one or more among them for the benefit of all. Figure 4.2 portrays these elements of successful practice that Mr. Peters honed and that were discussed in this chapter.

It is not my intention in characterizing Mr. Peters, to portray a sanctified, larger-than-life image of an elementary-middle school teacher. It is undoubtedly true that he demonstrated qualities of excellence in his chosen lifetime career, that he loved all his students, and enjoyed teaching them. It is also true that he had attributes that worked for him in his teaching--he could be kind, gentle, firm and fierce. But always he was fair, and his students recognized this. But he also had difficulties, tensions, and frustrations with the high turnover rate of students in the school, with unexplained absences, and with getting some of the students to share the vision of success that he held for them all. But he was charismatic, and keenly attuned to the needs of ethnic minority school populations, and his techniques and approaches are worthy of emulation.

Mr. Peters' success in creating an upbeat, nurturing atmosphere in the classroom helped turn around the behavior and increase the academic potential of his students. The fact that he believed in utilizing the cultural background in order to reach and connect with them, and to enhance their schooling experiences, made Mr. Peters' class a particularly good fit for the cultural-cognitive theoretical framework of my research study. It also coincided with the wisdom of empirical research undertaken in other ethnic minority student populations (Lee,

1991; Au & Mason, 1981 in Erickson, 1988). In addition, the new classroom environment supported and encouraged pride in academic achievement so that the students were motivated to respond positively to my requests for their involvement and participation. The new discipline and sense of mutual respect and cooperation that existed in the classroom made the collaborative work and discussion that formed a part of my study possible. Finally, his thinking was innovative and he welcomed the opportunity for his students and himself to learn from active research.

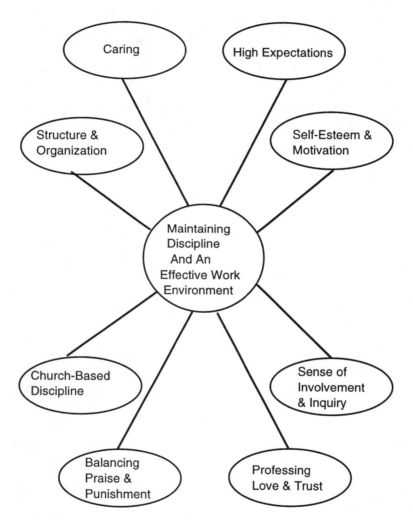

Figure 4.2. Elements of Successful Practice in an Ethnically Diverse Middle School Classroom

PART II

NARRATIVE STRUCTURAL ANALYSIS, RESEARCH DESIGN AND METHODS

CHAPTER 5

STRUCTURAL ANALYSIS OF THE SIX STUDY NARRATIVES

At the very least educators should help children fulfill their expectations about stories. We can do this by giving children stories that have sufficient structure for them to grasp. We should relieve them of the burden of coping with themelessness.

John T. Guthrie, 1985

Overview

The structural analysis of the narratives selected for this cognition-comprehension study is central to its conceptual foundations and to the design and analysis of the work. It is therefore the main theme that underlies Part 11 of the book, the chapters that comprise the Narrative Structural Analyses and Research Design and Methods. Chapter 5 is devoted largely to a structural analysis of the narratives, while Chapter 6 focuses more directly on issues of study design and method, with an emphasis on comprehension question construction and its interconnection with story structure. Two principles motivated this approach. Firstly, I believe that an analysis of the components vital to the structure of well-formed narratives--namely theme, character, plot, and setting--leads to a deep and thorough understanding of the narratives qua stimulus materials. Secondly, I propose that this process of structural analysis can be used to formulate a reliable system for the generation of comprehension questions based on the narratives. For example, questions that ask students to consider character qualities might issue from episodes in the narratives where that character's feelings reach a high level of emotional intensity as the plot line develops and peaks, revealing traits not previously alluded to. Or a question that asks students to problem-solve might be derived from an episode where a certain character's actions are portrayed negatively, thus opening up an opportunity for the reader to evaluate those actions critically, and to recommend an alternative course. This approach to question construction makes common sense, and is a natural and intuitive approach to comprehension questioning. But it tends to be used in a holistic, and sometimes "hit and miss" manner. Instead, I use this approach explicitly, systematically, and in a clearly articulated manner in this section of the book as a model for teachers and other practitioners.

In this chapter, the four sequential phases involved in the process of narrative structural analysis as used in the study are described in turn. They are 1) Selection of Narratives, 2) Exposition of Narrative Components, 3) Segmentation and Summary of Narrative Episodes, and 4) Production and Refinement of Narrative Map.

Phase 1: Selection of Narratives

During Phase 1, I selected six narratives for the study, based on a survey of dozens of stories. This process largely involved the weeding out of material that was unsuitable for my purposes (for several reasons including incomprehensibility of certain forms of dialect), then narrowing down the options that remained until I found material that matched the guidelines established for the study. My conceptual framework required narratives from two genres--traditional Black folk tales and contemporary African American short stories.

Many story collections carried tales organized around themes. Among others, there were supernatural tales, revenge tales, love tales, animal tales, origin tales, funny tales, people tales and heroic tales. I approached this task initially by finding one dozen stories from diverse genres that were distinctive from one another. Following this initial selection, I was aided in the final choice of tales by Kennell Jackson, a Stanford Professor of History and Afro-American studies who has a keen interest in African American folklore, Black culture and historical achievement (Jackson, 1996), and by Diane Ferlatte, a professional African American storyteller from Oakland, California. My final selection strategy for folk tales was guided by several factors, including authenticity, language comprehensibility, thematic relevance and sound story structure. Contemporary short stories were selected from the pool of African American short stories found in the students' past and current basal reader series. All story selections were made to conform to the design variable of readability level, and modified to meet the length requirement.

Authenticity

I considered folk tales to be "authentic" when they were preserved and reproduced in a manner that upheld the linguistic and thematic integrity of the original versions. Some folk tales trace their roots to far-away countries and are centuries old, while others, especially the Gullah tales, originated in the Southern states. But Gullah, a Southern Black dialect, is not readily understood by outsiders, primarily because it is a dialect of speech and not writing. As one folklorist acknowledges (Jaquith, 1981), the straight Gullah language can be "incomprehensible to the uninitiated" (Foreword). The reason is that the language is often reproduced idiosyncratically, and folklorists who use Gullah in recording stories (for example Dance, 1978) sometimes produce excellent renditions in collections that are linguistically difficult to read and understand. I tried to avoid this obstacle in selecting stories for the study.

Language Comprehensibility

Other folklorists try to retain the flavor and spirit of the original tale, without compromising the comprehensibility of the stories. They rely primarily on Standard English and include instances of Black dialect usage to maintain the integrity and authenticity of the original version. The vernacular is maintained as an important cultural marker, but idiosyncratic versions are avoided. Tales are usually recorded directly from the oral tradition and only such changes made as are needed for clarity and understanding. Following these guidelines, I chose tales from the work of folklorist Julius Lester (Lester, 1989), whose principles for folk tale collection seemed to reflect these guidelines. In her introduction to *The Tales of Uncle Remus* (Lester, 1987), Baker suggests that Lester "(told) Black folktales perfectly, (because) he used the voice and language of Black people." In his own words, he described the language he uses as "a modified contemporary southern Black English, a combination of standard English and Black English where sound is as important as meaning" (Lester 1987, Foreword).

Thematic Relevance and Good Structure

I made selections that I thought would be thematically relevant and interesting to urban youth for both the folk tale and non-folk tale genres, intending to keep the students involved and engaged. Themes of selected stories involved the conflict of child-parent relationships, the lure of truancy, the intensity of a young love affair, the agony of losing one's best friend, the struggles of a physically disabled youth, and the challenges of adolescence. In addition, I looked for tales with a strong structural base in keeping with the general significance of story structure to well-formed narratives (Lukens, 1976, Applebee, 1979), to folk tales in particular (Propp, 1977; Bower, Black & Turner, 1985), and to the overall conceptualization and design of the study.

Length and Readability Level

Finally, I selected folk tales that fulfilled the requirements of the design variables of length and readability level. I was able to modify the length of stories (see Note 1) where necessary to fit the stipulations of short, medium, and long stories, but paid careful attention to finding stories that corresponded to low, average and high readability levels (see Note 2). The three folk tales I decided on according to these guidelines were: *The Woman and the Tree Children* (S#1), an African (Masai tale), *Brer Rabbit Falls in Love* (S#3), (an African-American tale), and *Why Apes Look Like People* (S#5), (also an African-American tale). The three contemporary narratives selected were *The Runaway Cow* (S#2), *Remembering Last Summer* (S#4), and *Ride the Red Cycle*

(S#6). As the odd versus even numbers suggest, the folk tales and contemporary narratives were alternated in the design so that Story #1, a folk tale was followed by Story #2, a non-folk tale, and so on.. The number designations therefore reflect the order in which the stories were presented to the children.

Table 5.1 provides the titles and other design characteristics (story genre, readability level, and length) of the narratives I selected for use in my study. All of the stories carried illustrations that I reproduced in color and attached to the end of each narrative, making the "ethnic" quality of the stories discernible in both the auditory and visual modalities.

Story #	Story Genre	Readability Level	Length (# words)
S#1	African folk tale	RL 4	690
S#2	Basal Reader	RL 3	860
S#3	Af.Am. folk tale	RL 4	1553
S#4	Basal Reader	RL 4	1590
S#5	Af.Am. folk tale	RL 5	1819
S#6	Basal Reader	RL 5	1982

Table 5.1. List of Stories used in the Comprehension-Cognition Study.

All the stories met the requirements of the conceptual framework in terms of their readability levels (which were calculated on the original, full length versions), except for Story #1, The Woman and the Tree children. Ideally, this story should have been a Grade 3 readability level in order to match the level of the other selection in the first dyad, Story #2. But those who helped select the stories agreed that this narrative should be retained because of its structural and thematic excellence. Its inclusion was also justified because it was significantly shorter than the second story, a factor that might serve to compensate for its slightly higher readability level. The first two stories thus had a readability level of Grade 3-4, the second set had a readability level of Grade 4, and the third pair of stories had a readability level of Grade 5.

The six stories used in the study are included in the Appendix. S#3 and S#4 appear in their original unabridged form for copyright reasons.

Phase 2: An Exposition of Narrative Components

The structural foundations of each narrative selection is analyzed in turn, and the principal differences between the two narrative genres in the study design--folk tales versus non-folk tales--are discussed.

Generally, in folk tales, narrative features represent the archetype of person and behavior--the elements of theme, plot, character and setting dramatize immeasurable possibilities. Characters tend toward prototypes--they have a larger-than-life dimension that require "the willing suspension of disbelief". They may involve supernatural events or figures, talking animals and trees, and so on. Themes are didactic and moralistic, and the plot line tightly drawn. Usually the tale has survived the rigorous test of time because of the significance of its message and the skillful interweaving of narrative elements. There is no room for superfluous characters; every folk tale personality has a distinct role to play. Folk tales are also characterized by an appealing literary style that includes repetition, rhyme and rhythm, and other embellishments common to the oral genre.

By contrast, the non-folk tale or contemporary narrative is generally not influenced by the same rules. Their themes are relevant but realistic, their characters familiar, and the plots and setting connecting them are often within our immediate literary and experiential reach. The author tends to be more concerned with the message of the moment, as it were. The story line is built around a specific theme in a particular time and place, and the onus of creating archetypal characters is often not as prevalent. The fabric of structure need not be as tightly circumscribed around the narrative elements of character, plot, theme and setting, yet the short story succeeds because these structural elements are strong.

These distinctions may appear more dichotomous than they really are, however. Often the above characteristics are discernible in the two genres in a general way, but they are not always obvious and distinctive. For instance, a folk tale may occasionally seem to fit more closely into the mold of the non-folk tale, and vice versa. In both genres, the plot line is defined by its rising and falling action, since most good stories have a moment of climax and denouement.

THE FOLK TALES

The Woman and the Tree Children (S #1)

In Story #1 (S #1) *The Woman and the Tree Children*, the old woman is more than a specific person in a specific place and time dealing with specific circumstances. Her character is the instantiation of a human prototype. She represents the reality of human error and the pain of the resulting tragedy, namely the loss of the children she has waited for all her life. In this African folk tale, the narrative elements of character and theme are therefore archetypal. The old woman is not allowed another chance at motherhood once she makes her first slip. Her one mistake, yelling at the kids, earns her a life without the children she yearned for so much, and dooms her to perpetual sadness. Such absolutism is typical of the folk tale genre and supports its didactic and moralistic purpose. The message is sharp, strong and clear--happiness is not to be taken for granted because it can be snatched away as quickly as it was bestowed. The story of the *Olode* folk tale mentioned in Chapter 2, is similar to *Tree Children* in terms of the thematic base on which the story is built. In fact, the existence of many versions of the same folk tale is not an uncommon phenomenon, although there are obvious differences here. In both tales however, the moral we take away is that the good things in our life that are hard-earned are to be nurtured and valued. It behooves us to be cautious and careful when we achieve happiness lest we lose all, since happiness is fragile.

In addition to the universality of its theme, the plot dimension in *Tree Children* also emphasizes the child's perspective, a feature that I felt would capture the imaginations of the study participants. In the story, the children are wronged by the mother figure, and then become embroiled in a parent-child conflict, a situation familiar to adolescents and pre-adolescents. In *The Woman and the Tree Children*, the affective dimension is also prevalent, as the sadness of the children, reinforced by their teary-eyed depiction in both their characterization and the illustration, pulls at our heart strings. The setting changes from the warmth of home to the distant density of the forest and then back home again, only this time the mood is somber.

Brer Rabbit Falls in Love (S #3)

The other folk tales in the study, *Brer Rabbit Falls in Love* (Story #3) and *Why Apes look like People* (Story #5), also have a larger-than-life appeal. For example, in Story #3, the character of Brer Rabbit, the tiny animal who defiantly pursues his evasive young love and secures her, represents the triumph of the underdog in a complex world that is difficult to understand and negotiate. Brer Rabbit does not possess the outward trappings and power of a potential suitor. He is not handsome and rich, but he is smart, brave, witty, determined, and most of all--has feelings like a human being. He becomes sad and depressed because his love is unrequited and the arbitrary scratches he makes in the sand reflect his confusion and desperation. But before he allows his emotions to crash, he activates his crafty mind, and his strength of will and unabashed cunning lead him to think up a ruse that works. If the young lady wants a sign before she agrees to get married, she will get one, even if he has to be both its author and benefactor. At this point the story theme expands to include elements of superstition. He hides out near the house, and sings her a song through a reed. It is a big lie, but it is a strategy that works because it convinces the superstitious girl that her suitor is sincere, and once again the underdog triumphs and he wins the hand of his love in marriage.

There are scores of Brer Rabbit tales with this generic plot type, that is, involving courtship or cunning, but this one seemed particularly relevant to the at-risk student participants in my study. In days of old, the slaves (who brought many of the folk tales we now read from Africa) often resorted to trickery and cunning in attempts to outsmart their masters and alleviate the pain of subjugation. Similarly, the young, diverse students of poor ethnic communities are often forced to resort to creative and unique ways of overcoming adversity and disadvantages in their lives. Characters like Brer Rabbit have thus become heroes and symbols of the power of persistence and the triumph of the underdog over the wealth and dominance of the establishment. Of course, the analogy is not perfect in this story, since Rabbit is not up against a powerful and oppressive master in this particular case, as he is in some others, but he is nonetheless confronted with a difficult situation, and uses his wits to overcome it. The setting in this story is the outdoors and the home of Miz Meadows' daughter, but it might just as well have been the rough circumstances of the students' challenging urban surroundings and communities.

Why Apes Look Like People (S #5)

In Story #5, *Why Apes Look Like People*, the camaraderie with the character of God and his intervention on behalf of the animals is another symbol of the triumph of the disadvantaged and disfranchised over the rich and powerful. There are two standards of behavior presented in this folk tale--right versus wrong or good versus bad. The dichotomies are painted vividly; as in Story #1 above, the dimensions of exaggeration and excess in folk tale character portrayal are stylistic and effective. The forest animals are happy and healthy. Committed to family, they coexist according to the laws of God and nature. On the other hand, the humans, or man-animals (as they are somewhat degradingly yet justifiably called), are ironically depicted as aggressive, violent, and selfish. They pollute the environment, murder harmless creatures when they hunt, and cause their creator God to be sad and disappointed. But they are wealthy and worldly; their possessions are glamorous and attractive and the downtrodden forest animals ask God to transform them into man-animals to give them a chance to protect themselves against their constant threat, and to match up with the power and prestige of the humans. God agrees, but changes his mind at the last minute when he is disillusioned by the new-born greediness of the forest animals who plan to buy fancy new cars and lead promiscuous lifestyles just as men do, once they are changed into man-animals. As a result very few of the animals are allowed to change.

The lesson here is that we should not envy our neighbors their possessions, because their acquisition might bring us misfortune. In a real sense, Story #5 is an old-fashioned morality tale in which the dominant theme that emerges is the fundamental but age-old Chaucerian proverb: Radix malorum est cupiditas--gluttony is the root of all evil. The characters are portrayed in roles that support this theme, as do the plot development and narrative setting. Predictably, the students aligned their support with the innocent forest animals and alluded in their analyses to the need for self-respect, self-direction and self-appreciation in both the literary and the real world. *Why Apes Look Like People* is known as an "origin" tale, a type common in the folk tales of many cultures.

NON-FOLK TALES

The Runaway Cow (S #2)

The first non-folk tale, Story #2, *The Runaway Cow,* is a narrative about a cow named Annette and her devotion to her primary caretaker, Julie. Annette's brother Louis wishes the cow would let him ride on her back just as she lets Julie do, but Annette is a very smart, temperamental cow who rejects any other mount but Julie's. Pete, who has skipped school for the purpose, tries daringly, but is thrown. Although the rustic setting can be alluring, this story probably has the weakest structural base of all the selections. For that reason, it presents the sharpest contrast from the prototype perspective, with the folk tale genre. Apart from the protagonists Annette and Julie, and the truant Pete, the other seven characters in the story are rather poorly drawn--they are not all essential to the successful unfolding of the plot, and the constellation of characters undermines the story structure. One of the narrative analysts (G.B., a Stanford English Professor) who helped with the segmentation of stories into episodes, dubbed it "effete". By the end of the story, one still wonders if the author really needed some of the characters who are included in the narrative (comprehension question #11 actually gave the students an opportunity to address this question). For example neither Louis, Mr. Lovelace, nor the two men seem to advance the plot of the story significantly. But the thematic issues--both the topic of truancy and the theme of the unwavering devotion of a pet--are age-appropriate and relevant, and this factor combined with Annette's feisty and alluring character portrayal, earned the story its inclusion in the final selection.

Remembering Last Summer (S #4)

The next non-folk tale in the study, Story #4, *Remembering Last Summer*, focuses on multiple themes: the value of friendship, the pain of departure, the agony of a dead pet, and the difficulty of facing the inevitable in life. Interpreted through the eyes of a young girl, this story is built around topics that are meaningful to pre-adolescents. The characters are sensitively portrayed, and a unique characteristic of this story is the cross-gender affiliation which it portrays. The protagonist, a girl, "hangs out" with her best friend Bobby, who is a boy in a relationship that is entirely platonic. The girl also has a close relationship with her grandmother. These are some of the features of the story that I felt would be interesting to its readers. This story seemed a good match with the students, given the predominant role that a grandparent (often a grandmother) plays in the upbringing and life of many of the student participants, and the place of esteem and respect that she holds in the culture of African Americans and other ethnic groups.

The plot line rises and falls with the grandmother. She sits in the rocking chair on the porch, and "spends most of her time reading, taking care of her plants, and knitting." The protagonist boasts dispassionately, "I must have a jillion sweaters." But by the middle of the story she has intervened into the center of the drama to fix the torn emotions of her granddaughter whose favorite pet dog Pepper has died sadly and suddenly. By the end of the story, she brings about a happy ending by planting a dogwood tree on Pepper's grave which blossoms regeneratively in the early Spring. The gesture prompts a reaction of healing from the girl: "Then we laughed, and I gave her a big hug. Grandma is one of the most terrific friends I've ever had." Finally, in this particular story, the setting is also congruent with the cultural experiences of the study's ethnic minority student participants. The image of children and adults "hanging out" on the front steps during the warm summer months is reminiscent of many scenes in the community of East Tall Tree where my study is based.

Ride the Red Cycle (S #6)

Story #6 *Ride the Red Cycle* is the story of a determined Black youth, Jerome, who makes his dream to ride a bicycle become a reality despite the fact that he is physically disabled and wheelchair-bound. It is a moving story whose theme I thought the students would empathize with because it addresses some of the issues that arise when an individual is different from the majority. It deals with themes of struggle and frustration--of growing up disabled, and the impact of this circumstance on the dreams and aspirations of a pre-adolescent boy. I thought the students would identify with the character of Jerome and engage meaningfully with the narrative, because many of them might have experienced similar feelings of alienation in their lives. Jerome felt alienated from the rest of his family and friends because of his physical handicap, a fact that his character grapples with; the students would have experienced feelings of alienation as a result of growing up "poor" and "ethnic", compared with the wealthy White San Francisco Bay Area communities which surround them.

There are also other dimensions of theme, character and plot that made this story a suitable selection. As the plot unfolds, and Jerome starts on the path to achieving his dream of riding off into the streets of his neighborhood triumphant on his new three-wheeler, the author unleashes a web of complex character interactions. Jerome fights with his younger sister Liza because she reminds him that it is ridiculous to think he could ride a bike when he can't even walk yet. His older sister Tilly is much more sensitive to his condition and often defends him. As a result, she is more his buddy, and she kindly helps him through the painstaking process of learning to master his new bike. Yet he is sometimes bratty in his behavior towards her, and the episode in which he runs over her feet with his wheelchair is an enigmatic part of the plot. Meanwhile, the thread of his relationship with his mother and father adds another dimension to the fabric of the story. His father is ambivalent to the doctors, and is positive and supportive of him; his mother obeys the doctors who are conservative in their prognosis of Jerome's progress and who recommend against the bike. She is openly critical of her son; she wishes Jerome were more grateful to everyone for their help, and less demanding.

The realities of family conflict and cooperation amidst the backdrop of a difficult situation made Story #6 an appealing one. Finally, the cordial setting of the neighborhood block party and Jerome's final coup in riding off on his bike promised to make reading the story a familiar, rewarding and fulfilling experience.

Phase 3: Segmentation and Summary of Narrative Episodes

Following the selection of the narratives and an exposition of their components, I devised a plan for capturing their essential elements of character, theme, plot, and setting in a way that would lead to a mapping and graphic portrayal of these features. The graphic would represent the unique structure and development of each story dynamically. More importantly, for purposes of the present study, it would be used as an heuristic for generating comprehension questions that were integral to the structure of the narratives. The unit of analysis used for the *Narrative Map* was the episode. The technique of episodic segmentation therefore marked Phase 3 of the narrative analysis process.

After this was done, I summarized the narratives using the episodic segmentation to trace the development of the story through its critical stages--from the introduction of the problem, through the response, to the action taken and its final outcome. In this section, I explain how I achieved this process, and present the summaries that were based on the episodes.

A considerable amount of thought characterized this phase because of its procedural complexity, and its ultimate importance to the study questions. I enlisted the help of eight educators in the Humanities to do the groundwork. They included 2 Linguistics professors, 1 English Literature professor, 1 Education professor, and 4 Ph.D. students, 2 of whom were former English Literature teachers, and all of whom were currently pursuing degrees in the division of Language, Literacy, and Culture. They were all members of the faculty or student body at Stanford University. Each analyst started with an original, unabridged version of the six narratives. They read through each story, marking the points in the stories at which they felt episodic breaks occurred.

The analysts also marked the episodes that in their opinion, signaled points of high and low emotional intensity in the narratives. While doing their analyses they used a numeral, 1, 2, or 3, (1 marked a low level of emotion, 3 a high level) to indicate levels of emotional intensity they felt the characters in all the episodes reached. I planned to use this feature to calibrate the level of high affect that would be represented in the final story map. I also asked the analysts to jot down in the margins any clues that they used in determining where the episodic breaks fell. When they returned the completed narratives to me, I compared the various episodic segments that they had indicated for each story.

In general there was a high degree of agreement both in the number of episodic breaks assigned to each narrative, and in the places in the story that marked them. Where there were discrepancies, I devised a way to resolve the differences while maintaining the integrity of the analysts' work. For example, one analyst consistently marked both minor and major (his terms) episodic breaks in the narratives. After careful consideration, I decided to eliminate the minor breaks since I observed that the major episodic divisions corresponded with the divisions of most of the other analysts (the minor divisions however were useful in helping me decide which parts of the texts to omit in tailoring the excerpts to fit the length variable in the research design). Where there were other discrepancies, I was guided by the majority opinion of the informants in making decisions about where to place the final episodic breaks. In the final analysis, the total number of episodes per story ranged from four (Story #1) to eight (Story #5).

Next, for the record, and for keeping track of the process, I documented the clues that the analysts used for the divisions, based on their jottings and observations and on my own insights. Episodic breaks tended to be signaled by a key word or phrase, sometimes by the beginning of a new paragraph, and sometimes by a change of setting--a shift in time, place, character or scene, like a play in different acts. The analysts found that an episode was sometimes easy to identify and sometimes more difficult depending on the flow of the particular story.

Following the segmenting of the stories into episodes, I undertook to construct comprehensive summaries using the episodic segments as tools for chunking story content. Tables 5.2 to 5.7 represent comprehensive summaries of the six study narratives. The "physical characteristics" of the narratives are described at the beginning of each table. The first column identifies the episode; the second column highlights character and theme using the episode as the segmenting feature. The asterisk at the beginning of any segment signifies an episode of intense emotion, either positive or negative. The third column highlights the setting and plot providing the structural backbone of the story. As mentioned above, this is where the progression of the narrative is indicated beginning from the presentation of the problem to the response through the action taken, and concluding with the resolution of the problem and the final story outcome.

The Woman and the Tree Children by Julius Lester
Origin: African (Masai) Folk tale
Length: Short
Readability Level: Grade 4
Type: Supernatural (Magical) Tale

	Character & Theme	Setting & Plot
EP 1	A very unhappy old woman thought that a husband and children would make her happy.	*At home.* Protagonist is introduced. Problem is raised.
EP 2	The medicine man helped her get some children by filling pots from a sycamore tree with fruit. Then he sent her for a walk.	*Deep in the forest.* Second character is introduced. Promises to help protagonist solve her problem. Response.
EP 3	* When she returned the house was full of happy, hard-working children. She was very happy.	*At home.* The woman's problem is solved. Action.
EP 4	* Then one day, one of the children did something wrong and the woman yelled and insulted them and left to visit a friend. When she returned, the children were gone and she became sad and lonely again. She asked the medicine man for help once more but he failed to respond and she lived sadly forever afterwards.	*At home.* The protagonist transgresses, the solution dissolves and the problem reappears. *Deep in the forest.* Outcome.

Table 5.2. Comprehensive Narrative Summary (Story #1).

The Runaway Cow by Eleanor Lattimore
Origin: Non-Folk Tale
Length: Short
Readability Level: Grade 3

	Character & Theme	Setting & Plot
EP 1	* Annette the cow led a peaceful life. Julie Brown treated her well and in return the cow was very kind to her. Julie's brother Louis was jealous of their relationship.	*The shed door in the meadow.* The protagonist and two supporting characters are introduced. <u>Problem</u> is raised.
EP 2	* One morning at school, Louis wished he could ride on Annette's back like his sister did. Suddenly the children noticed that Pete was riding Annette and was thrown.	*The schoolyard in the meadow.* <u>Response</u>.
EP 3	* Two men came to his assistance but Pete was not hurt. They reprimanded him.	The character in danger gets help. <u>Action</u>.
EP 4	* Louis wondered how Pete succeeded in getting on Annette's back. Julie explained that Annette thought it was she, and Granny offered that the cow was smart.	*At home.*
EP 5	Pete never tried to tide the cow again. He became a good student.	Pete learns a lesson. He changes. <u>Outcome</u>.

Table 5.3. Comprehensive Narrative Summary (Story #2).

Brer Rabbit Falls in Love by Julius Lester
Origin: African-American Folk Tale
Length: Medium
Readability Level: Grade 4
Type: Trickster tale

	Character & Theme	**Setting & Plot**
EP 1	One springtime it was so beautiful that people were rapidly falling in love.	*A beautiful spring day.* Background information.
EP 2	* Brer Rabbit fell in love with Miz Meadows' daughter, and as a result became pale and wan. He told her he was afraid that she might reject him.	*At Miz Meadows's place.* Protagonist is introduced. Miz Meadows and the girls are introduced. <u>Problem</u> is presented.
EP 3	* Brer Rabbit sat by the creek and returned a song to the girl who said he looked lovesick.	*By the creek.* Second (supporting) character is introduced. Gives vital information to the protagonist. <u>Response</u>.
EP 4	* The girl said she was waiting for a sign before agreeing to wed but so far no spell worked. She was offended when Brer Rabbit hinted that he was interested in her.	*Outside Miz Meadows' house.* Protagonist uses information as a catalyst for achieving his own ends. <u>Action</u>.
EP 5	* Brer Rabbit thought up a scheme to give her a sign, crept up to her house, and tricked her with a song.	*Near the path.*
EP 6	* The girl accepted the mysterious song as a sign and the next morning they met and planned marriage.	*By the big pine.* The protagonist and the girl met and are to be married. <u>Outcome</u>.

Table 5.4. Comprehensive Narrative Summary (Story #3).

Remembering Last Summer by Sheila Stroup
Origin: Non-Folk Tale
Length: Medium
Readability Level: Grade 4

	Character & Theme	**Setting & Plot**
EP 1	My old dog Pepper and my neighbor Bobby Nelson were my best friends. The three of us did everything together. Grandma is great too.	Background information. Protagonist and supporting characters are introduced.
EP 2	* Everything was fine. Then one day Bobby and family moved to Ohio. First I was mad, then I became sad. Pepper tried to comfort me.	*At home.* <u>Problem</u> is presented.
EP 3	* Then one night while we were playing, Pepper fell over and died. Daddy wrapped him up in a rug and we buried him outside. I became immensely numb and sad afterwards.	Another <u>problem</u> is introduced. Favorite pet dies. <u>Response</u>. Protagonist is dejected.
EP 4	* Grandma invited me to sit on her lap, rocked me, hummed to me and comforted me. We walked by the river, and on the way home Grandma planted a tree on his grave.	Grandma soothes protagonist. <u>Action</u>.
EP 5	* It is Spring already. Today after school, I followed Grandma to the backyard. We hugged and laughed as we admired the pretty flowering dogwood tree.	<u>Outcome</u>. Protagonist is happy once again.

Table 5.5. Comprehensive Narrative Summary (Story #4).

Structural Analysis of the Six Study Narratives

Why Apes Like People by Julius Lester
Origin: Folk Tale; Length: Long
Readability Level: Grade 5
Type: Origins Tale

	Character & Theme	Setting & Plot
EP 1	* After God made the world, only animals lived in it. They lived cautiously, sensibly, and happily until one day a deer got shot by a human.	*The forest.* First character is introduced. <u>Problem</u> is raised.
EP 2	Meanwhile the father deer overheard the birds talking about one of their kind getting shot also.	*The forest.* <u>Problem</u> remains.
EP 3	Then the hawk observed the curious behavior of a human. The animals discussed the strange creature's behavior with the other animals and decided to call a meeting.	*The forest.* <u>Response</u>.
EP 4	The Rabbit chaired the meeting, and all the animals agreed to send representatives up to heaven to ask God about man.	*The forest.* <u>Action</u>.
EP 5	* Animals complained that man was upsetting forest's balance of life. God grew sad.	*Visiting God in heaven.*
EP 6	* God then reassured them that everything would be okay when they returned to the forest. But man's behavior worsened.	*Back in the forest.*
EP 7	* The animals returned to God and asked him to make them as powerful as man. At first God agreed. But the animals' behavior deteriorated. God became depressed, disappointed.	*Back in heaven.* <u>Outcome</u>.
EP 8	God then changed his mind. As a result, only a few animals were able to benefit from the plan to change into man-animals. That is why only the primates look like people today.	<u>Outcome</u>.

Table 5.6. Comprehensive Narrative Summary (Story #5).

Ride the Red Cycle by Harriette Robinet
Origin: Non-Folk Tale
Length: Long
Readability Level: Grade 5

	Character & Theme	**Setting & Plot**
EP 1	* Jerome hated the fact that he was different. He was a physically disabled youth, took special classes, and everyone always tried to help him. He felt stifled by it all.	Background information sets stage. <u>Problem</u> is presented.
EP 2	* Jerome asked his father for a tricycle. He dreamed of riding fast and impressing the public. His mother worried about doctors' warnings against it; his father agreed to it.	*At the table.*
EP 3	* Sister Tilly, his advocate, accompanied them to the bike shop. Overcome with excitement at his new bike, and oblivious to his sister's feelings, Jerome wheeled his chair over her foot. This upset her.	*At the bike shop.* <u>Response</u>.
EP 4	* Papa worked hard at outfitting the bike for Jerome, while Mama was nervous about it, and thought him ungrateful. But with Tilly's aid and devotion, he practiced hard and learned to ride well.	*Ay home. Outdoors.* <u>Action</u>.
EP 5	* At the block party, Jerome performed wonderfully on his bike. He bowed with flourish, and said thanks to his whole family including Mama, something that was previously difficult for him to do. The crowd applauded mildly.	*At the neighborhood block party.* <u>Outcome</u>.
EP 6	* Then Jerome got up and walked and everyone clapped and cheered. His dream had come true and his entire family was delighted.	<u>Outcome</u>.

Table 5.7. Comprehensive Narrative Summary (Story #6).

Phase 4: Production and Refinement of Narrative Map

The final stage of narrative structural analysis involved the production of a graphic or Narrative Map, resulting from the refinement of the processes involved in Phases 2 and 3 above. Using the episodic analysis as its foundation, the Map presents a graphic portrayal of narrative structure. Figures 5.8 to 5.13 below display the structural features of each narrative in turn. A comprehensive key is attached to each map.

Because of its dependence on symbol, the graphic is a more elegant and economical version of narrative structural analysis than its preceding manifestations, yet it incorporates additional dimensions and structural elements that are significant to stories. The Map depicts the salient characteristics of story, including the subtler nuances of character interaction and involvement. It also includes the affective component that often drives story. The Narrative Map uses symbols, lines, and variations of shade to represent the scope and sequence of narrative structure. It is a conceptual device that is potentially useful in understanding the grammar, structure or composition of a story. In the present study, it is used as a tool to guide the process of comprehension question construction for the six narratives involved in the study (details provided in Chapter 6).

The Narrative Map: An Explication

Using the separate episodes numbered EP 1, EP 2, and so on as the units on the X-axis, and the individual narrative characters identified by name as the units on the Y-axis, I created an outward frame or shell in which I would build the structural features of the narratives. Next I filled the cells--in columns under the separate episodes (EP 1, EP 2 etc.) and in rows beside the individual character units (Woman, Medicine Man, Tree Children, as in Story #1) with rectangular icons in a character-by-episode entry that represented all the episodes that the narrative contained, and all the characters portrayed in the story. Each icon represented the intersection between a specific character and a corresponding episode in the narrative text such that the graphic now contained the fundamental elements of the structure of a story--the episodic segments in which plot, theme, and setting are embedded, and the characters portrayed.

In the next phase of analysis, I focused on the centrality of the characters' involvement in each episode, their interaction with other narrative characters, and the level of emotional intensity they displayed in the dramatic action of each episode. If the character was significantly involved in a particular episode, I drew a continuous heavy horizontal line next to that character's name from the beginning of any specific episode, and continuing through to the end of the episode with a break in the middle of the line to position the icon representing that character's involvement in the episode. A heavy horizontal line therefore depicted maximum character involvement in an episode. By the same token, a broken horizontal line depicted a character's minimal involvement in a particular episode. In that case, a line was also drawn next to a character name from the beginning of any specific episode, continuing through to the end of that episode with a break in the middle of the line to position the icon reflecting that character's involvement in the episode.

A character was judged to be maximally involved if his or her dramatis persona played a major role in an episode. Usually the protagonist was maximally involved in many episodes since the narrative builds around him or her. Other characters tended to be maximally involved in particular episodes that featured them as affecting the action in one way or another, but usually not in all the episodes of the drama. In some episodes where the supporting characters are not featured, their name might still be mentioned or their role alluded to, but their actual involvement in the episode remains minimal. Such a character was judged to be minimally involved. For example in Story #1, The Woman and the Tree children, the author focused on the old woman in every episode of the story, and her role was critical throughout. Not so in the case of the medicine man or the children whose characters peaked and diminished depending on the episode that was being highlighted.

Maximal interaction between characters was depicted by a solid vertical line extending from the character icon in the first episode where the character has an interaction with another character to the icon of the character(s) with whom he or she interacts throughout that episode. Minimal interaction between characters was depicted by a broken line similarly extending from the character icon in the first episode where the character has an interaction with another character, to the icon of the character(s) with whom he or she interacts throughout that episode. A character was judged to be interacting maximally with another character when there is a confrontation that has significant consequences for either or both parties. A character was judged to be interacting minimally with another character when the confrontation is of little or no consequence or when it never actually occurs but is merely suggested. For example in the first narrative Story #1, the woman gets very angry with the tree children in the third episode when they do something that upsets her. As a result, she screams at them in anger:

> It is no wonder you did that. You are nothing but a child of the tree. You are all nothing but children of the tree! One can't expect any better from children born out of a tree (see Appendix, Story #1, E.3).

The outcome is that the children run away from home. In my narrative graphic therefore, the woman and the tree children are deemed to be interacting maximally in this episode. In the final episode when the woman returns to the medicine man and asks him what she should do, he simply shrugs his shoulders and says he does not know. Then the woman leaves. In my analysis, that interaction between them was judged to be minimal. There is no verbal communication between them (although the non-verbal signal may be deemed significant, especially since his reaction in fact ends up affecting the old woman's entire future), and the medicine man's attitude clearly displays a lack of interest.

Next, I inserted a fully shaded rectangular icon to indicate that a certain character displayed high affective intensity in a particular episode while a partly shaded icon meant that that character displayed low affective intensity in a particular episode. I used the information and numbered jottings of the story analysts about the level of emotional involvement the characters showed, plus my own intuitions to determine whether characters displayed high or low affect. Finally, I indicated the display of positive emotions (for example, happiness, excitement, love) by drawing in an arrow that pointed upwards vertically from the pertinent episode by character icon. I indicated the display of negative emotions (for example, sadness, anger, weakness) by drawing in an arrow pointing downwards vertically from the pertinent icon. A horizontal arrow indicated a pre-existing affective state. In all cases, the upper-case letter printed next to the arrow named the emotion. For example, in the first story, *The Woman and the Tree Children*, the S in EP 1 indicated that the old woman was sad at the beginning of the story, while the H in EP 3 indicated that she was happy, as were the children. A key indicating the meaning of the letters appears at the end of each map.

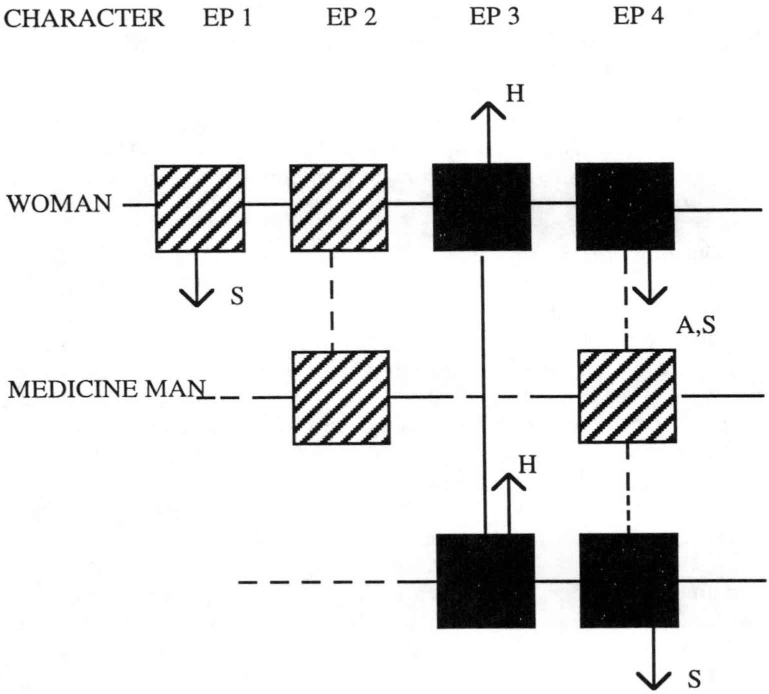
CHARACTER
EP 1
EP 2
EP 3
EP 4
WOMAN
MEDICINE MAN
H
S
A,S
H
S

S=Sadness H=Happiness A=Anger

Figure 5. 8. Narrative Map-- The Woman And The Tree Children (Story #1).

Structural Analysis of the Six Study Narratives 89

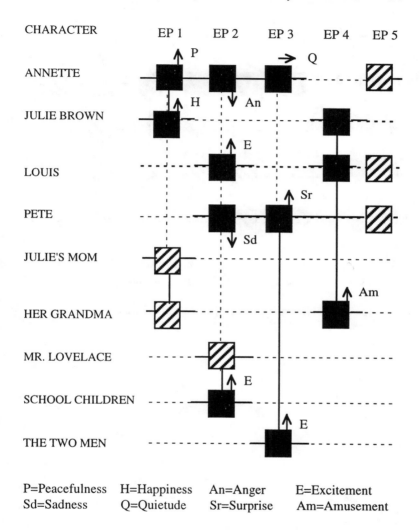

P=Peacefulness H=Happiness An=Anger   E=Excitement
Sd=Sadness   Q=Quietude   Sr=Surprise Am=Amusement

Figure 5.9: Narrative Map--"The Runaway Cow" (Story #2).

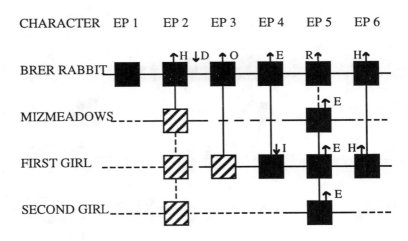

H=Happiness D=Depression O=Overjoyousness
E=Excitement I=Indignation R=Reinvigoration

Figure 5.10. Narrative Map-- Brer Rabbit Falls in Love (Story #3).

Structural Analysis of the Six Study Narratives 91

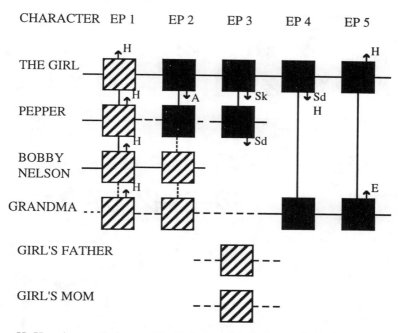

Figure 5.11. Narrative Map--Remembering Last Summer (Story #4).

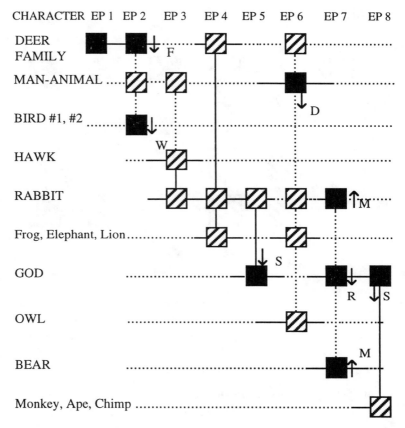

F=Fear W=Worry D=Destruction S=Sadness M=Materialism
R=Reassurance S=Sadness

Figure 5.12. Narrative Map-- Why Apes Look Like People (Story #5)

Structural Analysis of the Six Study Narratives 93

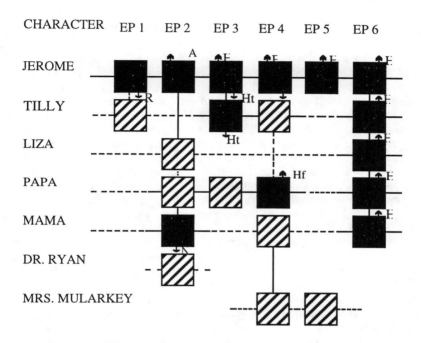

R=Resentment Ap=Apprehension N=Nervousness H=Happiness
Ht=Hurt E=Excitement Hf=Hopefulness

Figure 5.13. Narrative Map--Ride The Red Cycle (Story #6).

Distinctive Characteristics of the Narrative Maps

Each graphic creates a portrayal of narrative schemas. It builds on previous work on Story Grammar, for example Bower's tree structure diagram (in Guthrie, 1985), in capturing the essential elements of a story, and in showing the scope of an entire narrative in a single picture. It also extends the concept of Story Grammar beyond this point. In using the Character-by-Episode as the unit of analysis, the graphic maintains the integrity and substance of the narrative. Based on the map, it is possible to relegate various facets of a story to a numeric representation much like Bower does using terms like Attempts, Outcomes, State, Goal, Subgoal and so on. Instead the Narrative Map uses episodic analysis to portray all of these slots comprehensively, and symbols (lines, shading, arrows) to weight thematic features. As explained above, the graphic also depicts the level of affective involvement of the characters and highlights the degree of interaction between them both across and within episodes. Both the portrayal of emotion and of character interaction, nuances that are critical to narrative structure, are innovative in the graphic, and are afforded prime importance.

Another distinction is that in the narrative map, the concept of higher and lower nodes previously advocated (Pearson and Camperell, 1985; Van Dijk and Kintsch, 1985) can also be represented. Higher nodes would correspond to the nodes that are on the first tier or uppermost and leftmost in the narrative map. Similarly, lower nodes would correspond to the nodes that are on the lower tiers that mark the later episodes and that are rightmost where applicable. The hierarchical system therefore operates in a more transparent and hopefully more readily discernible fashion than it does in earlier tree diagrams, although it continues to be generally true that the higher nodes carry the information most central to the motivations and actions of the characters in the story. Finally, the presence of the letter codes representing the character affect also introduces more of the essential vitality of the narrative into the graphic.

From Structural Analysis to Question Construction

After completing the narrative analysis, my aim was to generate comprehension questions based on the stories--questions that were rooted conceptually in their essential elements. I did achieve this aim in that all the comprehension questions were linked in some measure with the dynamics of the final narrative map (and ultimately with the thrust of my research questions).

For example, the general questions (Q1-Q2) sought to find out what narrative elements the students liked most as they read each story. They thus encouraged the students to be reflective about the narratives. The literal meaning questions (Q3-Q5) were constructed from the early and late episodes in the story structure--from the higher and lower nodes as it were, where much of the introductory and culminating information are given. The third question category, the interpretive reading and critical evaluation group of questions (Q6-Q9) was designed with a focus on the episodes of dramatic tension depicted in the narrative graphic--the episodes of maximum involvement and character interaction. The final category of creative reading questions (Q10-Q11) asked students to imagine they were author, and modify the content of the final outcome or resolution in any way they thought feasible. The next chapter gives a complete description and discussion of the study comprehension questions.

Chapter Summary

This chapter focused on the selection of the six narratives identified for the comprehension and cognition study, and on the analysis of their structural components. Firstly, information on factors that influenced the selection process was provided. Next followed an exposition of the narrative elements of each selection in turn, using the categories of folk tale and non-folk tale as distinguishing features in analyzing the stories from a structural perspective. Thirdly, the narrative structural analyses were refined towards the production of a Narrative Map, both a conceptual tool, and a practical device. This graphic was the highlight of the chapter. It is also central to the entire study. The process of its production was detailed, tracing from the initial episodic segmentation of the stories to the final comprehensive narrative map. The innovative and distinctive features of the Narrative Map were discussed, and the chapter ended with stipulations for generating comprehension questions to be used in the study in a way that would connect them purposefully to the structure of the stories selected.

CHAPTER 6

RESEARCH DESIGN AND METHODS

What is a real question? Real questions connect. School questions are often artificial. The teacher asks the question, the student's job is to answer, but the teacher knows the right answer. It's a game. A real question is one where the questioner is genuinely interested in learning something from someone else...The essence of real discourse is unpredictability and authenticity.

Robert C. Calfee, 1995

Research Design

The research design of this study builds around the materials--ethnic narrative texts in combination with strategically constructed questions (See Figure 2: Conceptual Framework). These are the primary variables in the design. The narratives--both folk tales and non-folk tales--are interconnected with the comprehension questions by way of their vital components of Character, Theme, Plot, and Setting. The comprehension questions are subdivided into four categories--General

Questions (Q1-2), Literal Meaning Questions (Q3-5), Interpretive Reading and Critical Evaluation Questions (Q6-9), and Creative Reading Questions (Q10-11), in a multi-layered question design. Except for the General questions which focus on participants' holistic reactions to the stories, each comprehension question is derived systematically from a predetermined episode in the narratives. As Table 6.1 demonstrates, the comprehension questions connected with both the element of narrative structure and with the underlying research questions (the appeal of ethnic texts, the importance of higher-order questions, and

Narrative Factors	Comprehension Question Categories	Characterization of Questions
Character Theme Plot Setting (Language)	Q1: General Q2: General	First Impression/Rating Reactions to narrative components (character, theme, plot, setting)
Character Theme	Q3: Literal Meaning Q4: Literal Meaning Q5: Literal Meaning	Derived from an early episode Derived from a late episode
Character Values Character Actions Character Qualities Character Feelings	Q6: Interpretive Reading and Critical Evaluation Q7: Interpretive Reading and Critical Evaluation Q8: Interpretive Reading and Critical Evaluation Q9: Interpretive Reading and Critical Evaluation	All questions derived from episodes showing high levels of emotional intensity, and/or Maximum involvement of characters in episodes, and/or Maximum interaction between characters
Plot-line	Q10: Creative Reading Q11: Creative Reading	Derived from a late episode or coda

Table 6.1. Interconnection of study materials with study design and research questions.

so on), the one element dynamically reinforcing the other. The questions used as exemplars in this chapter are taken from Story #1, the folk tale entitled "The Woman and the Tree Children".

The study combined both quantitative and qualitative research methods. I used a multivariate analysis of variance to analyze the study outcomes (See the upcoming Chapter 7 on Quantitative Results), and qualitative excerpts and analyses to reinforce the findings and outcomes of the quantitative section of the study (see Chapters 8-11 on Qualitative Results). In subsequent chapters, quotations drawn from almost every student participants' work are provided as qualitative instantiations of quantitative results. Throughout the book, readers will notice that sample responses represent the work of students across ethnicities and achievement levels, and across both genders for the study classroom. Instruments in the design included questions and interviews. Further details of the research procedures are outlined below.

Methods: Questions, Scoring Procedures, Study Proceedings, Interviews

General Questions, Q1, Q2--Category 1: Description and Scoring Procedures

The two questions in the first category of "General" questions, Q1 and Q2, are reprinted in Table 6.2. These metacognitive questions, replicated verbatim for each narrative text, were intended to record the students' immediate and unvetted reactions to the stories. I wanted to provoke an on-the-spot reaction to one of the crucial factors in my study design that connected with the first of my research questions, the effect of using ethnic texts. Question 1 was ranked on a Likert Scale ranging from 1 to 6. The rankings assigned by the students were then totaled for all 25 study participants, and the mean calculated for each story. In focusing overtly on the essential elements of each narrative in question 2 (character, theme, plot, setting), I was attempting to make a preliminary assessment of students' reactions to story features that were to be examined more thoroughly in subsequent questions. Scoring for Question 2 proceeded simply by assigning a score of one for each narrative component which a student indicated he or she liked in each story, and a score of zero for each component that he or she did not like. Again, the tokens were added and averaged over 25 students to find the mean (see Chapter 7 on Quantitative Results for details).

> **General Question Q1:**
> On a scale of 1 to 6, rate how much you like this story. Circle the answer that most shows the way you feel.
>
> | 1 | 2 | 3 | 4 | 5 | 6 |
> |---|---|---|---|---|---|
> | Not at all | Very little | More or less | Much | Very much | Very very much |
>
> **General Question Q2:**
> People sometimes like stories because they like what the store is about (it's <u>theme</u>), or they like one or more of the people in the story (its <u>characters</u>), or they like the way the story unfolds (its <u>plot</u>), or they like the place in which the story was set (its <u>setting</u>), or they like the way it was written (the <u>language</u>). People also dislike stories for some of these same reasons. Explain why you like or do not like this story.
>
> | | **Like** | | **Do Not Like** |
> |---|---|---|---|
> | _____ | Theme | _____ | Theme |
> | _____ | Characters | _____ | Characters |
> | _____ | Plot | _____ | Plot |
> | _____ | Setting | _____ | Setting |
> | _____ | Wording | _____ | Wording |
> | _____ | Other (explain) | _____ | Other (explain) |

Table 6.2. General Question Category

Literal Meaning Questions Q3, Q4, Q5--Category 2: Description and Scoring Procedures

The three multiple-choice questions in the second category of Literal Meaning questions, Q3, Q4, and Q5 (Table 6.3), were designed to establish whether students would earn lower scores on the questions that focused on their literal and memory skills than on the questions in the next category that focused on their interpretive frames. One assumption behind this inquiry--others are explored in Chapter 8--was that the "stiff" answers and rigid predictability of these memory-based questions would be unappealing to these students who would be more motivated and engaged by problem-solving types of questions. These literal meaning questions conformed to the traditional, basic skills type of question in both form and function. In accordance with my conceptual framework the questions required a literal level understanding and comprehension of decontextualized prose.

There are two features that distinguish the literal meaning questions from all others. Firstly, question 3 was derived from the beginning or second episode of the story, while question 4 was derived from the last or penultimate episode in the narrative structure. This conceptual approach was maintained in constructing these two recall questions in all six stories. In addition, throughout the study, all the options in the multiple-choice answer consisted of plausible possibilities extracted from the relevant episode from which the question was framed. Among them, there was usually an implausible decoy option. Question five (Q5) was similar to the previous questions, question three (Q3) and question four (Q4) insofar as it was multiple-choice, but it also served as a bridge to the next category of questions in the comprehension test, the interpretive reading and critical evaluation Questions Q6 through Q9. It required a little more than mere recall; to answer it correctly, students needed some inference, because although the correct answer lay within the text, it was not supplied in a straightforward manner. Question five therefore straddled the second and third segments of the comprehension study, falling conceptually between the Literal Meaning category and the Interpretive-Critical Evaluation Reading questions. The decision to group it with the direct recall questions was based on the strength of the similarity in form of questions 3 through 5, and the partial similarity in function of question 5 with questions 3 and 4.

Finally, the multiple-choice format of questions 3, 4, and 5 typified contemporary standardized tests such as the CTBS (Comprehensive Test of Basic Skills), which is the established instrument of assessment in reading comprehension for elementary school students. There is a slight variation in the multiple-choice question format as used in this study, however. In addition to the basic question stem and four or five options in the answer category, this multiple-choice question design included a richly triangulated assessment system. It was organized around an estimated best, worst, or possible answer choice for each of the five answer options supplied, based on the students' recall of the textual material. Even though these questions were more like the recall questions of the traditional Basal reader therefore, they yielded a richer data set that would serve to inform and strengthen my subsequent analysis. Since students were instructed to give only one "best" answer, this approach gave the same data as a conventional "one correct answer" approach, while providing additional insight into how students were thinking and reasoning as they tackled each question.

I relied on the consensus of six advisors (three college undergraduate students, two graduate students and one professor) in determining the best, worst, and possible answers for all the options in scoring recall questions Q3, Q4, and Q5. Only responses that yielded either a unanimous agreement (100 % reliability) or a total of five votes out of a possible six (83 % reliability) were retained in the final study questions. All other options were discarded in order to maintain a high degree of reliability in the options identified as correct answers. When grading the scripts, the correct or "best" answer was consistently awarded a score of three points, the "worst" options earned one point, and the "possible" answers gained 2 points. Although the total number of points varied depending on the distribution of the "worst" and "possible" answers in specific questions, the raw score totals for each of questions 3, 4, or 5 consistently totaled either 15 or 16 points. The students' final scores were all converted to percentage points for the purpose of comparison and analysis.

Literal Meaning Question Q3:
Why did the old woman think she had lived an unhappy life?

	BEST	WORST	POSSIBLE
a) Because she had grown old	___	___	___
b) Because she had no husband and children	___	___	___
c) Because she had no friends	___	___	___
d) Because she had a husband but no children	___	___	___
e) Because she was a wicked old woman	___	___	___

Literal Meaning Question Q4:
What happened one day that made the woman yell at the children?

	BEST	WORST	POSSIBLE
a) One of the children laughed too loudly	___	___	___
b) One of the children dropped a glass	___	___	___
c) Nothing happened at all	___	___	___
d) The woman was tired and irritable	___	___	___
e) Something happened, but we are not told	___	___	___

Literal Meaning and Inference Question Q5:
Where do you think the children went to when the woman returned home the second time and found the house empty and lonely (p. 3)?

	BEST	WORST	POSSIBLE
a) Back to the sycamore tree	___	___	___
b) Out to buy groceries	___	___	___
c) Up to heaven	___	___	___
d) Back to the medicine man	___	___	___
e) To visit their mother's friend	___	___	___

Table 6.3. Literal Meaning Question Category

Interpretive Reading and Critical Evaluation Questions Q6-Q9, Category 3: Description and Scoring Procedures

The third category of questions, Q6 to Q9 represented in Table 6.4, comprised the question category on interpretive reading and critical evaluation. The questions that came under this category gave students the opportunity to engage with contextualized questions that were open-ended, and that encouraged readers to relate their understanding of the texts to their own backgrounds and experiences. They allowed readers to negotiate meaning from and with the texts, filtering it through their own ideas and voices. I hypothesized that these questions would enhance the students' sense of the adequacy of their own intuitions, perspectives and interpretations. They were the kinds of questions that required processes of argumentation and problem-solving to which students were constantly exposed in their own communities and which they could discuss with interest and enthusiasm.

Unlike the literal meaning or recall questions in the previous category, these interpretive reading and critical evaluation questions were not expected to have only a single correct or "best" answer. Although the answers would be evaluated according to pre-determined rubrics and standards of excellence, their correctness would be influenced by textual interpretations grounded in the judgment processes, thoughts, experiences and original ideas of individual readers.

There were other ways in which the questions that fell under the interpretive reading and critical evaluation category differed from the literal meaning questions. While the latter were entirely multiple-choice, questions six through nine were to be answered in paragraphs or short-essay answers. Lines were drawn in on students' answer sheets immediately following each of these questions to facilitate the required response. Further, questions 6 through 9 were drawn from the "action" episodes in the narrative. The source of material for these questions came from the nodes with symbols in the structural analysis graphic that depicted dramatic tension--either maximum character involvement, maximum character interaction, or high affective intensity (see Narrative Maps in Chapter 5). These questions therefore required higher order cognitive skills: critical thinking, evaluation, concept development, reasoning, analysis, and synthesis.

I secured the aid of six advanced undergraduates (three male and three female) in scoring the scripts of the students for questions six through nine. Raters attended a workshop session during which I trained them in using the rubrics established for scoring short-essay answers. They worked in pairs so that each script was read and assigned a score by two different readers. Where there was disagreement between raters, I encouraged open discussion of the particular issues involved until the raters reached consensus. I will now go on to provide further details about each of the questions in this category and the rubrics established for evaluating the answers.

Moral Judgment Question 6: Description and Scoring Procedures

Moral Judgment Question 6 investigated the students' development of moral reasoning and conduct. They were asked to make a moral judgment about the behavior of certain characters in the narratives, and to defend and justify that judgment. Students were asked to make connections between moral issues that arose in the narratives and in their larger world experiences. They were able to reflect on their own personal value systems, and to exercise their potential for empathy and sympathy towards others. This question also interconnected nicely with the underlying thematic issues of morality in some of the narratives especially the folk tales (Story #1, The Woman and the Tree Children and Story #5, Why Apes Look Like People). This feature further served to synthesize text with question and to strengthen the study design.

Raters assigned a score of one, two, or three to the given answers to Question 6 according to the following rubrics. A stated choice of right or wrong plus a well-developed explanation earned three points. A well-developed explanation might include an example or examples from the narrative, and-or from the student's background of experience, an offer of advice, or a suggestion of an alternative line of action. The "rightness" or "wrongness" of a character's actions were to be weighed against a conception of morality that included both justice and compassion. A stated choice of right or wrong plus an underdeveloped or incomplete answer earned two points. A stated choice of right or wrong plus a poor answer earned one point. A poor answer was one that simply restated the problem without contributing to the development of its solution, or one which was illogical or circumlocutory. A stated choice of right or wrong plus no reason earned zero points.

Raters were asked not to deduct points for mechanical mistakes such as spelling and punctuation, or for errors of grammar, since the objective of the study was to investigate the more substantive aspects of the students' comprehension and literary appreciation skills. In this segment of the study, the students' knowledge, ideas and feelings were the most important facets of their writing. The inter-rater Reliability score on Question 6, averaged over all stories, was 86%.

Favorite Character Question 7: Description and Scoring Procedures

Throughout the study, question 7 was the Favorite Character question. Question 7 was the question that asked the students to identify the character in each story whom they liked the best. My purpose in asking this question was to give students the opportunity to articulate the qualities they admired in a character whom they identified as their favorite. They were invited in their answers to say in their own words, why they liked the selected character.

Characters are one of the enduring facets of a good narrative because, among other things, they are the vehicle the author uses for developing the theme. In reading narratives, children identify with one or more of the characters because they resonate with the author's portrayal of the person's thoughts and actions and their outcomes. As a result, they are able to make deductions about the particular character that they admire or dislike. My aim in composing Question 7 was to give students an opportunity to participate in this kind of close engagement with narrative character creations in discussing the qualities or characteristics of their favorite character in each story.

The key element I was looking for in their answers was not so much which characters they selected, but the explanations they provided for their choices. Raters scored the answers to question 7 according to the following rubrics: a maximum score of three points was awarded for a thorough or extensive explanation; two points for a mediocre explanation; one point for a poor explanation, and zero points for no explanation. An explanation was deemed thorough or extensive when a student chose a favorite character and then gave adequate reasons (two or more) followed by full elaborations for that choice. An explanation was considered mediocre when a student chose a favorite character but did not support that choice with substantial evidence. The student may simply have listed one or two character qualities and stopped there. A poor explanation occurred when a student chose a favorite character, then followed up with a reason that was circumlocutory, illogical or irrelevant. The inter-rater reliability score on question 7, averaged over all stories, was 84%.

Character Feelings and Qualities Question 8: Description and Scoring Procedures

Character Feelings and Qualities Question 8 was similar to the previous question 7 in that it also focused on the dimension of narrative character. However, I included question 8 in order to plumb the students' intuitions about feelings, a salient dimension of character portrayal in narrative text, and an important affective ingredient of real-life personalities. Question 8 had two parts. Part 1 asked: "How do you think X felt when Y happened?" Here students were given the chance to select three qualities (from a list of twelve) that most matched their evaluation of a particular characters' feelings, but were also encouraged (orally and at every session) to add their own descriptors in writing up their answers. In creating the list, I took measures to ensure that students would give it substantial thought before making a decision. I manipulated the list so that at least half of the qualities listed were inappropriate given the thrust of the character's role in the narrative, and the other half represented subtle nuances of character quality that required careful thought in order to make a good choice. Part 2 asked students to explain their answer, "X felt this way because..."

The strategy for composing Question 8 was consistent throughout the study. It was crafted from episodes in the narrative map where characters depicted high levels of affective intensity, a context which provided an ideal set of dramatic circumstances around which to fashion such a question.

Raters scored the answers to this question according to the following rubrics: three points were awarded for a thorough answer; two points were awarded for a mediocre answer; one point was awarded for a poor answer, and a student who did not answer the question or was way off the mark, scored zero points. A thorough answer was one that showed thought, engagement with the story, and reflection in answering the question. In order to gain this score, students were required to select three qualities that best described the feelings of the particular character in question, and then demonstrate explicitly and in a reasoned way, why they made this selection. An answer was evaluated as mediocre when a student selected three qualities, and went on to supply pieces of factual information from the story randomly, without using it to develop a meaningful cause and effect explanation. A poor answer was one that failed to select three qualities, and did not elaborate on the one(s) selected in a way that made the answer convincing. It referred to an answer that did select three qualities, but instead of organizing them into a coherent Part II response, offered only one piece of insignificant detail from the passage, and made no attempt to develop a sound answer based on the character qualities selected. An answer earned zero points when no attempt was made to answer the question, or when the answer simply made no sense. The inter-rater reliability score on question 8, averaged over all stories, was 88%.

Deductive Reasoning Question 9: Description and Scoring Procedures

Deductive Reasoning Question 9 was the last question in the Interpretive Reading and Critical Evaluation segment of the study. In keeping with the underlying orientation of this question segment, the driving principle behind question 9 throughout the study was the requirement to think critically and reason deductively. This was a broader conceptualization than questions 6,7, and 8, which focused on moral judgments and narrative characters, and it allowed me more freedom in composing the question. I could examine any aspect of the narrative that was unique to a particular story, and that had not been previously explored in Questions 6, 7, or 8. In terms of its focus, then, question 9 was perhaps the most eclectic question in the study from one narrative to another.

For example, question 9 in Story #1 asked about the character and actions of the Medicine Man, who had not yet been spotlighted. Question 9 in Story #2 explored the credibility of the final episode or coda and asked students to critically assume the author's perspective. Question 9 in story #3 focused on the author's use of figurative language as a literary flourish, and required students to decipher its meaning. Question 9 in Story #4 asked students to attempt an explanation of how the human psyche responds to emotional pain, in this case, through denial. Finally question 9 in Story #5 and Story #6 required students to make inferences about the motivations for the actions or responses of specific characters much like question 9 in Story #1 did.

Question 9 also served as a barometer of the level of difficulty that the students could cope with in questions requiring higher-order thinking skills. Some of the questions (for instance question 9 in Story #2) definitely required the kind of complex literary analysis and appreciation that students at much higher levels of endeavor engage in, and some students did have trouble in coming up with an answer in such cases, although some were able to find the appropriate answer quite comfortably.

The rubrics used to grade Question 9 were as follows: A full score of three points was awarded to answers that showed that the student engaged with the text maximally in answering the question. Such an answer typically showed depth of insight and analysis, and included examples either from the text or from the students' own experience to support the claim(s) they made. A score of two points was awarded to answers that showed that the student understood the question and had a sound grasp of the text as it related to or involved the question. Examples were adequate, but lacked the spark of originality. A score of one mark was awarded to answers that showed only minimal engagement with the question. The answer was typically perfunctory, as was the example provided to support the claim that the student made. Finally, a score of zero marks was awarded for no attempt to answer the question, or for an attempt that was devoid of any substance. Inter-rater reliability on question nine, averaged over all stories, was 92%.

Moral Judgment Question Q6:
Was it right or wrong for the woman to lose her temper and scream at the children?
Right---------- Wrong----------
Give a reason for your answer. It was right, OR It was wrong, because...

Favorite Character Question Q7:
Who is your favorite character in the whole story? (Circle one)
        a) the medicine man
        b) the old woman
        c) the tree children
Explain why you like this character. I like this character best because...

Character Feelings/Qualities Question Q8:
How do you think the children felt after the old woman got angry and told them she could not expect any better from them because they were nothing but "children of the tree"? Circle three of the qualities that best describe how they felt.

    SAD   WANTED   HUNGRY
    BETRAYED   ANGRY   ALONE
    DIRTY   ALONE   COMFORTABLE
    LOVED   CLEAN   UNWANTED

Why did the children feel this way? Give a reason for your answer. They felt this way because...

Deductive Reasoning Question Q9:
Early in the story the medicine man made the woman choose between a husband and children. Later, after the children went away and she went back to him, he said he could not help her. Why do you think he said so? He said he could not help her because...

Table 6.4. Interpretive Reading and Critical Evaluation Question Category

Creative Reading Questions Q10, Q11, Category 4: Description and Scoring Procedures.

There were two questions in the category of Creative Reading. The first question, Problem Solving Question 10, asked students to think up an original solution to a problem that one of the characters faced in the story. The second question, Student-as-Author Question 11, empowered students to take on the persona of the author and suggest endings to the stories that were different from the ones given by the original authors. The Creative Reading questions comprised the final category of the comprehension questions for each story. These two questions were unique in that they were the only two questions in the study that students were allowed to answer collaboratively following group discussion. Each group selected a scribe, who was responsible for recording their opinions. Everyone was given a chance to make a contribution in the group process. Group sessions were recorded on tape and later transcribed. There were five students in each group (see Chapter 11), and the understanding was that because they would each earn the group score, they were individually responsible for their own full participation in the group process. Raters used these data in addition to the scribe's notes to assign scores to each group for questions 10 and 11.

There were many reasons for including a group work segment in the study. Firstly, I wanted to explore the Vygotskian perspective (Tudge, 1990) with which I agree entirely, based on my own experience, that children can improve and increase their learning if allowed to interact with each other cognitively. Vygotsky believed that in group situations where levels of individual knowledge vary, children could teach each other through active discussion and argumentation, and help each other make cognitive strides towards their zone of proximal development. Perret-Clermont (1980) had a similar idea. He conceptualized peer collaboration as "a process of active cognitive reorganization induced by cognitive conflict" most likely to occur "in situations where children with moderately discrepant perspectives are asked to reach a consensus" (p. 162). In addition, the opportunity to work together in groups also allowed me to observe the quality of inter-ethnic relationships that existed in the class. This information was valuable in its own right, and also as a connection with my inquiry into the effect of ethnic literature in a richly multi-ethnic classroom situation. The outcome of the group work segment of my study validated these potential advantages of peer group collaboration.

Students were visibly excited during these sessions, and became actively engaged in argumentation and discussion as their levels of motivation increased. Individuals who were more knowledgeable than others in specific arenas (for example rules for composing raps and rhymes or ideas for devising alternative story endings) helped other group members along, and as a result, by the end of the group process, students had usually acquired knowledge that they did not have before. In addition, group sessions generated an atmosphere of friendliness and openness reminiscent of the core ideas of cooperative learning strategies articulated by Elizabeth Cohen of Stanford University.

Question 10 was worth three points. Typically it asked: "What would you say or do" to help comfort a particular character who was in need of emotional support. Students were given a point each for recording something they would say and something they would do in such a situation. A third point was awarded if the support that they offered to the needy fictional character was positive and sympathetic. The third point was generally denied if students offered negative and potentially harmful counsel. The third point was still awarded however, if the harmful or unsympathetic counsel was well-written and argued. The justification was that I was not interested in morality per se here as I was in the case of question 6 above, but in reasoning. For example, if in response to question 10 of Story #2, a student said that he would not do anything to help Pete once he was thrown from the cow and landed in the meadow, but he would make sure he was not hurt, then just walk away and leave him, telling him that sometimes hard things happen to teach people a lesson for the future (an answer we actually did get), that student would be awarded a third point.

Question 11 was also worth three points. Typically the question asked: "How would you end the story if you were the author and had a chance to write a different ending? Three points were awarded for a novel ending that demonstrated imagination and insight. A paraphrase of the original ending with some elaboration or modification earned two points. One point was given to an answer that offered what was essentially the same ending, if the student could justify the retention of the author's ending in a credible manner. A straight repeat of the author's original ending without justification earned zero points. Interrater reliability for question 10 averaged over all stories, was 80%; for question 11, it was 75%.

> **Problem Solving Question Q10:**
> How would you treat your tree children if you were the old woman in the story? Write about what you would say to them or do with them after they broke your special dish.
>
> **Student-As-Author Question Q11:**
> The end of the story goes: "And she lived in sadness the rest of her life" (p. 3). How would you end the story if you were the author and had a chance to write a different ending?

Table 6.5. Creative Reading Question Category

Study Proceedings

The administration of the stories and comprehension questions proceeded as follows. Mr. Peters agreed to read each story aloud, as the students followed along. He read and acquainted himself with the story preceding each class session. During the testing sessions, each student received his or her own copy of the narrative and comprehension questions. Each of the six narrative texts was color-coded in blue, pink, green, yellow, orange and magenta consecutively, and in each case there was an illustration from the original story on the last page. The illustrations usually depicted African or African American characters, except in Story #5, which was an animal folk tale. The students listened very carefully throughout the reading, then answered the comprehension questions (which I read aloud), on individual "worksheets" printed on white paper. Students spent an average of forty-five minutes on the task of answering the complete set of eleven comprehension questions following the reading of each story. After reading the narratives, Mr. Peters had very little involvement with the students for the rest of the testing session. Although he usually remained in the classroom throughout the session, he mainly kept order, helped the students find their groups for the last two questions, and so on.

When the study was first conceived, my plan was to have the students themselves read the story, and answer the comprehension questions that followed. However, I subsequently modified my plan for the following two reasons: 1) The aim of my study was to investigate comprehension ability, and not decoding skills. The two primary components of reading are decoding-spelling and comprehension, and I wanted to explore reading comprehension. 2) From my involvement in the classroom, I knew that a few children would have difficulty reading the extracts fluently within the assigned time, and I wanted to give all students a chance to participate. The fact that at the conclusion of the experiment all the participants turned in fully completed answer sheets seems to have justified my decision in this regard. In so doing, students demonstrated that they were able to engage with and respond to the stories. They also showed that because their reaction to the study materials, instruments, and coordinators (their teacher and me) was essentially positive, performance and good discipline came fairly easily.

Comprehension question sessions were generally held at two week intervals. At the end of each session, I collected twenty-five scripts, one for each student in the class, and had them graded. The students were generally happy to see me, a condition that was probably not unrelated to the fact that I shared out candy and juice following each session. Following the administration of each story, I transcribed and coded the data recorded, including data from tape recordings, noting down from the narratives any interesting insights or "nuggets" that showed up as I went along, as a preliminary to the final data analysis and interpretation of the study.

Student Interviews

In addition to comprehension questions which formed the core of the study, the study instruments included individual and small group interviews designed to provide additional qualitative data that would reinforce the basic quantitative study. To this end, the interviews were also constructed around the original research questions. The protocols are included below.

Student interviews were conducted after the completion of the main cognition and comprehension study. When they were done individually, they lasted for about twenty minutes per person; when done in student pairs, they lasted for approximately a half an hour. Interview sessions included written questionnaires divided into three sections. The primary purpose of these sessions was to derive information that connected back with the main focus of the study and research questions. For example, Questions 1 to 4 which comprised the first section, contained basic bio-data, and also provided important information pertaining to students' ethnic background and language habits. Such data were vital to this study that sought to determine the efficacy of using ethnic narratives as a literary motivator. Interview data also supplied a basis for understanding student factors such as achievement levels, details of reactions to the narratives and comprehension questions, and so on. Questions read as follows:

1. Name? Date-of-birth? Home language?
2. Where were you born and which family members do you live with?
3. How many years have you lived in East Tall Tree? Attended Lantana School?
4. What books, novels or magazines do you like to read?

Questions 5 to 8, which focused on the narratives, comprised the second section of the student interviews. The questions were somewhat reflective, and prompted the students to think about their personal reasons for identifying one particular story as their least or most favorite (an area also explored in Questions 1 and 2 of the comprehension test). They were also asked to suggest reasons why their peers liked certain narratives more or less than others. Section two of the interview-questionnaire therefore aimed at brainstorming student ideas about their preference (evidenced by their ratings of the stories), for ethnic literature over mainstream literature, and their stated appreciation of literary texts that validated their ethnic and cultural background. The questions in the second section of the interview-questionnaire read as follows:

5. Of the six stories in the study, which story did you like the best, and why?
6. Of the six stories in the study, which story did you like the least, and why?
7. Overall, the class rated story #6, Ride the Red Cycle the highest, that is, they said they liked that story more than any other story in the whole set. Why do you think the class liked this story so much?
8. Overall, the class rated story #2, The Runaway Cow the lowest, that is, they said they liked that story less than any other story in the whole set of six. Why do you think the class disliked this story so much?

Questions 9 and 10 comprised the third and final section of the student interview and questionnaire. They focused on some of the special features of the narratives that contributed to their ethnic flavor. This section therefore also connected with the main thrust of my research study. The questions investigated the students' thoughts and reactions to the use of special linguistic features in the form of African American Vernacular English (or Ebonics) in some of the stories, and also to the use of ethnic characters in the form of Black illustrations in most of the stories. The responses that the students gave would be important not only in understanding their attitudes to these important dimensions of the narratives, but also to the larger philosophical issues that they represent. For example, the desirability of incorporating some form of dialect use embedded in texts as in the present study, in the education of ethnic minority students, would be one such issue. The final two questions read as follows:

9. Several of the stories contained some dialect, for example, "I ain't been feeling too well." (Story #3); "Won't be nobody as dap as me nowhere." (Story #5); "John, physical therapist say it be good leg motion." (Story #6). What do you think about the use of dialect in these stories? In general do you like this feature in stories? Why or why not?

10. Did you like the illustrations at the end of each story? What did you like (or not like) about them?

Teacher Interviews

The teacher interview protocols are included in Appendix B. Data from teacher interviews were collected during two sittings with Mr. Peters. The interviews covered questions that provided information both on Mr. Peters' experiences as a veteran teacher, and on various aspects of the comprehension-cognition study conducted in his classroom. I asked questions that investigated issues of discipline and Mr. Peters' philosophy of teaching in general and his approach to teaching narrative reading and comprehension in particular. During the interviews, I asked Mr. Peters how he felt about the idea of using ethnic folk tales and contemporary literature as motivational texts for his students, and how he felt about incorporating authentic and thought-provoking questions in comprehension exercises. Interview questions were divided into four separate areas--Background and General Information, Approaches to the teaching of Narrative Comprehension, Questions on the Study Narratives and Comprehension Questions, and Questions on the Effects of the Cognition-Comprehension Study. The interview thus served to gather more information on the larger questions of the Study, a significant amount of which was subsequently incorporated into the Study (see Chapter 4 on the general background and contextualization of the study).

Chapter Summary

In this chapter I discussed the research design and methods used in my Study. Details of the comprehension test questions were given, including an explanation of the four categories of questions in the study--General, Literal Meaning, Interpretive Reading and Critical Evaluation, and Creative Reading questions. In describing these categories, I discussed the way in which the questions within each category were conceptualized and constructed, and the procedures for scoring them. The inter-rater reliability index for the questions was given where appropriate (for questions 3 through 11, since "general questions", questions 1 and 2 were not subject to scoring). Finally, further proceedings of the study were discussed, including details of the actual administration of the stories and comprehension questions. Details pertaining to the purpose and orientation of the student and teacher interviews and questionnaires were also provided.

PART III

DATA ANALYSES AND INTERPRETATION

CHAPTER 7

QUANTITATIVE RESULTS: AN OVERVIEW

Yes, if minority people are to effect the change which will allow them to truly progress we must insist on "skills" within the context of critical and creative thinking.

Lisa Delpit, 1995

This chapter reports the results of the quantitative analysis of the study. It is an omnibus analysis of the entire comprehension question set which was comprised of four different question categories. First I present the main outcomes, then elaborate on each finding in turn, providing supporting details from the data set to explain them. Both descriptive data and inferential statistics are used to portray the results. The chapters that follow this one provide qualitative results as instantiations of these quantitative outcomes.

Quantitative Results and Outcomes

The study outcomes were as follows:

1) There was a significant effect of question category. There were differences in student achievement between question categories such that students earned higher scores on higher-order questions of interpretive reading, critical evaluation and creative reading, than on lower-order questions of memory and literal recall.

2) There was a significant effect of story length. Students earned higher scores on questions that were based on the longer, more complex stories than they did on questions that were based on the shorter, simpler texts.

3) There was no significant effect of the narrative genre variable. Students expressed as much liking for the folk tales as they did for the non-folk tales, and their performance relative to the two genres showed no significant difference. They did not seem to discriminate between these two variables in any discernible way.

4) There was a significant effect of student gender. There were significant differences in participant achievement by gender on comprehension questions. In general, girls attained higher scores than boys. In addition, girls and boys approached certain social issues that showed up in questions (such as caring and nurturing) in distinctly different ways.

5) There was no significant effect of ethnicity. Students of all the diverse ethnicities represented in the classroom--African American, Hispanic, Tongan, Samoan and Fijian--demonstrated appreciation for the opportunity to work with ethnic literature that represented the cultural heritage of the African American group with whom they showed solidarity.

Question Effects: Outcome of Question Category

Figure 7:1 demonstrates the outcome of question category. It is a display of the mean scores earned for all 25 participants on each of the four separate question categories over six stories. Aggregate scores are expressed as a percentage of the maximum possible score and are calculated for each narrative. One outstanding trend is that the scores on the higher-order comprehension questions in the third category of Interpretive Reading and Critical Evaluation questions--Q6 to Q9--were consistently higher than the scores on the lower-order comprehension questions in the second category of Literal Meaning questions--Q3 to Q5. Students scored a mean of 79% of the maximum possible points on higher-order thinking questions 6 through 9, marking their highest mean score of all four question categories. By contrast, they scored their lowest scores on the recall or literal meaning questions, a grand mean of 60% of the maximum possible points on questions 3 through 5. Mean scores on individual stories reinforce this trend with consistency. Total mean scores on the Creative Reading question category (designed to be conceptually similar to the preceding interpretive reading questions) amounted to 75%, also significantly exceeding scores on the literal meaning questions.

Note that the mean percentage scores for the interpretive reading questions Q6 to Q9 are all in the high range from Story #1 to Story #6. Similarly, the mean percentage scores for the creative reading questions Q10 and Q11 are also generally high (except for one outlier, Story #2, which is discussed later). Contrastively, the mean percentage scores for the literal questions Q3 to Q5 are all in a comparatively lower range from Story #1 to Story #6.

These descriptive results corroborated my predicted outcomes of the comprehension question categories. As hypothesized, the students did better on questions requiring interpretive thinking, critical evaluation, and creative reading than they did on the literal meaning questions. Their performance on questions requiring advanced thinking skills such as inference, imagination, and argumentation, and that tapped into their areas of experiential and background knowledge, outstripped their performance on questions that required mainly low-level skills such as memory.

QUESTION CATEGORIES. 1-2 General. 3-5 Literal Meaning. 6-9 Interpretive Reading-Critical Evaluation. 10-11 Creative Reading.

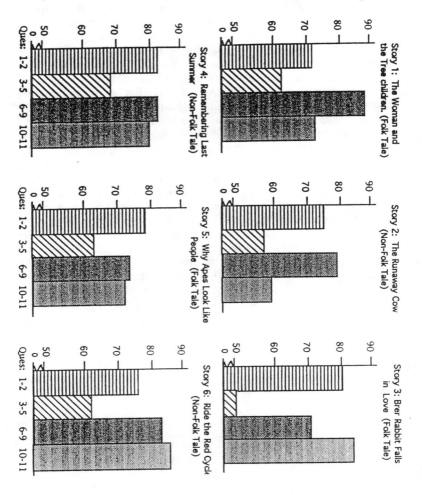

Figure 7.1. Effect of Question Category. Percent Maximum Score for each of Six Stories

Narrative Effects: Outcomes of Story Length

In addition to question effects, the data also showed significant story effects. As Figure 7.2 demonstrates, the trend of student scores in relation to the variable of narrative length differed with question category and story genre. But in general, however, there was a dominant tendency for participant scores to rise from one story length category to another as story length increased. This is an important outcome because it holds implications for the level and range of student abilities and cognition. Again, the numbers are aggregate mean scores representing the percentage of the maximum possible score that all twenty-five students earned across six stories.

For example, the achievement curve on the folk tale genre for both recall questions 3 to 5 and interpretive questions 6 to 9 slopes downward from the baseline scores established for short stories to scores achieved for medium long stories, then slopes upwards again for long story scores. The scores decrease from the short stories score of 65 to the medium stories score of 50 then rise again to 60 for the long stories score in the former case, and from 87 for short stories down to 70 for medium stories and up again to 73 for long stories in the latter case.

Another trend, the inverse of the one described above, is that the scores sometimes rise from the baseline short story score to the score for the medium long stories, and then either curve downward slightly or plateau for the long stories. The case of student performance on the recall questions 3 to 5 for the non-folk tale genre, and on the creative reading questions 10 and 11 for the folk tale genre instantiate this phenomenon. In the former case, scores begin at 55 on short stories, advance to 68 on medium stories and plateau at the same score of 68 on long stories. In the latter, scores increase from a base score of 73 up to 83 and back down to 73 again.

Despite the tendencies described above, there are many more cases of rising scores or of scores remaining high after beginning an upward trend. As Figure 7.2 demonstrates, there was a total of nine such cases, counting each movement from one mode to another for all story genres and all question categories, compared with a minimum of two cases of falling scores as story length increased. Moreover, there were consistent increases between short, medium, and long stories in three specific cases that were statistically significant (p <.01). All these cases were instantiated in the non-folk tale narrative genre and occur across all comprehension question categories. For example the length effect on non-folk tales was significant for the literal meaning questions

Q3 to Q5, where scores increased steadily from a mean of 54 on short stories to 65 on medium length stories to 72 on long stories. The length effect on non-folk tales was also significant for the interpretive reading and critical evaluation question category, Q6 to Q9 over all six stories. Scores on this genre ranged from an aggregate mean score of 77 on short stories, increased to 83 on medium long stories, and stabilized there showing the same score of 83 on long stories. The length effect on non-folk tales was also significant for the creative reading question category, Q10 to Q11 over all six stories. In this case, percentage scores increased from 60 on short stories, to 80 on medium stories, topping out at 85 on long stories.

In order to fully grasp the meaning of these narrative length outcomes, it is important to remember that the shortest story was 689 words long while the longest story was 1982 words long, almost three times longer. Also the shorter stories were "easier", registering a readability level of 3 or third grade, while the longer stories were "harder", registering a readability level of 5, equivalent to fifth grade. An effect of length therefore indicates increased cognition of participants, not only because of increase in the physical facet of story length, but also in terms of the more abstract quality and increased complexity inherent in the longer stories in this study (see Chapter 5).

These results ran counter to my original hypothesis that students would earn higher scores on the shorter, less complex stories because they would be simpler and therefore easier to understand. The results of the length effect variable on the data demonstrate trends in the opposite direction. Students in fact did better as the difficulty level of the stories increased both in terms of story length and story complexity. The greater significance of these results are discussed in Chapter 12.

Quantitative Results: An Overview

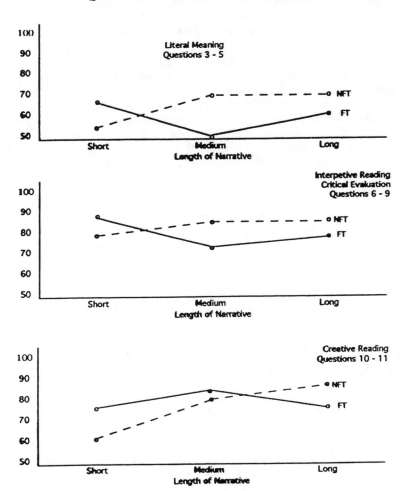

Effect of length: Percent maximum score for each of six stories by genre and question category.

FT — Folk Tale NFT — Non-Folk Tale

Note: p < .01 for stories showing significant length effect

Figure 7.2. Effect of Length

Narrative Effects: Outcomes of Story Genre

As Table 7.3 shows, raw scores assigned to the study narratives showed no effect of genre, that is, the data showed no effect of the folk tale versus the non-folk tale genre variable. The source of this outcome were Questions 1 and 2 in the General Questions category. Here I asked the students to rate each story on a Likert scale from 1 to 6 according to their response to that particular story immediately following its reading (question 1). Then they were asked to indicate what element(s) of the story they liked or did not like--theme, character, plot, and setting. I also included language and-or dialect as a facet here (question 2) because of my interest in the weight that it carried for students.

Table 7.3 represents the outcomes of these two questions. The numbers are the total scores that the students gave to each of the six narratives in the study. A score of six was the highest possible per student for question 1, and 150 (25x6) was the highest possible maximum aggregate score for each story. A score of five was the highest possible score per student for question 2, and 125 (25x5) was the highest possible maximum aggregate score per story.

QUES. # Raw Totals	FOLK TALES		NON FOLK TALES			
n = 25	#1 Tree Children	#3 Brer Rabbit	#5 Why Apes Look	#2 Run-away Cow	#4 Rem. Last Sum...	#6 Rid Red Cycle
Ques. 1 359/358	116 Mn. 4.6	122 Mn. 4.9	121 Mn. 4.8	115 Mn. 4.6	122 Mn. 4.9	121 Mn. 4.8
Ques. 2 303/306	90 Mn. 3.6	105 Mn. 4.2	108 Mn. 4.3	99 Mn. 4.0	111 Mn. 4.4	96 Mn. 3.8

Table 7.3. Raw Scores assigned to Study Narratives for General Questions 1 and 2 showing no Effect of Genre

Demographic Effects: Outcomes of Gender and Ethnicity

The results show that the students liked both the folk tales and the non-folk tale narratives equally well. For question 1, the total aggregate score for the folk tales was 359 compared with a total of 358 for the non-folk tales. In addition, the aggregate averages that these scores represent for the folk tale stories are 4.6, 4.9, 4.8, scores that are matched exactly by the mean score for the non-folk tale stories or 4.6, 4.9, and 4.8 respectively. This effect was counter to the outcome I anticipated. My hypothesis was that the distinction between folk tales and non-folk tales would have a significant effect--that the students would enjoy the folk tales more than the non-folk tales because of the cultural muscle of the former. This turned out not to be the case.

The outcome of Question 2 reinforces this pattern. Again the folk tale scores came quite close to the non-folk tale scores; students earned an aggregate of 303 on the former, and 306 on the latter, reflecting mean scores of 3.6, 4.2 and 4.3 for folk tales, and 4.0, 4.4 and 3.8 for non-folk tales.

The final variables analyzed were the demographic factors of ethnicity and gender. The data showed effects of gender, but no effect of ethnicity. I analyzed these variables by means of a repeated measures analysis of variance. The means, F-ratios and levels of significance for these variables, are displayed in Tables 7.4 and 7.5 for those categories of comprehension questions that show significant effects. Table 7.4 displays the effect of ethnicity and gender for Interpretive Reading and Critical Evaluation Questions 6 to 9, and Table 7.5 displays these effects for Creative Reading Questions Q10 and Q11.

In both tables, the demographic factors are listed along the columns; the text factors along the rows; the final row indicates the residual. The raw score means and score scales for each narrative on which the analysis is based are as follows for Interpretive Reading and Critical Evaluation questions 6 to 9: Raw Score Means: Story #1--2.6, Story #2--2.3, Story #3--2.1, Story #4--2.5, Story #5--2.2, Story #6--2.5 (Scale of 0-3). For Creative Reading questions 10-11 they are: Story #1--4.4, Story #2--3.6, Story #3--5.0, Story #4--4.8, Story #5--4.4, Story #6--5.1 (Scale of 0-6).

The effect of gender is significant for most of the questions--for both the Interpretive Reading and Critical Evaluation Questions 6 to 9, and the Creative Reading Questions 10-11 ($p < .01$). This finding replicates numerous studies showing an effect of gender on reading and writing. Girls generally do better than boys, especially in the elementary and middle grades of school. The hypothesis that I made as I embarked on this study, that there would be an effect of gender in the data was therefore validated. My intuitions were fueled both by these general trends, and also by my observations as a participant in the classroom.

What is interesting about the gender effect, however, is the intriguing way in which it shows up in the responses to certain questions pertaining to social issues, as a fundamentally different approach between girls and boys. I discuss this phenomenon in the next chapter.

F-RATIOS

Source	df	B-S	Length	(Linear)	Folk	LxF	(lin x F)
Mean	1	*	1.5	1.5	3.1	5.4	6.6
Eth	1	0.2	0.6	0.0	0.0	1.4	2.5
Gender	1	8.1	0.2	0.2	2.3	0.8	0.3
EthxGen	1	0.5	0.2	0.3	0.1	0.1	0.1
Resid	21	.742	.185	.207	.127	.188	.181

For Gender, (F = 8.1, **p** <**.01**); For Ethnicity, (F = 0.2, p = 0.6)

Table 7.4. Effect of Ethnicity and Gender for Interpretive Reading and Critical Evaluation questions Q 6 to Q 9

F-RATIOS

Source	df	B-S	Length	(Linear)	Folk	LxF	(lin x F)
Mean	1	*	7.3	5.7	0.2	5.5	9.3
Eth	1	0.5	5.6	0.8	0.8	0.8	1.1
Gender	1	8.7	0.5	0.0	1.9	0.2	0.2
EthxGen	1	1.4	.4	0.5	.0	0.2	0.2
Resid	21	2.78	1.52	2.14	1.7	1.07	1.21

For Gender, (F = 8.7, **p** <**.01**); For Ethnicity, (F = 0.5, p = 0.6)

Table 7.5. Effect of Ethnicity and Gender for Creative Reading questions Q 10 and Q 11

The performance of the ethnicity variable was orthogonal to the behavior of the gender variable. The data showed no effect of ethnicity for any of the comprehension question categories, including both the Interpretive Reading and Critical Evaluation questions 6 to 9, and the creative reading questions Q 10 and Q11 where the gender effect was dominant. My hypothesis that there would be an effect of ethnicity in the outcomes was therefore not validated. It was not the case that the Black students did better than the other students of color in the classroom, namely the Latino, Tongan, Samoan and Fijian students.

Chapter Summary

In this chapter, I reported the main quantitative results of the study, from the perspective of narrative, demographic, and question factors. I used both descriptive statistics and analyses of variance to portray the outcomes of the effect of question category, story length, narrative genre, gender and ethnicity. These results were cast against the background of my original research questions.

The question category analysis showed that students earned higher scores on the higher-order thinking questions than they did on the lower-order ones. This is a result that I predicted early in the study, mainly because of the goodness-of-fit between such questions and the study participants. The story length analysis showed a significant effect, an outcome that ran counter to my hypothesis, but one that sends an important message about the level of narrative complexity that weak readers are capable of comprehending. Again, the fact that the students responded with equal appreciation for both folk tales and non-folk tales did not support my original hypothesis that they would favor the culturally based narratives, although the results showed that students valued the opportunity to interact with ethnic literature. The analysis of variance showed a significant effect of gender, an outcome that replicates a common phenomenon in literacy studies. Finally, the lack of an ethnicity effect showed that the diverse students who participated in the study all appreciated the ethnic literature materials that I used. The remainder of the study provides a qualitative analysis and in-depth examination and discussion of these results and outcomes.

CHAPTER 8

NARRATIVE GENRE AND LITERAL MEANING QUESTIONS

Many teachers today recognize how important it is for children to see themselves--their experiences, their cultural traditions, their histories-- reflected in the literature that is read and discussed in the classroom. These books present children with a rich variety of real and imagined situations, characters, and themes that reflect the diversity of African American experience and that help make the act of literacy meaningful to children's lives.

Terry Meier, 1997

General Questions 1, 2: Effect of Genre

An analysis of the study data showed no effect of the narrative genre variable, that is, students seemed to like both folk tale and non-folk tale types of story equally well. This outcome is perhaps most dramatically portrayed in the students' responses to General Questions 1 and 2 of the comprehension study questions, and subsequently in interview questions based on various aspects of the stories such as the illustrations. As a reminder, General Question 1 asked the students to rate how much they liked each story on a scale of 1 to 6, while General Question 2 asked students to identify which story components they liked or did not like, making their selections from the elements of theme, character, plot, setting (and also language). The results revealed remarkably comparable ratings for both Questions 1 and 2 across narrative genres. For Question 1, average rankings assigned to folk tales and contemporary narratives were identical for each group of stories--values of 4.6, 4.9, and 4.8 for each folk tale and corresponding non-folk tale, while for Question 2, the calculated mean scores for narrative components though not identical, were again similar across genres--values of 3.6, 4.2, and 4.3 for the folk tales, and 4.0, 4.4, and 3.8 for the non-folk tales (See Figure 7.3 in the previous chapter).

In the analysis, three factors emerged as potential reasons for this outcome: the structural elements of the narratives, the use of dialect features in the language base of the stories, and the presence of ethnic characters in the story illustrations. These were the factors that students identified as positive and appealing characteristics of stories in both genres. The students' perception of the variables in the two genres as heterogeneous may thus have contributed to an erosion of possible effects of the narrative genre variable as originally perceived. Firstly, it turned out that the students found the structure of the narrative components appealing in both the folk tales and non-folk tales. In addition, the fact that the narratives consistently communicated an overt ethnic core element through the use of dialect and illustrations, seemed to hold particular significance for the students, and to influence their largely positive reaction to the stories. An important facet of the narrative genre outcome is the deep meaning that this ethnic flavor in the narratives seems to have held for the students and its implications for the teaching of narrative comprehension. This outcome is investigated in this chapter and also in Chapter 12.

Despite the identification of the appealing factors outlined above, still it might be difficult to articulate exactly why the students warmed to the stories in the way that they did. This is so, primarily because the psychology of interest is an elusive phenomenon, and one that previous researchers in the fields of both psychology and education have sometimes found difficult to pin down. There are strong leads for us to follow, however, and some of the potential contributing factors that showed up in my study have been found to exist in previous work.

For example as far back as 1979, Jones found that text characteristics such as pictorial narratives and narratives containing elements of the child's natural language are powerful motivational contexts for children's reading, and can be manipulated to affect interest in and understanding of reading materials. More recently, the Ebonics controversy has caused teachers, other educators and linguists to focus once more on the salience of Black Language and Literature. In doing so, Meier (1997) contends that Black texts, either written by African American authors, and-or representing Black experiences, traditions, and histories, are important to children's literacy development for another reason as well. In a special issue of *Rethinking Schools* devoted to discussing the power, language, and education of African-American children, she suggests that such texts provide powerful linguistic models for children to draw on in developing their own speaking and writing abilities. To drive her point home, she cites the case of the literary scholar Henry Louis Gates Jr., who describes his adolescent encounter with the work of James Baldwin as life-shaping and life-transforming as he bathed his mind and intellect in the cadences and figures of Black culture portrayed therein.

A strong sense of this deep-seated and positive kind of reaction to the texts is present at an almost visceral level, in some of the students' reactions to the narratives they read. This quality seems to empower their reactions to the texts, even when their remarks are somewhat vague. The positive factors that they identified in the stories are discussed below in the following three sections: 1) Issue of Narrative Structure, 2) The Language Factor, and 3) Issue of Illustrations. Structure and language are examined as deep-structure phenomena while illustrations are explored as a less substantive, but as it turns out, almost equally important surface-structure feature.

Issue of Narrative Structure

Both the folk tales and contemporary narratives contained strong structural elements. In each case, the themes addressed issues that were developmentally appropriate for the student participants. For example, the folk tales addressed themes of parent-adolescent conflict (S #1), teenage puppy-love experiences (S #3), material wealth versus moral uprightness (S #5). The non-folk tales addressed themes of pet-animal devotion and youthful daring (S #2), the pain of losing one's best friend (S # 4), and the stigma of physical disability in youth (S #6).

Some of the students' remarks indicated that there were other narrative features including and beyond theme, that they may have found attractive. Following are samples of their comments chosen from all the stories:

Folktales

S#1: The Woman and the Tree Children
I like this one because it gets to you deep inside (African-American male).
I like this story because it shows responsibility (African American male).

S #3: Brer Rabbit Falls in Love
The main reason I like it is because it has talking animals and Brer Rabbit has problems telling people he love them just like people (Latino male).
I like it because it is about facts in life. The story is about a rabbit falling in love. Someone is falling in love right now. I like it because it is romantic (African American female).

S #5: Why Apes Look Like People
I like this story the best because ape look like people and it is very funny (Tongan-Samoan female).
I like this story because to me it is the best story of all you came to read in our classroom (Samoan male).

Non-Folk Tales

S #2: The Runaway Cow
I like this story because it is like life, sometimes people like you and sometimes they don't (African American male).
I like this story because the cow only likes the person that treats her like a good and only friend (Fijian female).

S #4: Remembering Last Summer

I like this one because it showed friendship and courage. The girl really cared for her dog and before her dog died her best friend had moved away (African American female).
I like it because it was about black people and it was also during the summer (African American female).

S #6: Ride the Red Cycle
I like Red Cycle the best because it tells about the way people tease other people who are handi-capped it is not fair (African American female).
I like #6 the best because it has really great setting and great characters (African American female).

These comments show that the students warmed to both the folk tales and non-folk tales for a variety of reasons, many of which pertained to their basic narrative qualities. They report that they found the folk tales deeply touching, realistic, and enjoyable, while they found the non-folk tales familiar, true-to-life and representative of the unfairness of life. The original contrastive features in the two sets of stories therefore turned out to be shared between genres. In fact the reaction of one of the students to one of the folk tales, S #1: *The Woman and the Tree Children*, shows clearly that the distinction between the two genres is a more complex issue than previously envisaged. One student attributes authorship of this folk tale to a specific (and maybe even modern author) suggesting that he did not get the distinction between traditional folktales which have no specific author, but carry instead the handed down wisdom of the past, and contemporary narratives, which are usually attributable to a specific author even if "anonymous". That student's remark was as follows:

> It is a good plot or story, and whoever wrote this I give them a two thumbs up for writing such a beautiful and great story. I like the medicine man because he help the woman get her some children. (Student #7)

This kind of complexity helped cloud the results insofar as a genre effect were possible, and the use of dialect and ethnic illustrations in both sets of stories helped solidify this overall effect.

The Language Factor

Both the contemporary narratives (for example Story #6) and the folk tales (for example Stories #s 3 and 5) contained the dialect known as African American Vernacular English or Ebonics. This is an important observation because, as I point out above, the students seemed to perceive the use of dialect in the stories as a significant and positive factor. As instantiations of this language-based overlap, examples of dialect use in folk tales and non-folk tales are provided below:

Folk-Tale #3: Brer Rabbit Falls in Love

"You sho' 'nuf in bad shape."
"Don't make no difference to me."

Folk-Tale #5: Why Apes Look Like People

"There's a new animal down there, that. . .ain't got no hair."
"Won't be nobody as dap as me nowhere."

Non-Folk Tale #6: Ride the Red Cycle

"Papa, uh wannn-n tha' un," he called out.
"But Dr. Ryan say that leg real stiff."

In all the excerpts quoted above, the dialect used contains examples of syntax typical of African American Vernacular English--for example, the use of double negatives in the folk tales, and the omission of the final "t" consonant and the use of the zero copula in the non-folk tale. It is plausible to assume that the students recognized this familiar dialect usage as a potent cultural dimension, and that it also factored into their appreciation of both the folk tale and non-folk tale narratives in which it occurred. Students' comments corroborate this conjecture. Note that 24 out of 25 of them said they liked the use of Black dialect in the stories. Some of their reactions follow:

I like it because it is like I am in the story. It helps the story a lot because it makes the story younik=[unique] in its own way; people have to hear there own way of talking (African American male).

I like it because dialect makes the story more interesting. Yes, because it helps the story sound like real people are talking (Latino male).

Because it puts excitement in it (the story). It helps the story by making it enjoyable (African American male).

I like the dialect because it puts a lot of feelings in it (Fijian female).

Because it was my kind of talk. I enjoy reading dialect stories and also I think it help the story (African American male).

I like it because it gives people who aren't that culture and know nothing about it a chance to see how other people are. I like dialects that are like African American not just because that's what I am, but because it is funny how they be talking--like I just did (African American female).

Students therefore acknowledged that the use of African American Vernacular English in stories had an important psychological impact on them. Apropos of the comments made earlier, one effect seems to have been that dialect use made them feel personally involved and invested in the narrative drama. They also felt that the use of dialect in text validated their own individual vernacular dialect, increased language tolerance and promoted multiculturalism. Finally, students said that the incorporation of dialect in the stories simply made them more interesting and enjoyable.

Interestingly, the students' teacher also reacted positively to the incorporation of dialect in the stories. Mr. Peters thanked me "for including a question like this one--just a great question." When I asked him why he liked the "dialect" question, his reply was:

"Because it taps into anther modality. You see, these kids learn through many different modalities. This is the oral modality. You see, they love it. They do very well here. This is great. This is great."

This was thus the kind of classroom where the teacher showed great respect for the students' vernacular dialect as a manifestation of their culture, and where as a result, the students felt motivated and encouraged to demonstrate their appreciation of it in the stories they read (for further comments on the efficacy of dialect use in teaching literacy, see Rickford & Rickford 1995). Note that although the majority of these comments are made by African Americans, they are not restricted to students representing that ethnicity; comments are in fact distributed across ethnic boundaries. This quality of cross-ethnic cultural appreciation emerges increasingly in the data in this study, and is dealt with in the discussion of the effect of ethnicity in the chapter that follows.

Issue of Illustrations

Another plausible explanation, and one which might just as easily have clouded the distinction between the two narrative genres, is the fact that ethnic illustrations occurred in both kinds of stories. Of the total of six stories, five of them contained full-page color prints of the original narrative illustrations depicting African-American characters and personalities (Story #5 was an animal story). As was the case with their reaction to dialect, the students again expressed appreciation for the incorporation of Black illustrations into the texts. Their reaction to this factor was overwhelmingly positive across all six stories. Following are some of the reactions they offered. Note again that an impressive total of 23 out of 25 students, again across ethnic boundaries, supported the use of Black illustrations:

I like the way they are made and everything. AND THERE ARE BLACK PEOPLE (Student's emphasis, African-American female).

Some of them were nicely dron [= drawn] and others were just funny (Latino male).

The illustrations made me like the story better (African American female).

They brought out some thought out of the story (Tongan-Samoan female).

I like it because it makes me feel that I am really a black girl (African American female).

Although all the students do not refer specifically to the Blackness of the characters in the illustrations, only to the enjoyment of those illustrations, they seem to have made the students feel included, and to have invested them with feelings of dignity and self-worth. Some students gave a more superficial yet consistently positive reaction when they said the illustrations were nice or funny, while others even claimed that the illustrations raised the cognitive potential of the stories. But overall, student reactions were positive.

Paradoxically then, though there was a lack of the narrative genre effect (and in addition to everything else, the small number of stories may have compounded the tendency for this outcome), the performance of this variable does seem to teach an important lesson: that students of ethnically diverse backgrounds enjoy stories that are structurally sound, and that in some way reflect their ethnicity and culture (of which language is a significant part). It seems that students feel validated and experience enhanced self-esteem when they have the opportunity to read stories with these characteristics. This is an area that needs further systematic investigation and analysis. Such research would increase our knowledge and understanding of the text factors and characteristics that impact literacy learning and comprehension, and also help settle some of the dust that the Ebonics controversy seems to have stirred up.

Literal Meaning Questions 3, 4, 5: Effect of Question Category (Lower-Order Questions)

Students earned their lowest scores of all the comprehension questions in the study on questions 3 through 5, the literal meaning questions that comprised the second category of the comprehension test. As Figure 7.1 in Chapter 7 demonstrates, performance on these lower-order thinking questions was considerably lower than performance on the higher-order thinking questions that comprised the third and fourth categories of questions. Students earned a total of 60% of the maximum possible points on the literal meaning questions, compared with a total of 79% of the maximum possible points on the interpretive reading and critical evaluation questions 6 through 9, and a total of 75 % on the creative reading questions 10 and 11.

Background to Questions 3, 4, and 5: Purpose, Crafting, Expectations, and Outcomes

Purpose and Crafting

Questions 3, 4, and 5 were designed as basic recall questions. In all six stories, these questions opened with a traditional question marker "Why" or "What", and posed a question that required the reader simply to "recall" or retrieve from the text, points of detail previously expressed in the story. The correct answer lay always within the story, often in a sentence or paragraph in virtually the same words that were used in constructing the questions--hence the category title, Literal Meaning. The standard routine in answering this particular type of question, is to seek out the relevant episode (or paragraph, or sentence) in the text from which it was crafted, and root out the appropriate response.

For example, Question 3, Story #1: "The Woman and the Tree Children" read "*Why* did the old woman think she had lived an unhappy life?", and four of the five options provided in the multiple choice answers were all taken directly from the story. In fact the correct answer, option (b)--Because she had no husband and children, appears in the story in the same episode (Episode 1), immediately following the statement that indicates she felt that she had lived an unhappy life.

Question 4 was similar in its approach and derivation. For instance Question 4 of Story #5: "Why Apes Look Like People" asked "*What* did they (the forest animals) go (up to heaven) to see God about on their previous visit?" The correct answer, option (a)--They wanted him to stop wintertime, appears in the text, again in the same episode (Episode 5) in which the particular phrasing used in the question appears.

A typical Question 5 was also text-based, but it sometimes required a small measure of inferential thinking. For example Question 5 of Story #2, "The Runaway Cow" asked: "Why did Mr. Lovelace dismiss the class after he saw the runaway cow? and the correct answer, option (d)--Because the children were being distracted by the cow, is readily given in the information that appears in the text, also in the same episode (Episode 2) in which the information given in the question appears.

The recall questions throughout the study are therefore ostensibly simple and straightforward. They require no more than the ability (and motivation or desire) to surf the text until one comes upon the correct answer, and then mark that option down. They do not require the more advanced reading skills of high-level inference, elaboration, interpretation, synthesis, and so on that the subsequent questions Q6 through Q11 in the Interpretive Reading and Critical Evaluation and the Creative Reading categories of the comprehension study require.

The purpose in asking these questions was to gather data on the strategies and techniques that the students who participated in the study, and more generally students like themselves, use in the complex process of retrieving information in narrative reading comprehension. To this end, students were given the opportunity to select which one of five possible options they considered the best choice for each question in this category, and also to indicate which of the remaining answers were possible based on the information given in the text, and which ones were the worst options. Three points were awarded for the "best" answer, two points for a "possible" answer, and one point for a "worst" answer. My thinking here was that such data would lend itself to deeper examination and analysis, and would augment the knowledge that already exists in the field in this arena, as it would help inform theory.

Expectations

One of my hypotheses upon embarking on this study, was that the students' score on these "lower-order" recall-type questions would be low, in part because of their cultural unfamiliarity with this pedantic mode of questioning. I use the word "cultural" to refer to the general tendency that some students demonstrate (many usually come from lower income and ethnic minority communities) in treating authentic questions that seek genuinely unknown information with more seriousness and attention than information that is readily available and-or obvious to all. An anthropologist who has done work in poor black communities has also observed this propensity, and discusses the phenomenon in comparing the difference in modes of questioning at home and at school (Heath, 1982b). Based on such previous research and on my own years observing its validation in elementary classrooms therefore, I expected the study participants to select responses to the questions in this category based on their individual interpretations of the text, rather than on the details and specifics that the author supplied in the narrative. By the same token, I predicted that the students would gain higher scores on the more challenging "higher-order" thinking questions because of their interest in "real" authentic questions, and their propensity for deduction and argumentation.

As Figure 7.1 in the preceding chapter generally demonstrates, my hypothesis turned out to be correct in both cases. The reasons underlying this outcome are seemingly straightforward on one level, but they become multi-faceted and abstruse upon closer examination and analysis. The approaches, orientations and rationalizations that precipitated the low scores on the recall questions 3, 4, and 5 are examined below.

Outcomes

It is interesting to take a look at some of the questions in the literal meaning question category that precipitated the lowest scores in the study. They are analyzed thoroughly below. In general, the trends that show up in the students' responses coincide with the basic orientations towards recall questions recorded in the research literature on narrative reading comprehension. But their answers also suggest other interesting dimensions to text-based questions which are important, especially considering the fact that these are largely the kinds of questions that show up on standardized tests that measure comprehension in the elementary school. The notion of the levels effect in story hierarchy (Guthrie 1978), whereby the information that appears high in the structure of the text is predicted to be recalled with greater precision than the information that appears lower in the text structure is borne out in this study. On the average, students recorded comparatively higher aggregate scores (64%) on question 3 which were crafted from the first and second episodes than they did on question 4. These earlier episodes corresponded with the higher nodes in the narrative structure where critical information pertaining to the essential narrative components of theme and plot tended to be introduced. Students earned lower aggregate scores on question 4 (54%), which were formed from the later (final and penultimate) episodes in the narrative structure, generally containing information less central to main developments in the story. More specifically, in all three cases (Question 3 of Story #6, #4, and #1) where scores topped out at above 70%, the questions had the additional boost of having their "best" answer coincide with the main idea or story theme.

For example, question 3 of Story #6 asked, "Why was Jerome upset that people were always helping him?", and the best answer, option (b) stated: Because he never got a chance to make things happen himself, which was essentially the main idea behind the story. The reason why the majority of students (twenty-one out of twenty-five students or

84%) got this answer right, could be because they encoded the theme as a powerful or central force in the story structure.

On the other hand, as I mentioned before, students were not as capable of answering recall questions correctly when they required that they retrieve specific detailed information and facts from the story. This trend was especially true when these details were located in the lower levels of the narrative structure, and were not obviously connected to the story in a thematically important way. These recall questions required that students lift detailed pieces of information out of context and in isolation from the broader and more substantive issues of the narrative. An obvious explanation for this situation would be simply that the students were such poor readers and decoders, that they were not able to return to relevant passages in the text and retrieve the particular information they needed to answer the questions correctly. After all, recall questions tend to require this ability more so than other kinds of question. This is a very attractive explanation, and one that undoubtedly holds some truth, but this possibility fades in light of the vast numbers of students who "fell" for the same "incorrect" answers, including the better readers in the group. We are therefore forced to look beyond solutions of this nature in our investigation.

The ability to comb text for the right answer to basic recall-type questions is a skill that students who are school-savvy learn well. I have been told by some of my current college-level students, for example, that when answering multiple-choice test questions in elementary and high school, they would simply read the question carefully, and then scan the text for the phrase, or line, or passage that carried the exact words of the question in order to find the correct answer. Some argue that it was even possible to answer some of these questions without ever actually reading (or understanding) the relevant passage or text from which the question came. In addition to this dubious quality, there is also an "I'm gonna try and trip you up" element to these questions that tend to appear in standardized tests and that often require almost a kind of practice in academic chicanery to understand and respond to correctly. Further, as already stated, these questions tend to be less interesting and engaging, hence less motivating to constituents of poor readers.

These are just some of the issues that must be examined in attempting to understand the students' response to the literal meaning segment of the study, and scrutiny of some of their answers is valuable. We will examine their answers to questions on which they scored most poorly (50% or less of the maximum possible points). These are Story

#1, question 4 (44%); Story #2, question 3 (49%); Story #3, question 3 (49%); Story #2, question 4, (50%); Story #3, question 5 (49%); and Story #6, question 4 (50%). Some of these are examined closely below.

Discussion

Story #1, Question 4

By far the lowest score of all was recorded for Story #1, question 4. The question asked: "What happened one day that made the woman yell at the children?" The correct answer is prompt (e) "Something happened, but we are not told". The source of this answer is the final Episode 4 in the story where it states that "one day, something happened. It does not matter what. It was nothing important. Perhaps...Perhaps etc."(see quotation below; see Appendix for entire text). To the experienced reader, the answer is obvious, and all of the study advisors who helped select each question unequivocally identified this option as the right answer. Not so the students. Only 2 out of 25 checked it. Most of the other students opted for choice (a), that one of the children laughed too loudly--10 students, or choice (b), that one of the children dropped a glass--16 students, or choice (d), that the woman was tired and irritable--11 students.

Now this question is a particularly enigmatic one, because ironically, the general impression gleaned from a reading of the story, the big picture if you will, and the one that the students take with them, is that *something* specific did precipitate the woman's anger. It is the details or the little picture that prove otherwise on careful consideration. The stylistic repetition of one reason after the other, for the old woman's anger and subsequent yelling at the children, pervades Episode 4 in the narrative structure. The words that:

Perhaps the woman had not slept well the night before, and was feeling tired and irritable that day. *Perhaps* something she had eaten was hurting her stomach. [Perhaps] one of the children laughed too loudly for the woman's ears, dropped a dish or a glass and broke it, or something else. . .(Episode 4, page 2).

serve to conjure up the irrefutable impression in the students' minds that something did happen. As a consequence, they chose the answer that in their perception, represented the stronger thematic proposition.

Note further that the particular wording of a question in this category may also have contributed to its complexity and level of difficulty. For instance this question requires that students have the ability to sort out the meaning of the abstract adverbial "perhaps" as introducing speculative possibilities as against hard statements of fact. Indeed, the one factual statement that we do have here, is, paradoxically, the one that tricks us--"something happened. It does not matter what". So we know that something happened, but we do not know what that something was. Instead we are told that "it does not matter what." The concrete nature of this information is therefore compelling in the way in which the data are presented, but also for another reason.

One might also argue that students chose the answer that conformed with their story schemata or mental structure of how the world works. It is a reasonable deduction to make that the woman yelled at her children because they broke her precious dinnerware (the option that got the highest votes--16 students out of 25). This is a reality that most children have experienced at one point or another in their lives (even adults can reflect back on at least one such occasion in our childhood), and therefore one that would suggest itself most naturally to the students. This background of experience undoubtedly contributed to their reactions to this question. However, the answer that was deemed correct for this question, was derived from a single, isolated point of detail, "it does not matter what" (Episode 4, p.2).

Story #6, Question 4

Story #6, question 4, is another example of the fundamental impact of one's mental map on the process of understanding a story--the notion that the way one perceives, organizes and adapts to the environment is based on one's cognitive experiences which are in turn influenced by an individual's schemata (Athey, 1985). The question, derived from Episode 4, asked: "Why was there an eerie quiet after Mrs. Mullarkey announced that Jerome Johnson was next on the program?" Most of the students (18 out of 25) correctly chose as the "best" answer, option (e): "Because nobody knew what he was going to do and they were afraid that he'd mess up." But they lost points on this question when 19 students checked that the option (b), "because they thought he would be great" was a possible answer as was option (d), "because Mrs. Mullarkey had great faith in Jerome" (13 students).

The text stated unequivocally that " the kids on the block had already decided that Jerome would never ride" (Episode 4) and Mrs. Mullarkey, the neighbor, was clearly skeptical of the disabled Jerome's ability to control a bicycle: "'Boy's gonna kill himself on that, Mary!' Mrs. Mullarkey whispered." These excerpts therefore ruled out the possibility of either option (b) or (d) quoted by the students above as viable answers. However, the students nurtured a great deal of sympathy for Jerome's character (most respondents chose him as the favorite character on Favorite Character Question 7), and maybe at a deep and even unconscious psychological level, wanted to see him succeed. In answering the question therefore, they may have allowed their mental scripts or frames to take preeminence over the details of the story. They were snagged by the lure of their inner feelings and dispositions towards the story.

Story #3, Question 5

Story #3, Question #5 further demonstrates this point. It asked the following question: "Why do you think the girl tried to pretend like she was out taking a walk and happened to come that way when she went down to the big pine the morning after she got the sign?" Only about a half of the students (13 of them) recognized the right answer (option e), that is, that she did not want Brer Rabbit to think that she was overly excited about getting married to him (again an answer that all the study consultants agreed on readily), whereas almost as many students (11) chose the decoy answer as the correct one--Because she didn't want Miz Meadows to find out (option d). My guess is that the answer happened to coincide with the students' cognitive framework and probably with their experiences too. The decoy answer said that the girl did not want Miz Meadows to find out about what she was doing. This answer is really an unlikely one since the text shows clearly and at many points that Miz Meadows was very open to the possibility that one of the girls might fall in love with Brer Rabbit. In fact, one might even say that Miz Meadows was conspiring to help bring about this match, "Have you told the girl you in love with her?" (Episode 2), and so on. But faced with the same situation, the students would probably imagine a scenario in which the girl tried to hide her impending love-affair from her mother. It is conceivable then, that they were led in their choice of response by their perception of the mother-daughter adolescent relationship based on their prior real (or vicarious) experiences. Furthermore, the issue of (formal) language usage discussed in the analysis of Story # 1, question 4 above, again applies here. Note that this is a very linguistically complex question in that the main clause contains several embedded clauses: "Why do you think...when...after...?"

Story #2, Question 3

Finally, students' response to Story #2, question 3 provides an excellent demonstration of their general approach to the literal meaning category of questions. The question asked: "Why did Julie's mother and Granny think that Julie had a charm over Annette?" The answer to this question is given in the sentence that Annette's "large eyes looked at Julie very gently, and she never stamped her hoofs or swished her tail around if Julie were nearby" (Episode 1), contained in option (b) in the answers--"Because Annette's large eyes looked at Julie gently". However, only nine students got this answer right. Most of them-- twenty-one--felt that the best choice was option (a), "Because Annette led a peaceful life." Now Annette did lead a peaceful life, and Julie's "special care" *was* the main source of her happiness, but the story supplies a more specific and immediate reason, namely the way she looked at her caretaker. Again, the students preferred to focus on the fundamental meaning of the story, rather than on the minutiae of the clause. Again, as it were, the devil is in the details.

One might argue that these students need to be trained in the fine-grained techniques of recall questions, in order to perform better on these types of question. This is true, indeed a laudable and essential pursuit, and one that will be necessary if they are to score well on traditional standardized assessment tools often designed to test the kind of literal-level meanings germane to this question genre. But the problem may not be simply an additive one. Students were often observed to be carefully browsing through the text before selecting their answer. They were also quite capable of invoking detail when they needed it to support a point or to pursue a certain line of argument in answering subsequent questions that required interpretive reading and critical evaluation. But their cognitive processes worked best when they were able to engage with the story, express their feelings and negotiate their understandings with the narrative content. When comprehension involved a two-way flow between author and reader, as in the case of the higher-order thinking questions in subsequent question categories 3 and 4, students' scores improved. They seemed more interested in and motivated by the authentic life-based questions that arose from *their* understanding of the text than the text-based recall questions that were rooted in the author's encoding of story particulars and points of detail.

Heath's work (1983) with children in the Piedmont Carolinas bears this out. She explained that while the more mainstream White Roadville children would "excel in class when they [were] requested to recall a straightforward account or to retell a lesson" (p. 298), the less mainstream Black children could not "lift labels and features out of their contexts for explication" (p.353), but instead were able to "link seemingly disparate factors in their explanations, and to create highly imaginative stories" (p. 353). A possible explanation could be that the rich and complex discourse processes and interactions that mark the pulse of inner city and other ethnic communities enrich and support these tendencies that are revealed in the classroom.

Ethnic minority students who are at risk for academic failure do not seem to find purpose, interest, and motivation in the staid routine of memory type questions. In order to maintain interest in school (note that the high school drop-out rate in East Tall Tree is upwards of 70%), and encourage continuing attendance, these students need to be engaged in classroom activities. One source of interest could be the kinds of comprehension questions that they are asked to think about and answer. Teachers could conceivably place greater emphasis on the interactive type of questions that draw on the wealth of personal experiences that most of these students have had by the time they are in the middle grades at school. Such a strategy would give them increased opportunities for success in school and a more solid base on which to incorporate training in answering the old-school, traditional type of recall questions that they need to develop skills in also. Interest in classroom based questions and activities would also encourage "buy-in" to the idea of school so needed among these populations. As Calfee and Patrick suggest, students could more profitably be involved with "a literacy curriculum that promotes reading and writing as cognitive competencies, rather than behavioral skills, that support learning as active and reflective rather than passive and rote," (Calfee & Patrick, 1995, p.51).

Most of the remaining recall questions on which the students earned low scores resulted from this focus on processing the main idea of a story, and on engaging their cognitions with the complex thematic and narrative issues rather than on the minutiae that often form the core of literal-meaning questions. They focused on the meanings they were able to negotiate from their interactions with the text (Heath, 1983; p.196), rather than on ascribing supreme authority to the word of the text. This tendency supports the concept of a "hypothesis-driven" rather than "data-driven" approach to narrative comprehension that story grammarians describe (Anderson, 1985). It also reminds us of the complexity of the mental processes of recall and memory that service the process of reading comprehension. Unlike the common impression that these kinds of questions are simplistic and easy--another reason that poor readers are so often saddled with them--these analyses demonstrate the complex and multi-faceted nature of narrative recall. But the word of the text is important also, both in answering comprehension questions, in other multiple-choice situations, and also in real life situations. An understanding of students' techniques and strategies in dealing with these questions is therefore instructive especially since given the above analysis, it seems likely that failure to answer literal meaning questions must not necessarily be interpreted as ignorance on the part of some students. Van Dijk and Kintsch (1985) captured the essence of the complexity of students' thinking processes in the following statement:

> Recall is not mere reproduction, but involves reasoning and explaining. In other words memory and hence recall are essentially reconstructive, and are based on rationalizations of different sorts, and on the current knowledge, interests, and emotional attitude of the subject with respect to the story and its content (p.795).

Chapter Summary

In this chapter I discussed the results and outcomes of General Questions 1 and 2, and Literal Meaning questions 3, 4, and 5 in the comprehension question set. With respect to the General questions, I analyzed the effect of story structure, language, and illustrations on the students' enjoyment and appreciation of all of the narrative texts including both folk tales and non-folk tale selections. With respect to the Literal Meaning questions, I compared the scores that the students earned on this lower-order question category with the scores that they earned on the two higher-order comprehension question categories of interpretive reading and critical evaluation. I demonstrated that students recorded the lowest scores of all questions on the literal meaning segment, and that this result confirmed my original hypothesis that the students would find the task of answering the questions in the recall question category "correctly" a challenging one. This was an outcome that I had predicted, arguing that these students with their particular academic, cultural and socio-economic backgrounds and propensities, tend to have weak skills of identification and decontextualization, but strong skills of argumentation and contextualization. An in-depth analysis of students' answers to the Literal Meaning Questions 3 through 5 was undertaken, tracing trends and patterns that showed up in the data, linking them with prior research findings, and suggesting additional explanations and new perspectives.

CHAPTER 9

INTERPRETIVE READING AND CRITICAL EVALUATION QUESTIONS

The history of literacy shows that education has not, for the most part, been directed primarily at...personal growth and development. Rather it has stressed...different sorts of behaviors and attitudes for different classes of individuals: docility, discipline...for the lower classes...verbal and analytical skills, 'critical thinking'...for the higher classes.

James Paul Gee, 1990

Effect of Question Category for Higher-Order Questions: Interpretive Reading and Critical Evaluation Questions 6, 7, 8, 9.

In this chapter I analyze and interpret the results of Questions 6 through 9, the category of questions that I asked the students to answer in the "Interpretive Reading and Critical Evaluation" segment of the comprehension study. I demonstrate the strength of their answers to the questions in this category that caused them to earn scores that were significantly higher than the scores earned in the previous literal meaning question category, and indeed in all the question categories. Students earned an impressive total of 79% of the maximum possible points on these questions. This performance led to the effect of higher-order over lower-order questions that showed up in the data set, arguably one of the most consequential outcomes of the entire study. More important than the high scores themselves however, is the actual source of those scores--the high quality answers and depth of engagement and involvement that students' written work demonstrated. Throughout this chapter, I draw on a sample of student answers taken from both the folk tale and non-folk tale genres, selecting examples that are representative of the general thrust of responses. It is important to note that I have included examples from almost every student respondent in the sample (22 out of 25 students), while the ideas and orientations of all the student participants are represented. The abilities that I praise in the selected samples are therefore not restricted merely to a few "star" students (although some students obviously tend to give richer responses than others), but represent instead the strengths of all the study participants. This is an important consideration in terms of the general applicability of the comments made in this chapter.

Background to Question 6 through 9: Purpose, Crafting, Expectations and Outcomes

Purpose and Crafting

These four questions were designed to be distinctively different from the questions analyzed in the previous chapter in the literal meaning question category--different in conception, formulation and function. Whereas the literal meaning questions were text-based and tapped into recall or memory-type functions, these interpretive reading and critical evaluation questions were reader-based and required skill in making inferences, in deductive reasoning, in argumentation and in interpretation. Instead of depending on the author's schemata to help them understand points of detail in the story, students were now invited to filter text-based information through their own prisms of experience, understanding, and interpretation. While the formula for constructing the recall questions required that they be derived from the early and late narrative episodes, the interpretive reading and critical evaluation questions were all derived from the nodes in the narrative map that signaled dramatic tension. Such nodes represent an episode of maximum character interaction, a climactic episode, or an episode of intense character affect. These action episodes are typically characterized by the tension between right and wrong, good and bad--the essence of the moral dilemma. These questions were therefore structurally grounded in the "grammar" of the story, and in the open-ended analysis that questions six through nine demanded. In a real sense, they were the important questions--the ones that carried the lasting meaning that would be derived from the stories. Finally, whereas the literal questions were of the multiple-choice variety, questions six through nine required short-essay type answers.

A typical question 6 or Moral Judgment question was framed thus: "Was it right or wrong for character X to behave in a particular way Y? Students were asked to take a position, and defend it. The second part of the question asked: "Give a reason for your answer." A typical question 7 or Favorite Character question asked: Who is your favorite character in the whole story? Explain why you like this character best." Again in their response, students were expected to stake a claim, and provide a well-reasoned warrant in support of it. A typical question 8 or Character Feelings and Qualities question had two parts. Part 1 asked: "How do you think X felt when Y happened?" and Part 2 asked students to explain their answer, "X felt this way because..." Students were given the chance to select three qualities (from a list of twelve) that most matched their evaluation of the character's feelings, but were also encouraged to add their own "qualities" in writing up their answers. Finally, a typical question 9 or Deductive Reasoning question generally asked students to propose an explanation for someone's behavior based partially on the knowledge and information acquired from the specific story. There was some measure of internal variation among individual questions 9 based on the specifics of particular stories. But in general, students were required to draw on their powers of deduction and reasoning to answer them all. For example in Story #2, question 9 read: "At the end of the story we are told that Pete changes very much. 'When he came to school, he bent over his books like a real scholar.' Do you believe that he really changed this much? Explain your answer." Here, as in all other cases, students need to find a warrant for the belief that they claim. As far as possible, however, the four questions in this category were worded similarly throughout the stories for purposes of comparison.

Expectations

One of my hypotheses upon embarking on this study was that the students would become engaged and absorbed with these higher-order thinking questions because they would find them authentic, meaningful, and relevant to their own lives and backgrounds of experience. Consequently, I predicted that they would earn considerably higher scores on answering questions assigned to this interpretive reading and critical evaluation question category than they would on questions assigned to the preceding literal meaning question category. I argued that these questions posed the kinds of realistic situations and dilemmas that the students could immerse themselves in, consider, and problem-solve. I contended that the levels of discussion, interpretation, argumentation, and persuasion that these questions supported would stimulate cognitive engagement and afford students opportunities in reading literature that they would conceivably encounter in their own lives and communities.

My expectations were justified. As was demonstrated in Figure 7.1 in Chapter 7, students consistently earned higher aggregate percentage averages on questions six through nine than they did on questions three through five on all the stories. By contrast, as previously explained, they earned only 60% of the total possible score on recall questions 3 through 5 averaged over all six stories for all 25 students. Below I discuss trends in the students' responses that led to this outcome, marking the interpretive reading and critical evaluation questions 6 through 9 as high-scoring question types.

Outcomes and Trends in Student Responses

In general, students demonstrated their skills of argumentation and discussion in answering these contextualized questions. Achievement levels for each of these questions were very comparable and consistently high, ranging from 74% to 79% of average aggregate scores--79% on question 6, 74% on question 7, 90% on question 8, and 74% on question 9. Several themes emerged in students' answers.
1. In confronting issues of morality, they were adept at presenting their own point-of-view in argument, and a well-reasoned perspective with supporting details drawn either from the literary base or from their experiential base to substantiate it.

2. Participants consistently showed empathy for narrative characters in the role of the underdog, perhaps because the challenges those characters had to face in some way mirrored the challenges of their own lives.
3. Students showed skill in identifying and discussing the feelings and emotions of characters who found themselves in stressful and-or threatening situations.
4. Generally, respondents demonstrated their ability to argue and reason using strategies of deduction and inference in answering the questions in the interpretive reading and critical evaluation question category of the study. The ideas, analyses, and interpretations that they articulated in answering these higher-order thinking questions are discussed under the following four themes: 1) Issues of morality; 2) Empathy for the underdog; 3) Character feelings and emotions; 4) Argumentation and reasoning.

1. *Issues of Morality: Participant Perspectives*

The question of moral education in schools is an issue that has moved towards center stage within recent years, spurred on by the publication and popularity of former Education Secretary William Bennett's "Book of Virtues" (1993), and by several more recent articles on character education and the teaching of values (Doyle, 1997; Kohn, 1997). In a special article on "Teaching Themes of Care", Noddings (1995) also makes a case for the centrality and importance of these issues in our systems of education, and makes a plea for us to redirect the primary focus of our educational efforts towards themes of caring, arguably an extension of the more abstract and larger idea of morality:

> We would like to give a central place to the questions and issues that lie at the core of human existence. . . To have as our educational goal the production of caring, competent, loving and lovable people is not anti-intellectual. . . We should want more from our educational efforts than adequate academic achievement, and we will not achieve even that meager success unless our children believe that they themselves are cared for and learn to care for others (Noddings, 1995; p. 675-676).

In my own study, Question 6 in each narrative is a morality or a caring question. Like Noddings, I agree that these are issues of the utmost importance and that when possible, connections should be made

Interpretive Reading and Critical Evaluation Questions 155

between moral issues that arise in narrative textual analysis and students' larger world experience. As my study demonstrates, these issues can be intertwined in the very fabric of the language arts curriculum in the form of strategic comprehension questions that encourage thought and thoughtfulness about the self as a whole and autonomous entity, and about others as they impact and intersect with the self and with other people. Such questions offer students the chance to reflect on their own personal value systems, and to exercise their potential for empathy and sympathy towards others. The study participants responded to this challenge with a commendable display of justice, compassion, and caring.

For instance, Question 6 of Story #1: "The Woman and the Tree Children" read: "Was it right or wrong for the woman to lose her temper and scream at the children? Give a reason for your answer." I suspect that most of us adults would be relatively forgiving of the old woman, especially those among us who are parents and have had the experience of losing our temper, secure in the knowledge that we would soon regain it. Not so the students. Out of the total twenty-five students in the study, a massive twenty-three (92%) checked wrong, and only one checked right (one student checked both), their responses plainly filtering through the prism of a child's perspective. Student responses were recorded verbatim.

Sample Answers to Question 6, Story #1: The Woman and the Tree Children, (R=Respondent)

It was wrong because then there will be nobody to help her do the dishes, clean, and nobody to bring the cattle from the field. And also the kids would feel bad. And most of all she would stay unhappy. (R #8)

It was wrong because they didn't do anything for her to yell at those kids. They are just poor little inisant =[innocent kids]. She would want anybody to yell at her for no reason? (R #4)

It was wrong because the children didn't know that she was irritable and feel so weak. The best thing to do without screaming at the kids, will be, you have to tell them that you are tired, and they will know. (R #9)

It was wrong because the children did not know that there mother was irritable. So they just thought it was okay to laugh loudly. And if they knew they wouldn't have laugh very loudly so the woman would not yell. (R #16)

One of the two students who felt that the old lady could be forgiven for shouting, explained his choice in eloquent terms:

Because she was sick, irritable, and stressed, so she didn't really mean what she had told them, because, remember, <u>she</u> (emphasis) asked for the children." (R #20)

These are all responses that earned the full 3 points because they show both morality and compassion. Students' are alternately concerned with the common good (#8), with showing compassion for the Tree Children (#4), and with presenting a balanced opinion (#20). They take the moral high ground when they adopt the mother's perspective (#9, #16), especially when one bears in mind that these children themselves live in very challenging circumstances and have projected beyond their own situations into the ethos of the story.

As a second example, consider responses to Question 6 in Story #2: "The Runaway Cow" which read: "Do you think it was a good or bad idea for Pete to try to ride the cow? Give a reason for your answer." The students voted overwhelmingly against Pete's action. Twenty-two of them said it was a bad idea, while only three agreed that it was a good idea. The students who said it was a bad idea quoted concern for Pete's physical safety and for the safety of the cow as reasons. But they also took umbrage at the idea that he skipped school in order to steal a ride on a cow. Generally therefore, students upheld a position of moral responsibility in upbraiding and reprimanding Pete for making a bad decision. The few students who said it was a good idea gave reasons that hearkened back to the same premise, namely that Pete had made a bad decision and that he could stand to learn a lesson from this experience. These reactions are somewhat ironic, and rather poignant given the fact that statistics show that for a variety of reasons, some of these students are likely to drop out of school when they reach the upper levels. The irony lies in the fact that the reasons for the high attrition rates include the lack of opportunities for meaningful participation and involvement in classroom activities, such as these higher-order thinking questions and discussions provide.

Interpretive Reading and Critical Evaluation Questions

Sample Answers to Question 6, Story #2: The Runaway Cow, (R=Respondent)

It was a bad idea because he now=[know] that the cow was too heavy and picture if he fell and the cow ran over him he would either have broke his back or ribs. That is dangerous. I wouldn't do that because I have common sense. (R #13)

It was a bad idea because he could have gotten kill when the cow had thrown him off and he could have landed on his head. (R #24)

It was a bad idea because the cow might have ran into the bushes and maybe he might have been lost or something. (R #8)

He shouldn't have because he had no business getting on a cow anyways, and he did not even know what kind of cow it was. He should have been in school and not try to be out riding a cow. (R #5)

It was a good idea so he could learn his lesson. (R #18)

Finally, consider the responses to Story #5, question 6, which read: "Do you think it was right or wrong that God changed his mind after agreeing to turn the forest animals into man-animals? Give a reason for your answer." Almost all of the students (24 out of 25) said that God was right in changing his mind. Only one lonely voice dissented. Surprisingly, the students expressed no moral indignation in the fact that God's words were not binding, and that he failed to keep his promise to the forest animals. Perhaps because the character of God is awe-inspiring even in narratives, students hesitated to place any blame there. The more likely reason, however, was that they assessed the extent to which He was right or wrong based on the viability of his actions. Their approach was pragmatic rather than absolute. The opinion that emerged from their answers was that a promise should not be morally binding if circumstances change, and make its potential effect harmful. Students also expressed an antipathy towards greed and selfishness in life. One student captured the gist of the class' attitude in her rich vernacular--"The animals don't have to wear it (that is, God's kindness) out with bad men behavior" (Respondent #16). Following are some of the more comprehensive answers that demonstrate this kind of thinking:

Sample Answers to Question 6, Story #5: Why Apes look like People, (R=Respondent)

It was right because if they were greety=[greedy] then while they were animals, how would they react if they were people? (R #2)

I think it was right because then when they become people they pollute the air and do a lot of bad stuff to make the lord more unhappy. (R #8)

It was right because he was disappointed when the animals were talking about what they were going to do when they turned into man-animal. Also because you have to be proud of who you are. (R #9)

It was right because god tried to be nice to them and they took it for granted and started getting greedy and selfish and it was already enough wrong in the world. (R #25)

It was right because the man-animals messed up the world, they killed everything in sight. (R #20)

There was one final reason why the students felt that God was right in changing his mind about turning the forest animals into man-animals. They explained that people should always be proud of who they are and not yearn to change their identity. Students first indicated this strong sense of self in my individual interviews with them when they (representatives from the multiple ethnic groups in the class) said that they liked the study narratives because of the strong ethnic thrust (dialect, themes, illustrations and so on) that reflected positively on their identity as a group of students of color. They reiterated the necessity of a positive self-image and the importance of being an advocate for one's own kind in their responses to this question:

It was right because the forest animals were not man animals. People should be who they are, and not try to be someone else. The man-animals may not want them to be like them. Be yourself for who you are !!! (R #4)

I think it was right because they need to stand up to Man and tell him about himself. And they need to be there to stand up for their family. (R #7)

In upholding this philosophy, the students continue to demonstrate the same impressive level of moral reasoning pointed out above in my earlier analyses. They present convincing arguments that bolster their own moral framework, based on examples and counter-examples from the narratives.

2. Empathy for the Underdog: Participant Perspectives

The art of creating character is a complex but important one. Characters are the conveyors of theme, itself the most enduring facet of a good narrative (Heisinger & Wolf, 1989). They are therefore a vital facet for developing story. In reading narratives, children identify with one or more characters because they resonate with the author's portrayal of the person's thoughts and actions and their eventual outcomes. They are then able to make inferences and deductions about a specific character whom they admire or dislike. My aim in composing Favorite Character question 7 was to give students an opportunity to do just this. This question was intended to draw students into the heads and hearts of characters, and encourage them to analyze their attraction to any one personality they most favored. Throughout the study therefore, question 7 included a line-up of all the characters in each narrative, and the question asked students to select one as their favorite. It provided six blank lines on which students were asked to give the reasons for their choice.

Student answers to Question 7 were well developed. They were able to articulate the qualities that they admired in a favorite character with poise and clarity. In discussing these admirable qualities, students often forged links between the behavior of a character in the narrative, and their inner world of values and feelings. In general, the students chose as their favorite character an underdog, a character (whether human or animal) who was in a position of challenge and stress. Whether it was the tree-children who were abused by the old lady in Story #1, or the girl whose best friend Pepper died of a heart attack in Story #4, students consistently demonstrated an affinity to this "distressed" character type.

Given the difficult challenges that many of these students face in their daily personal lives, this preference for a character who is disadvantaged because of injustice or discrimination, is probably not merely coincidental, but related to students' perceptions of their own reality as disenfranchised and marginal members of society. Never did they like a character for superficial reasons such as external or physical appearance.

Their responses transcended this basic level of attraction and explored the higher domain of traits, behaviors, feelings and temperaments. In all cases, students provided compelling accounts of the qualities and traits that they found endearing in their favorite character choices. Participant responses to the favorite character question across the board, reinforce the importance of narratives that are relevant thematically and sociologically to the readers' life and background. The analysis of their responses that follows makes it clear that cognition, that is, the kind of knowing that comes with background and culture and experience, does in fact influence comprehension.

Story #1, question 7 read as follows: "Who is your favorite character in the whole story? Give a reason for your answer." Only three students picked the character of the old woman, the lead character, as their favorite. By contrast, most of the adult raters who read this story felt sympathy for the old woman (all but one who took the perspective of the students). Fourteen students embraced the character of the mistreated Tree Children while the three students who chose the Old Woman commended her character primarily insofar as she was connected with the children. Most of the students who chose the Tree Children pointed to their positive character qualities---kindness, goodness, and helpfulness. Similarity in age between the students and the tree children was also a factor in their attraction. Some of the responses read as follows The favorite character that the participants chose is indicated prior to the responses:

Sample Answers Question 7, Story #1: The Tree Children, (R=Respondent)

The Tree Children:

I like this character because they were beautiful and inisant. They looked sad and I like them. (R #4)

I like the tree children because they were nice, kind and helpful to the woman and to thereselves. (R #5)

They were good and they were the best part of the story. They were good, they make the bed, do the dishes and do all the chores. (R #9)

Interpretive Reading and Critical Evaluation Questions 161

I like the tree children because they were kind and they helped clean the house and they made her happy. (R #24)

They are probley my age and they help the old woman clean up and was kind to come into the old womans life. (R #11)

The Old Woman:

I like this character because she wanted to be a mother and she was determined to do that, but she made a mistake. (R #3)

I like the old woman because she was nice and kind. And she liked kids and wanted a husban[d]. (R #24)

Some of the students also chose the Medicine Man as their favorite character. Eight students, approximately a third of the class, said they liked him best. Interestingly, however, their stated reasons hearkened back to their liking for the character of the tree-children insofar as he was instrumental in their creation. Some students said they liked his positive character qualities, while others mentioned his link to the children in his role as the woman's source for acquiring them. In commenting on the extent to which he liked the story, one student probably voiced the opinion of the entire class when he said that he gave the author "two thumbs up for writing such a beautiful and great story." Following are sample quotations:

The Medicine Man

I like the medicine man because he helped the old woman. He helped the old woman get the tree children. He also could have got her a husband but the old woman did not want one. (R #6)

I like the medicine man because he is smart and helpful and he help out constently (=constantly) when she needed help. (R #12)

The medicine man helped the old woman get children. He told her to go to a tree and get the fruit and take it back to her house and go for a walk. Then when she came back she had some children at her house. (R #14)

It is a good plot or story, and whoever wrote this I give them a two thumbs up for writing such a beautiful and great story. I like the medicine man because he help the woman get her some children. (R #7)

Story #2, question 7 also asked students who their favorite character was. Thirteen students, more than half the class, chose Annette, the cow, as their favorite character. They also perceived Annette as the underdog in the story, since she was portrayed as a peaceful, loyal cow whom Pete took advantage of in trying to ride her "like a horse or mule". They took more pity on her plight than on Pete, the young rider who is thrown in the story. Following are some of their answers:

Sample Answers to Question 7, Story #2: The Runaway Cow, (R=Respondent)

I like this character because she was friendly to the person who takes care of her and because she knows who is who. The cow knows how to act in front of the person who really knows her, and not [the one who] just wants her for a ride. (R #21)

I like Annette the cow because she's pretty, and a gentle and loving cow. She never bothers anyone. So that's why I like Annette. (R #5)

Annette was exciting and I think that she was the main character in the story. I also liked how she thought, and how she threw Pete off of her. (R #17)

In Story #3, the strong favorite was the protagonist and underdog Brer Rabbit who earned twenty-one votes, while the remaining four votes went to Miz Meadows' daughter. Students described the character of Brer Rabbit in exciting terms, and seemed to identify with him in a special way. Both the boys and the girls saw him as an icon of the perfect teenager. He seemed to embody all the traits that young people aspire to as they approach adolescence. They admired his spunk, cleverness, confidence, and persistence, and empathized with his muddled, confused, love-sick state of mind. They thought he was smart and funny, "crazy" and loving, and applauded his unflinching pursuit of the girl he loved. Although the narrative portrays him as a former shady character who now "couldn't steal and couldn't scheme", the students concentrated on the reformed aspect of his character, and not his

Interpretive Reading and Critical Evaluation Questions

former nature. Their responses speak for themselves. This is a character with which the students identified maximally:

Sample Answers to Question 7, Story #3: Brer Rabbit Falls in Love, (R=Respondent)

I like Brer Rabbit because of all the "effort" he put into this story, and because I like rabbits. (R #2)

I like Brer Rabbit because when he was told that the girl didn't want to get married with him, he didn't give up. He kept trying. (R #6)

I like Brer Rabbit because he was interesting in the story, and he seemed to be a kind and a loving young fellow. (R #9)

I like this character because he was funny, and he was very, very, clever. And he stopped doing bad and really nasty things to people. (R #12)

I think Brer Rabbit had lots of courage to ask the girl to marry him. The girl insisted on a sign and she got a sign, and Brer Rabbit believed in himself and he got to marry her. (R #14)

Brer Rabbit is the main character in the story, and he is also crazy and loving, and will probably do anything to get someone's hand in marriage. In other words, he cares for the girl he marries. (R #17)

I like Brer Rabbit because he was smart to convince the girl to come down to the pine, and he was sitting there. (R #17)

In Story #4, the most popular choice for favorite character was the dog Pepper. Although Pepper was not introduced to the reader as a character in the role of the underdog, he assumes this role because he dies early in the story, seemingly undeservedly, after having been a faithful friend and companion to the protagonist, "one of the best friends I ever had". Almost half of the students--eleven--chose Pepper. The students who liked the character of the dog best of all, cited reasons that were consistent with the reasons discussed above in the other stories. They said they admired the special qualities of his character, his friendship, understanding and kindness, his loyalty and devotion to his owner. Students also felt sympathy for him when he died. Following are some sample responses:

Sample Answers to Question 7, Story #4: Remembering Last Summer, (R=Respondent)

The dog Pepper was real sweet and made a good friend. He understood people's problems and liked to play with other people. (R #17)

I like Pepper because he is a dog and dogs are loial=[loyal]. He was loyal throughout the whole time, even when he died. (R #1)

I like Pepper the dog because he had the best role and he was a good friend to everybody. I also like Pepper because I felt sorry for him when he died. (R #6)

The seven students who chose the girl as their favorite character, mainly valued the tight bond with her dog. One student upheld the love that existed between the girl and her dog as a model of the perfect relationship, and one that she and her classmates could stand to emulate:

I like the dog and the girl because they are the main ones and they show much love for each other, and that gives us kids something to think about. (R #8)

The students who voted for Grandma (also seven) as their favorite character, either appreciated her insightfulness and tactfulness in dealing with the girl's sadness and loss, or simply ascribed to that character, the positive connotations of the traditional caring, loving grandmother, so dear in many children's hearts:

I like the grandma because she could understand the girl's problem. She told the girl that people that died did not want their relatives or friends to be sad. They would always want them to be happy. (R #14)

I like Grandma because she was understanding and very helpful. (R #2)

I like Grandma's character because it is a good character, and because it is Grandma. (R #19)

3. Character Feelings and Emotions: Participant Insights

Question 8 gave students the opportunity to examine and intuit the feelings and emotions of narrative personalities who were confronted with stressful situations. A typical question 8 described a difficult moment in the narrative for any particular character, and then asked students to select three qualities that described the person's feelings and emotions during that difficult time. In constructing each question 8, a list of potential character qualities was provided from which the students were expected to choose three that best described the character in question. In general, students were good at selecting just the right qualities that reflected the feelings of characters at points of dramatic tension in the narratives. They also handled the task of explaining the reasons for their choice with excellence and ease, often taking the time to give detailed explanations to justify the selection of a particular character quality.

Students were skillful at describing the extremes of emotion in the narratives--both the nadir of despair (as in Story #1) and the zenith of elation (as in Story #3). The proverbial Wordsworthian "willing suspension of disbelief" seemed to take effect here as the students immersed themselves in the flow of the drama, and offered an emotional paraphrase of a particular character's experience. Students' responses to Stories #s 1, 3, and 4 are provided as examples of this skill.

Story #1, The Woman and the Tree Children, question 8 read as follows: "How do you think the children felt after the old woman got angry and told them she could not expect any better from them because they were nothing but children of the tree?' Choose three of the qualities that best describe how they felt, and explain why you think the children felt this way." In answering this question, the students empathized with the tree children, reflecting the depth of their sorrow and anguish at being "dissed" (disrespected) by their own mother. Students commiserated with the pain of degradation and the depletion of self-esteem that the tree children experienced with their mother's chilling words "you are nothing but children of the tree" and unleashed their emotions in their responses:

Sample Answers to Question 8, Story #1 : The Woman and the Tree Children, (R=Respondent)

I think they felt sad because they really thought she loved them. They were angry because they were so good and helpful. I think they felt unwanted because she yelled and was mad (R #5).

They felt sad, angry and unwanted because they tried hard to be nice to the woman and they even cleaned up for her and [still] she screamed at them (R #25).

They were sad and probly because they never been hollered at before and because she hollerd at them they probably thought she didn't want them anymore and that made them feel alone and unwanted (R #20).

The majority of the students chose "sad" (23 out of 25) and "unwanted" (23 out of 25) as qualities that described the way the children felt. "Angry" (8 out of 25) and "alone" (8 out of 25) were a far second among the most popular of choices. It is noteworthy that students did not depend on the descriptors with which they were provided in composing their answers to this question. They drew on their own funds of knowledge and added their own adjectives like "hurt", "helpless", "not-loved", and "homeless" to capture the despair of the moment. In their answers to question 8, students demonstrated that if text and question are thought-provoking and moving, they will themselves be inspired to be original and creative:

Dirty, hungry and homeless. They had a cruel mama and it made them think that they were homeless without a dollar to they name and had to eat fish out the sea (R #13).

In Story #3, question 8 read: "While Brer Rabbit was sitting by the creek, the girl he was in love with came by singing. The story says 'Brer Rabbit's heart started going pitty-pat, his ears jumped straight up in the air like antennae on a TV set, and he slicked down his hair real flat.' How do you think Brer Rabbit felt at this moment? Select 3 emotions that best describe how he felt, and say why you think he felt this way." In answering this question, students resonated with the thrill and beauty of first love. Although at the young age of 12 and 13, many of them may actually have had limited real-life experiences with romance, they would almost certainly have discussed and thought about these issues in their budding adolescence. Their ruminations and realities are expressed in some of the answers they gave:

Sample Answers to Question 8, Story #3: Brer Rabbit falls in Love, (R=Respondent)

Delighted, excited and cheerful. He like the girl, so when he sees her he always feel so cheerful, or he feels so happy, [even though] seeing someone you love without letting them know can make you very nervous. (R #8)

Delighted, excited and lucky. The woman that he love was coming and he wanted to look good for her. (R #11)

He felt hopeful that the girl would noties [=notice] him. He felt excited because of the answer he would get from the girl. He felt nervous because he proble thought that the girl will ignor him and walk away. (R #21)

He was excited that he saw the girl. He was nervous because he did not know how to tell the girl he liked her. He felt hopeful because he hoped that the girl might like him and would marry him. (R #14)

Brer Rabbit felt delighted, excited and cheerful. He got shot by her beauty. (R #2)

Story #4, question 8 read: "After her dog Pepper died, the girl said she felt the way 'your mouth feels after the dentist gives you a shot.' What do you think she meant? Circle 3 of the qualities that best describe how she felt. Why did she feel this way? Explain your answer." In their answers to this question, students show all too well that they understand the pain and permanence of death. They speak with a sense of pathos of its physical, emotional, and psychological trauma. Many of these young people have already experienced loss on a personal level as a result of the violence of the drug trade and gang warfare in their communities (Garbarino et al, 1992), and some of their answers reflect the struggles of coping with the harsh consequences. Following is a representative sample of their responses:

Sample Answers to Question 8, Story #4: Remembering Last Summer, (R=Respondent)

Numb, empty and weak. She didn't know what to do since [now] she had no real friend, and she felt empty because she lost both of them [her friends], and she felt weak because she needed someone to tell her feelings to. (R #17)

Empty, weak and tearful. I think she felt empty because then there won't be anybody making her feel better or maby she feel week cause all she is gonna do know=[now], is sit down and stuff. (R #8)

Sad, weak, tearful. I think she felt this way because he had been with her for a long time also that she didn't have anybody else to play with. (R #12)

Numb, weak, tearful. When you sometimes get a shot you get numb. You also feel weak. When you get a shot you feel tearful. You feel like crying. You feel like you cannot move because it might hurt very much. [That's how she felt] (R #14)

Sad, hungry and tearful. She was sad he died. She felt like eating something. She felt tearful. She felt like crying. She was very sad. (R #19)

Most of the students chose labels that emphasize the hollowness of death. The words "tearful", "empty", "weak" and "numb" were among the most popular choices. One of them, student #19, chose the epithet "hungry" to describe the girl's feelings after her dog died, while others also alluded to eating as a nervous psychological attempt to fill the chasm of emptiness--"sit down and stuff". This ability to apply their own thoughts and experiences with death to the story context, gave their answers a touching, poignant quality. Coincidentally, student #19 had had a close encounter with death only a few months prior to the study when his cousin was murdered in a drug-related incident. His response was therefore deeply rooted in reality.

4. *Argumentation and Reasoning: Examples from Students' Work*

Question 9 was the last question in the higher-order thinking category of questions. It was more broadly conceived than questions 6,7, and 8. This question had a "roving" quality to it, in that it was used to examine any aspect of the narrative that was unique to a particular story, or that had not yet been previously explored in the preceding

Interpretive Reading and Critical Evaluation Questions 169

questions 6, 7, or 8 of this category. In terms of its actual composition, it was therefore the most eclectic question in the study. In keeping with the interpretive and critical thrust of this question segment, these questions 9 also required that students use logical reasoning and sound argumentation in answering them.

For example, question 9 in Story #1 examined the character and actions of the Medicine Man who had not yet been spotlighted. Question 9 in Story #2 explored the credibility of the final episode or coda and asked students to pitch the narrative author's perspective against their own. Question 9 in story #3 focused on the author's use of figurative language as a literary flourish, and required students to decipher and explain its meaning. Question 9 in Story #4 asked students to explore the workings of the human psyche in its tendency to seek escape from emotionally painful incidents through denial. Finally question 9 in Story #5 and Story #6 required students to make inferences based on the particular behavior of certain characters. Following is an analysis of selected answers that students gave to Question 9. They are drawn from the last three stories, #4, #5, and #6.

Question 9 of Story #4 read: "When the girl's father told her that her dog Pepper was dead she shouted: 'No, you're wrong! You're wrong, wrong, wrong!' Why do you think she said that?" In answering this question, students gave well-framed reasons:

Sample Answers to Question 9, Story #4: Remembering Last Summer, (R=Respondent)

She loved her dog so much that she did not want to let him go. (R #1)

She didn't want Pepper to leave her like that. She didn't know that things you love and somebody you love sometime have to go. Just like her friend Bobby. That's why her grandmother didn't promise her not to leave. (R #9)

She said that because she thought that Pepper would live forever. She loved Pepper more than anyone because he made her feel better after Bobby left her. (R #21)

She loved Pepper in her heart and she hated to see him dead. If I had a pet like that I think I would say that also if I loved him [as much]. (R #25)

It is wrong, and I will not take this. (R #19)

Question 9 of Story #5 asked: "Why do you think the forest animals were so happy 'delirious with joy (p. 6)' when they found out that they themselves might become man-animals? Explain your answer." Students provided thoughtful and well-reasoned answers to this question also:

Sample Responses to Question 9, Story #5: Why Apes look like People, (R=Respondent)

They were happy because they wer told that everything is going to be alright, and they would have no worries. The reason [they were happy] is because then they themselves will be man. (R #3)

They were not going to get hurt if they were one of them. Then if they were man-animals, the man-animals themselves would not and could not hurt them. (R #4)

They were happy because they will be powerful and tough like man. They won't drink the dirty water and they will eat fresh food. (R #9)

They were happy because they could see how it felt being a man-animal. They could have all the previlages=[privileges] a man-animal had, and they would not be afraid they would die too. They would get powerful as the man-animal. (R #14)

They were happy because they were going to be man-animals and can dress in fansy=[fancy] clothes and drive fansy cars. And lady animals will like them. (R #16)

They were happy because they thought they would have all of the girls, and drive around in red corvets. They also thought that they would be driving airplanes, ships, and submarines. (R #24)

They were happy because one animal said that he was going to drive a convertible car and I guess they thought they were just going to live it out. (R #13)

They were happy because they want girls, and also they were being greedy (R #22)

Interpretive Reading and Critical Evaluation Questions 171

They were happy because if they were man-animals they wouldn't have to worry about getting killed or running out of food. They also could drive fancy cars and have girl friends when they are man-animals (R #25 gave both reasons).

Finally, Question 9 of Story #6 asked: "Why do you think Jerome's Mama called him 'contrary' and 'ungrateful' even though he had such a rough life? Give reasons for your answer." Answers to this question ranged from agreeing that Jerome's behavior was discourteous and that he therefore deserved his mother's reprimand, to a defense of Jerome's attitude in life and an aggressive denouncement of his mother's waning faith in him. A few students were able to look beyond peer support (the protagonist Jerome was a young man of about the students' age), and sympathize with Jerome's mother, in much the same way that some students did in sympathizing with the old woman who shouted at the tree children in Story #1, Question 6. Following is a sample of well-reasoned answers that demonstrate this range of responses.

Sample Answers to Question 9, Story #6: Ride the Red Cycle, (R=Respondent)

Jerome's mother called him these things because he should have shoud [showed] more thanks to the people who helped him in his life, like all his doctors, and the other people who tryed [tried] to make him feal [feel] good. (R #1)

Jerome's mother called him these things because he showed no remorse sometimes when he did bad things, or like when someone did something for him, he would not say thank you. (R #3)

Jerome's mother called him these things because he never say thank you to people who helped him. Jerome will not say thank you because Jerome never wanted them to do it for him. He wanted to do it himself and be pleased with what he's doing. (R #9)

Jerome's mother called him these things because she is very rude and unbelieving in her own son. She's a mean old witch. (R #5)

Jerome's mother called him these things because she was acting mean to him and hurting his feelings, and so I think he didn't even know what she was talking about. (R #13)

Jerome's mother called him these things because she was mad and sometimes when people are mad they say things they don't mean (R #2).

Discussion of Outcomes

The depth of answers that students gave, in responding to the questions in the interpretive reading and critical evaluation category of the comprehension study, is evidence of the positive effects of high quality comprehension questioning in the public school classroom. Answers were reproduced here exactly as given, but the presence of spelling and grammar mistakes should not detract from the powerful content of the responses. When a framework for teaching and questioning allows children to reflect on the many embedded contexts of their daily lives--family situations, personal and community challenges, issues pertaining to ethnicity, culture and language--then teachers have a chance to tap into and begin to understand children's understanding (Cochran-Smith, 1995). Students are then able to draw on their practiced experiences with a sense of knowledge and confidence. They then have the chance to breathe fresh air into comprehension sessions and not be stifled and suffocated by the onslaught of effete, low quality questions to which they are so often subjected. This is indeed, teaching "against the grain" (ibid; p. 510), and it can yield a big harvest.

Chapter Summary

In this chapter, I described trends in the students' responses to the interpretive reading and critical evaluation questions #s 6, 7, 8, and 9, and demonstrated ways in which their engagement with the kinds of questions in this category consistently yielded deep and thoughtful responses. These responses contributed to the effect of higher-order over lower-order questions in the data set. I used a representative sample of quotations and excerpts from students' writings, and showed that by virtue of the eclectic and open-ended nature of these questions, students were able to demonstrate their expertise and skills of contextualization, reasoning, and argumentation in answering them. The kind of experience-based thinking that helped resolve some of the complex situations presented in these questions, are not open to them when answering questions in the mode of the more restrictive literal

Interpretive Reading and Critical Evaluation Questions 173

meaning or recall question category. In the next chapter, I discuss ways in which this questioning dynamic also contributed to the effect of length that showed up in the statistical data analysis.

CHAPTER 10

EFFECT OF STORY LENGTH IN HIGHER ORDER QUESTIONS

Education is meant to develop "a critical spirit and creativity, not passivity...one does not particularly deal with delivering or transferring to the people more rigorous explanations of the facts, as though these facts were finalized, rigid, and ready to be digested. One is concerned with stimulating and challenging them."

Paulo Freire, Brazilian Educator

Background, Expectations and Outcomes

The variable of story length showed up as a main effect in the study data, embedded in the effect of question category--higher-order over lower-order questions. According to my conceptual framework, the narrative dyads (namely each folk tale and non-folk tale pair of stories) in the study varied both by length and readability level. Stories #1 and #2 were short, 690-860 words, Stories #3 and #4 were of medium length, 1553-1590 words, and Stories #5 and #6 were long, 1819-1982 words. Similarly Stories #1 and #2 were of a low readability level, about third grade, Stories #3 and #4 were of a medium readability level, about fourth grade, and Stories #5 and #6 were of a high readability level, about fifth grade. At the beginning of the study, my hypothesis was that the students would earn lower scores on the longer, more complex stories, and higher scores on the shorter, simpler ones. As struggling readers, I predicted that it would be an easier task for them to read and understand the shorter, less complex narratives and then answer comprehension questions based on them. This hypothesis turned out to be wrong. As Figure 7.2 showing the effect of length demonstrates in Chapter 7, there were many cases in which students did better on the longer, more difficult stories than on the shorter, simpler ones.

As it turns out, these cases are all instantiated in the category of the non-folk tale genre--where participant scores demonstrated a steady and continuing level increase from short stories through medium length stories, reaching their highest point at the level of long stories. This trend occurred across all three comprehension question categories: literal meaning, interpretive reading and critical evaluation and creative reading categories. Here I focus primarily on the interpretive reading and critical evaluation questions (six through nine), and creative reading questions (ten and eleven) to demonstrate one source of the length effect that showed up as significant in the quantitative analysis.

Such an emphasis is justified for two reasons. First of all, continuing a trend that already showed up more generally in the effect of higher order over lower order thinking questions, this interpretive reading and critical evaluation question segment marked the largest total aggregate percentage score increase of all three question categories of literal, interpretive, and creative type questions. There was a twenty-five percent score increase from short stories to long stories in this question category. Secondly, in both cases of interpretive and creative reading, students' scores topped out on Story #6, by far the longest story in the entire narrative selection set (at 1982 words, it was approximately three times as long as the shortest story). The fact that students earned their highest scores on this story on a total of five out of nine comprehension questions contributed to this length outcome (note that the two questions in the general question category are excluded because they are not comprehension questions per se). Student responses to three questions in the interpretive reading and critical evaluation category on which they earned the highest scores on Story #6--question 6, 7 and 9--and to two questions in the creative reading category on which this pattern repeated itself--questions 10 and 11 are discussed below. Sample answers from both categories of questions are also provided.

Interpretive Reading and Critical Evaluation Questions 6-9 and Creative Reading Questions 10-11: Effect of Length

In general, students gave high quality answers to Story #6 in responding to either the Moral Judgment Question 6, the Favorite Character Question 7, or the Deductive Reasoning Question 9. They also provided excellent answers to Problem Solving Question 10, and Student-as-Author Question 11. In all these cases, students consistently earned some of their highest scores in the comprehension study. On a scale of 0 to 3 (raw score), they earned an average aggregate of 2.72 on Q6, 2.48 on Q7, and 2.36 on Q9. On a scale of 0 to 6 (raw score), their average aggregate on questions 10 and 11 was 5.12. Students therefore earned approximately 80% or more of the maximum possible total points on each of these questions.

There are multiple explanations for this performance pattern--both story factors and question characteristics. The theme of Story #6, Ride the Red Cycle, was of a disabled, wheelchair-bound adolescent struggling to achieve his dream and succeeding despite all odds. It was one that the study participants embraced and held dear in their analyses, perhaps because of its relevance to their own personal situations in life. In addition, the characters portrayed in the story are realistic, familiar, and recognizable. Little sister Liza is a tease, big sister Tilly is his buddy, Mother is worry-worn and Father is proactive and positive. The element of verisimilitude is therefore strong throughout the story. Another story factor to which the participants were probably attracted was the level of emotional intensity that the story touched off. As the narrative map shows (Chapter 5, Figure 5.7), Story #6 has a constellation of nodes that symbolize maximum interaction between characters and high levels of emotional intensity throughout the story, narrative features that signal episodes of high drama. The final episode when Jerome rides off into the distance triumphant, to the loud applause of the entire neighborhood gathering, is the crowning moment of the story. In addition to the attractiveness of the narrative features, the appeal of the interpretive reading-critical evaluation questions and the creative reading questions which draw strongly on these dimensions of affect in the story, increased the positive interaction of the students with Story #6. Some interpretive reading questions have been discussed in the previous Chapter 9, and others are further examined here, while the creative reading questions are discussed in the following Chapter 11. The combination of story factors and question characteristics therefore contributed to the outcome of the length effect.

Interpretive Reading-Critical Evaluation Questions: Sample Answers and Discussion

Story #6, Question 6 read: "Was it right or wrong for Jerome to run over his sister Tilly's foot with his wheelchair and not say he was sorry? Give a reason for your answer." This is a tricky question, because unlike the other right-wrong or good-bad questions (Stories #1, #3, #4, #5), the protagonist in this story does not start out on an equal playing field with the other characters. He is a disabled youngster in a wheelchair, a situation that usually evokes a measure of sympathy. But the question is asking the students to think beyond Jerome's physical challenges, and pass judgment regardless on his actions and behavior. Even though Jerome lives in an environment where people show very little faith in him and give him sparse encouragement for his efforts, twenty-one students out of twenty-five agreed that Jerome acted wrongly. Only four students found his behavior justifiable. Some of the responses of the students who thought he was wrong follow:

Sample Answers to Question 6, Story #6: Ride the Red Cycle, (R=Respondent)

I think that it was wrong because it could of hurted her. He did not even think to say sorry. Jerome is very ungrateful. He would not like it if someone ran over his feet with a wheelchair. (R #4)

He was wrong because brothers and sisters should not be mean to each other, especially if you don't say sorry. I think that is not nice. (R #8)

It was wrong because he didn't have to take his madness out on his sister. (R #17)

It was wrong because she was on his side when he said he wanted his bike and everyone else laughed at him. (R #25)

One of the students who thought Jerome was right said:

It was right because he was so excited to see the bike and he was happy to see something new in his life and try to make his friends feel good. (R #13)

And a student who argued that he was both right and wrong offered the following explanation:

It was not his falt[fault] because he was excited, [but] it was not nice of him not to opplige [apologize]. (R #1)

 These are all answers that earned the maximum possible score of 3 for providing reasonable and well-argued inferences and interpretations. In these answers, students demonstrate an impressive level of moral reasoning. They alternately refer to the Golden Rule, "Do unto others as you would that they to you should do", the solemn bond of the sibling relationship, or the inappropriateness of misplaced anger and ingratitude. They also try to see the situation from Jerome's perspective, and they sympathize with him. Nonetheless he is scolded for failing to take the opportunity to compensate for his mistake and make amends by apologizing. Students thus demonstrated a high level of engagement with the moral and psychological issues pertinent to this story.

 Story #6, Question 7 asked: "Who is your favorite character in the whole story? Explain why you like this character best." In Story #6, consistent with the established pattern of identifying with the character in the role of the underdog discussed in the previous chapter, the majority of the students--sixteen out of twenty-five--chose Jerome as their most favorite character, while eight students chose either Jerome's father, Papa, or his big sister, Tilly. This outcome is striking because it shows that the students are able to pronounce judgment on a character for doing something wrong, and yet reserve the right to admire his essential nature. Despite the aggressive act against his sister (he ran his wheelchair over her foot), the character of Jerome aroused feelings of sympathy and understanding in the students. They cataloged a distinctive array of traits that they recognized and admired in him. Students commented on his independence, his perseverance, his determination, his motivation, and his sense of self-efficacy:

Sample Answers to Question 7, Story #6: Ride the Red Cycle, (R=Respondent)

Jerome is my favorite character because everybody is always picking on him, when he can do things himself. So then I feel sorry for him, I would like to be on his side, and personally be his best friend. (R #4)

Jerome he needed help and he got it and he improved on it. With courage he improved on his walking. If he keep on going, he will improve more. (R #16)

Jerome had a lot of faith in himself. He tried to do his best in everything. He did all he could to ride the tricycle. He also wanted to do things for himself. (R #14)

Jerome tried his hardest to ride his bike, and he couldn't, but then he made a plan so he could make his legs push the peddles. So he practiced and practiced until he finally made his legs push the peddles to move the bike. (R #20)

Jerome wanted his dream to come true. He tried his hardest to ride his bike and he tried to talk and walk. (R #11)

Some students even engaged in some psycho-analysis:

He was nice and he was really trying to make his way in life, but he didn't really get enough attention, so he try to be bad. (R #14)

Jerome was believing in himself and he didn't stop or give up on his dream because people do things for him and people hardly believe in him. Jerome has a bit of self-esteem, that's why he learned how to ride a bike. (R #9)

The students who chose Jerome's Dad, Papa as their favorite character, admired his faith in his son's ability to overcome the obstacles in his life:

Papa had faith in Jerome when he said he wanted a tricycle and he went out and bought Jerome a bike and fixed it so that Jerome would be comfortable on it and so he couldn't fall off. (R #25)

Story #6, Question 9 asked: "Why do you think Jerome's Mama called him 'contrary' and 'ungrateful' even though he had such a rough life? Give reasons for your answer." Samples of students' mature answers to this question are already discussed in Chapter 9, and will not be repeated here, except for the answer given by Respondent #2, which I have singled out for discussion because it was particularly insightful and sophisticated.

Sample Answer to Question 9, Story #6: Ride the Red Cycle, (R=Respondent)

Jerome's mother called him these things because she was mad and sometimes when people are mad they say things they don't mean. (R #2)

This response demonstrates an almost adult level of insight and understanding. In this answer, the respondent is cautioning against a hasty castigation of Jerome's mother by reminding us that it was probably her anger that she was giving vent to with her mean words, and not really her true feelings. This is the kind of behavior that we can all identify with; it thus receives our empathy, as the response reminds us that "To err is human; to forgive divine."

Creative Reading Questions: Sample Answers and Discussion

Story #6, Question 10 came from the creative reading category of questions. It read as follows: "While Jerome was struggling to master his new tricycle, the kids on the block had already decided that he would never be able to ride. The story says they thought "he had been fun the way he was; if only he would be satisfied with himself". How would you help him through this difficult time? What would you say or do?"
Students' advice again showed thoughtfulness. They understood that Jerome yearned for independence in his life, that he needed this to feel good about himself, and so they offered him encouragement and support.

Sample Answers to Question 10, Story #6: Ride the Red Cycle, (R=Respondent)

    SAY: I would say that the only way to get through this illness is to believe in himself and have strong self-esteem.
    DO: I would go with him everywhere and don't do anything for him until he want me to. Jerome want to do something for himself, why not make him do it. (R#9)

    SAY: You are going to be able to ride. Don't give up on yourself.
    DO: Then I would stay and help him ride his bike to show him that nothing is impossible. (R #12)

    SAY: Don't give up. Keep trying to persaver = [persevere]. Believe in yourself, have faith, have hope.
    DO: Help him practice with him help him learn how to walk so he can improve on riding his bike. (R #16)

    SAY: Don't give up, just try. You can do it. Believe in yourself. Don't listen to what other people say.
    DO: Support him, help him, make him believe in his self. (R #17)

    SAY: Never let people put you down. Have a lot of faith in yourself. Try and try and you will get it.
    DO: Help him out. See that he would do it and finish it. Have faith in him so he can do anything he want. (R #21)

    SAY: Never give up. Don't let anyone put you down. Keep trying. Don't get discouraged.
    DO: Encourage him. Help him try to ride the tricycle. Keep him motivated. Try to make sure he never gives up. (R #25)

    Question 11 of the same story read: "The story ends with Jerome dreaming again--this time about maybe being able to run his own bases next summer. How would you end the story if you were the author and could write a different ending? Write a few sentences that give the story a different ending." Following are some of the answers that earned full marks for their imaginativeness and creative potential:

Sample Answers to Question 11, Story #6: Ride the Red Cycle, (R=Respondent)

If I were the author I would let Jerome walk again and let him fully recover from all his pain. (R #1)
He would be able to run bases by his self. People would not tease him anymore. His life would be happier and he would not be cripple because he would work out more. The End! (R #4)

If I were the author I would end it by letting him be normal again like his original life was. That's how I would end it. (R #5)

A few years later Jerome would master his bicycle and would start to recover from everything that he had problems with. (R #20)

I would end it with Jerome learning how to walk without the help of those brasis = [braces] on his legs. (R #24)

Discussion of Outcomes

The preceding student responses and analyses demonstrate that these students have the ability to interact confidently with tough issues in stories, and to negotiate their way through complex levels of text. Their critical, interpretive and creative abilities are evidence that they can handle fairly sophisticated questions and reading material, and therefore deserve to be exposed to more in school. The combined results of the length effect coupled with the effect of higher-order questions reinforce this reality.

Chapter Summary

In this chapter, the story and question factors that contributed to the main effect of length, one of the outcomes of the quantitative analysis of the study, were discussed. Examples from the study data in the form of students' responses to particular questions provided qualitative support for these results. Finally, recommendations were made concerning the need to keep low-achieving students reading and interacting with challenging materials and questions, despite the fact that their current reading levels might be low.

CHAPTER 11

CREATIVE READING QUESTIONS, AND EFFECT OF ETHNICITY AND GENDER

Hanging out only with people who are like you is like keeping your boat in the harbor...You'll be perfectly safe, but you won't go very far in this world.

Johnnetta B. Cole, 1997.

This chapter has two foci. Firstly, comprehension questions 10 and 11 are analyzed. This question couplet comprises the category of questions that students answered in the final or Creative Reading category of the study. Their answers to these questions earned them scores that were significantly higher than the scores earned in the literal meaning question category, although not as high as the scores earned in the interpretive reading and critical evaluation question category analyzed in previous chapters. These answers therefore also contributed to the overall effect of higher-order over lower-order questions that showed up in the data analysis. Samples of student answers that are typical, drawn from both the folk tale and non-folk tale genres, are therefore provided.

Secondly, the outcomes of the variables of ethnicity and gender that showed up in the quantitative analysis of the study data are examined, again using qualitative excerpts. These too are drawn from answers to the creative reading questions, but answers gleaned from the interpretive reading and critical evaluation question category are also included when they highlight ethnicity and gender issues. Since the ethnicity variable outcome pervaded the entire data set, examples that portray the gender outcome are also used to demonstrate the behavior of the ethnicity variable in the analysis.

Creative Reading Questions 10 and 11: Background, Purpose, Crafting, Expectations and Outcomes

The two creative reading questions included Problem-Solving Question 10 and Student-as-Author Question 11. Both questions were meant to tap into the creative potential of the students. They therefore compared conceptually more with the interpretive reading and critical evaluation questions 6 through 9 than they did with the literal meaning questions 3 through 5 in that both these kinds of question required higher levels of cognition and creativity. For example, a typical question 10 was framed: "What would you say or do "to help comfort a particular character who was in need of emotional support ? A typical question 11 asked: "How would you end the story if you were the author and had a chance to write a different ending ? Write one or two sentences to replace the given ending." At the beginning of this study, my hypothesis was that students would earn higher scores on answering the questions assigned to the creative reading category (much as they did in answering the other higher-order questions 6 through 9) than they would in answering the recall questions, because they were more culturally attuned to this type of questioning. My expectations were verified. Students consistently gained high scores on the category of creative reading questions--an average aggregate of 75% of possible points on all six stories, second only to the interpretive reading and critical evaluation question category where the average aggregate was 79% (see Chapter 7, Figure 7.1). What is important is not simply the fact that the students' scores were high. The more important point is of course, that these scores are an indication of how absorbed and motivated students were with the ideas generated by these questions. Some of the sources of their engagement are identified below.

Positive Outcomes of Group Work

When answering questions 10 and 11, the students were encouraged to work together in groups (organized by their teacher) in order to pool their ideas and reap the potential benefits of peer group collaboration. Groups were heterogeneous in that gender, ethnicity, and achievement level were all mixed. The group dynamic created opportunities for increased achievement because students were able to learn from each other in a Vygotskian manner, in open discussion of issues that the questions raised. There were two variations on the group process. In answering question 10, students recorded their responses individually after sharing their insights with the group and benefiting from the process. In answering question 11, the appointed scribe recorded an answer that represented the entire group effort. The answer they arrived at was one they had come to following a period of interaction, discussion, and exchange of ideas. Unlike Question 10, Question 11 therefore required consensus among group members. However, the cooperative effort also seemed to precipitate stronger gender role differences than might otherwise have been evident, particularly with respect to question 10. This outcome is discussed later in the chapter.

Theme of Sympathy and Understanding

Another factor that contributed to the students' high achievement level on this question category, was the maturity of themes that emerged from their responses, by way of their sympathy and understanding. Story #4: Remembering Last Summer, question 10 read: "The day that her good friend Bobby Nelson moved was an 'awful' day for the girl. Write what you would say to her after he moved away, and what you might do to help her." Some of the answers read as follows:

Sample Answers to Question 10, Story #4: Remembering Last Summer, (R=Respondent)
SAY: I would say "Be careful out there! and say "Have a nice trip!"

DO: "Give him or her something to remind me of." (R #2)

SAY: I would say, "Don't worry because later on he might come back, don't cry."
DO: I would talk to her and take her for a walk to try to cheer her up! (R #4)

SAY: I would say don't worry he'll be back some day
DO: Try to get her mind off of the fact that her friend was gone. (R #11)

SAY: I will still be her friend when ever he leaves.
DO: I would try to get his phone number in Ohio so she could talk to him. (R #15)

SAY: I would say, "I hope you have a better life than you did here.
DO: I would give him something that he would want so he would remember me. (R #20).

SAY: You'll make new friends
DO: Keep his memories. (R #24)

    Students responded with a great deal of empathy to the girl's loneliness following the loss of her friend. The measures they say they would take to help her through this difficult time are sensitive and potentially effective. The detail and precision of the recommendations suggest that they thought the question through carefully. No doubt they themselves have experienced the loss of a close friend in a community where children often leave home to live with the other parent, a grandmother, or another relative somewhere out of state. Here again the element of authenticity in a situation may have factored into students' answers.

    Students continued to show sympathy and understanding in their response to Story #5: "Why Apes Look Like People" Question #10. It read: "At the end of the story, after God threw a thunderbolt from Heaven and broke the pot of oil, the forest animals were shocked and amazed that they could no longer become man animals. How would you help them at this difficult moment? What would you do or say?" Responses were of the following kind:

Responses to Question 10, Story #5: Why Apes Look Like People, (R=Respondent)

Creative Reading Questions, Ethnicity and Gender   187

SAY: Go and ask God to turn you into a man-animal. You don't have to force it.
DO: I would take them to God and explain the whole story. (R #4)

SAY: It wasn't meant for you to be man-animal. Be thankful for who you are.
DO: Treat them as if they are man-animals. Treat them as they want to be treated. (R #9)

SAY: I would say it was for your own good.
DO: I would try to cheer them up by being very nice. (R #12)

SAY: I would tell all of the animals that didn't get the oil, I would tell them to come in an opening in the morning.
DO: I would sprical = [sprinkle] all of the oil on them. (R #16)

SAY: You do not need to be a man-animal to live a nice life. You can swim all day and you don't have a curfew.
DO: I will go up to heaven and tell god why did you change your mind. (R #20)

SAY: I would say too bad.
DO: Ask god to give them one more chance. (R #24)

Again a definite thread of commiseration and sensitivity runs through these answers. The students' intention in all cases is to console and appease. The means to this end encompasses two extremes--from the plan to make representation to God on behalf of the troubled animals, to the plan to assume the role of God themselves in order to fulfill the wishes of the animals. In either case, the ultimate goal is the same-- a demonstration of concern leading to sympathy and understanding for the characters.

Further instantiations of this theme occurred in student responses to Story #6, Question 10. It read as follows: "While Jerome was struggling to master his new tricycle, the kids on the block had already decided that he would never be able to ride. The story says they thought "he had been fun the way he was; if only he would be satisfied with himself" (p.5). How would you help him through this difficult time? What would you say or do? "

Students articulated strong support for the character of Jerome as portrayed in the story. They showed a depth of understanding for the trials and challenges of his life as a disabled youth that belied their chronological age and level of maturity. Perhaps these children recognized themselves as the victims of society's low expectations, just as Jerome's world seemed defined by low expectations because of his physical disability, and were thus strongly invested in the theme of the story. Their counsel was thoughtful, wise and sound. They understood that the protagonist Jerome yearned for a measure of autonomy and independence in his life in order to feel good about himself, and they offered him encouragement and support. Following is a sample of their responses:

Sample Answers to Question 10, Story #6: Ride the Red Cycle, (R=Respondent)

SAY: I would say that the only way to get through this illness is to believe in himself and have strong self-esteem.
DO: I would go with him everywhere and don't do anything for him until he want me to. Jerome want to do something for himself, why not make him do it. (R #9)

SAY: You are going to be able to ride. Don't give up on yourself.
DO: Then I would stay and help him ride his bike to show him that nothing is impossible. (R #12)

SAY: Don't give up. Keep trying to persaver = [persevere]. Believe in yourself, have faith, have hope.
DO: Help him practice with him help him learn how to walk so he can improve on riding his bike. (R #16)

SAY: Don't give up, just try. You can do it. Believe in yourself. Don't listen to what other people say.
DO: Support him, help him, make him believe in his self. (R # 17)

SAY: Never let people put you down. Have a lot of faith in yourself. Try and try and you will get it.
DO: Help him out. See that he would do it and finish it. Have faith in him so he can do anything he want. (R #21)

SAY: Never give up. Don't let anyone put you down. Keep trying. Don't get discouraged.
DO: Encourage him. Help him try to ride the tricycle. Keep him motivated. Try to make sure he never gives up. (R #25)

Theme of Imaginativeness and Creative Potential

In answering creative reading question 11, the student-as-author question, students were quite original in their ideas. Story #1, question 11 read: "The end of the story goes: 'And she lived in sadness for the rest of her life' (p.3). How would you end the story if you were the author and had a chance to write a different ending?" Following are the group efforts:

Sample Answers to Question 11, Story #1: The Woman and the Tree Children

She was sad and wanted her children back. Now she promises never to leave them. One day they came back and they lived happily ever after. (Group #1)

If I was the author of the story I would end it like this, "then she died two years later and she [everybody altogether now, says the appointed scribe, and in unison the group says]:
'She want to be down
But she can't be down,
Cause she dead, she dead,
Yeah, baby'" (Group #2)

In the above response, members of Group 2 staged an immediate impromptu oral performance while working on this question. They could be heard practicing their verse in chorus; the catchy rhythmic pattern of the stanza is determined by the kind and number of lines. A quatrain, it is composed of one iambic and one anapest metric stress in each of the first three lines (iambic, anapest--line 1; anapest, iambic--line 2; anapest, iambic--line 3), followed by an iambic and unfinished anapest for a dramatic end in the final line 4. To "be down" means to be committed to someone or to be interested in that person's welfare. For the woman "to be down," she would have to have access to the tree-children whom she has lost, which she doesn't, hence "she dead" in the metaphorical sense, that is, her life has lost its meaning.

When the woman returned there was noone at the house. Then she visited the tree, and the kids went [back] home with her and they lived happily ever after. (Group #3)

I would have ended it by saying that she was really a witch. The other thing I would ended was that she lived happily ever after with her husband. (Group #4)

I would make the children come back to her room and apologize to her. Then she found a husband and had some children. She got married and had some children and lived happily ever after. (Group #5)

These answers demonstrate a wide range of dynamic suggestions for a different ending to the story. Notice that four of the five recommended conclusions have the standard formulaic ending, "and they lived happily ever after", reinforcing the concept of story structure that undergirds this study and that children have. Besides, the thematic and character-based variations of this formula demonstrate engagement with the story, and reflectiveness on the part of the students. The members of Group #2 adopt the form of the rap genre, the popular and "culturally congruent" youth music with which they resonate as adolescents. They also adopt some of its harshness, although the tone is joking rather than realistic.

Answers to Story #4, question 11 were also quite imaginative. The question read: "At the end of the story, the girl and her grandma have become very close friends ('Grandma is one of the most terrific friends I have ever had' p.5). Write one or two sentences to show how would you end the story if you were the author and had a chance to write a different ending? Here are some of their ideas:

Sample Answers to Question 11, Story #4: Remembering Last Summer

I would end the story like this: Grandma and I lived happily and became closer than ever. Grandma had gave good examples to the girl. (Group #1)

I would say, you see Grandmas are not so bad to be with. . . when you are feeling bad or anytime. And I would also say there's always someone to fall back on when you're down, like your Grandma. (Group #2)

I would end the story by giving her a [new] friend and also a dog, and letting someone live next door and let her or him be her best friend. Thank you. This concludes my presentation. (Group #3)

I would make a happy ending because I would make my friend come back and visit her and um, that's it. (Group #4)

I would go find some more friends and when I get older I would go visit my friend. And I would say everybody has friends but you always have to lose them. (Group #5)

Answers to Story #5, question 11 were similarly perspicacious. The question read: "The story ends with only a few animals being able to wash their faces, hands and feet in the drops of oil that remained after the pot broke. How would you end the story if you were the author and could write a different ending?" In response students wrote:

Sample Answers to Question 11, Story #5: Why Apes Look Like People, (R=Respondent)

Everybody would of [have] got to wash their faces, hands and feet in the drops of oil. Everyone would get a chance to get in the oil and be man-animals. Also God would no longer be depressed and sad and staring off in space. (Group #1)

The animals in the forest would be turned into man-animals. But some animals would be proud of who they are, so would not want to turn into man-animal. (Group #2)

I would write the pot was placed in a different forest, and that the pot of oil turned the forest animals into gold. (Group #3)

I would end the story with, "God saw that the animals would do anything to be human, so he changed his mind." (Group #4)

Their = [there] wasn't enough oil for everyone to wash their faces, but God saw that the only ones that were not being greedy were the monkeys, chimpanzees, apes, and gorillas, so he turned them into man people and they lived happily ever after. (Group #5)

The group answers captured the tension between wanting to grant individuals their wishes, and the students' desire to follow their own convictions even when they did not coincide with other people's wishes. Students chose different paths in resolving this conflict. They either granted people's wishes (Group #1), created an avenue to voice their own values and convictions (Group #2), or settled for a thoroughly imaginative, archetypal fairy tale ending (Group #3), as a kind of escape. Still, in each situation, the new story endings are unique.

Finally, question 11 for Story #2: "The Runaway Cow" read: "Why do you think the author included Louis in the story? Could she have written the story just as well without him? Give a reason for your answer." This was the most challenging question 11 in the entire study. It contributed to the uncharacteristically low score (59%) for the creative reading questions on Story #2. Although the question does require "creative reading" in that the students are encouraged to consider a different development of the plot than the one presented, it demanded a deep understanding of the roles and interrelationships of the narrative characters. In order to answer this question, students had to think reflectively and metacognitively. They had to assume the role of author in a manner that allowed them to make critical decisions with respect to the structural elements of the story--which characters are vital to the plot and other elements, and which characters play a minimal role and are perhaps dispensable. This was a very difficult question for the students, and the comparatively low score is evidence of this, but some of them were able to meet the challenge. Indeed a few responses were right on the mark:

Sample Answers to Question 11, Story #2: The Runaway Cow, (R=Respondent)

I think the author included Louis because if he wasn't in there, the story, they wouldn't am know that the cow was a one person rider and that nobody else could, and that's it. (R #1)

She wanted to tell us that Annette would only let Julie ride on her back--she didn't even let Louis, her brother, sit on her back. So how could she let Pete ride on her back? (R #14)

I think the author probably included him in the story see, because they probably wanted to make the point that Annette only leted Julie ride her, but he didn't really have to put Louis in anyway. (R #2)

Other students came close to the "right" answer, but explored alternative possibilities. Following are some of their ideas:

I don't know why he include him in the story... and he could have just written it just as well without him, because he's not that popular in the story anyway. (R #5)

The author could have written the story just as well without Louis because he really didn't do or say much. (R #17)

The author could have written the story just as well without Louis because that was the mean one, and it truly could have been better. I would have written the story in a good way and I would not have had Louis in the story. (R #3)

Students were thus able to figure out that Louis' role was marginal, and that it would have been possible to write the story without including his character, even though they did not specify the other alternatives open to the author. For example, they did not mention that the author could conceivably have communicated the information about Annette not tolerating any other rider than Julie in a single sentence, or via another character. The story was already overloaded with actors even as a non-folk tale, a major source of weakness in its underlying structure. At under 900 words and 10 characters, it far exceeded the average number of participants around which a short story is generally built. For example, the other story in the dyad, "The Woman and the Tree Children" contained about 700 words with only 4 characters. As a result, its structure is tighter, while the sense of density in Story #2 was only compounded by including yet another character.

Effect of Gender and Ethnicity: Gender

The data analysis showed a significant effect of student gender, but no significant effect of ethnicity ($p < .01$); that is, there was a distinctive difference in the performance level between girls and boys in terms of their achievement level as defined by the scores they gained in the study, while there was no perceivable difference in students' achievement scores according to or as a function of their ethnic background. The source of the gender differences in student achievement was multifaceted, but in general, the main distinction between the sexes in the study, lay in their approaches to certain comprehension questions, which for girls and boys, were qualitatively different. Firstly, students tended to support the actions and behavior of characters along gender lines, thereby demonstrating the power of gender-based identification at this stage in their psychological and emotional development. Secondly, girls demonstrated a greater sense of caring and nurturing for characters than the boys did, at least overtly. Thirdly, girls and boys approached the task of solving problems presented in the narrative differently. The girls' tended to view situations from a real life perspective, while the boys were more likely to view issues squarely from the point of view of the text. Girls showed more "warm fuzzies" as it were in their dealings with certain situations, while boys acted more "by the book". Fourthly, girls were more superstitious than boys, so that where narrative situations gave them the opportunity to exercise superstition, they came up with answers that reflected such a bias. Finally, in response to questions in the creative reading question category, boys seemed better able to compose verses, and produce language for rhyming and rapping. In many ways, therefore, this portion of my analysis reflected traditionally established gender-based norms.

Same Gender Character Identification

One way in which the tendency for students to choose their favorite character along gender lines became evident was in their response to Favorite Character Question 7. Although in a class of twenty-five, there is a built-in limit on numbers of students who could respond in this manner, still their preferences tell a story. For example Story #3 question 7 asked: Who is your favorite character in the whole story? a) Brer Rabbit, b) Miz Meadows, c) The girl he marries. Explain why you like this character best. In answering this question, all but one of the students who chose Miz Meadows' daughter as their favorite character were girls, the girls admitting that they saw a reflection of themselves in the character's cautious approach to love and marriage:

Sample Answers to Question 7, Story #3: Brer Rabbit falls in Love, (R=Respondent)

I like the girl he marries because she was smart and fun. (R #5, African American female)

I like the girl best because she checked him [out] before marrying him, and I really liked how she acted, and I would do the same thing she did. (R #8, Tongan female)

Similarly when answering the Favorite Character Question 7 in relation to Story #2, the Runaway Cow, all four students who chose Pete as their favorite character were boys, who found his daring to be an attractive quality. Again, mostly girls--three out of four students--chose Julie.

Sample Answers to Question 7, Story #2: The Runaway Cow, (R=Respondent)

I like Julie because she was a good and helpful person to her father, and because she treated that animal the way she would want to be treated. (R #2, Tongan-Samoan female)

I like this character because she is the main one and I always wanted to be the main character in a story or song. I wish I was! (R #7, African American female)

I like Pete because he wanted to ride on the cow's back and Pete was sad, because the cow only let Julie ride on her back. (R #10, African American male)

I chose Pete because he is the one person in this story who tried something that noone else has tried to do before. (R #1, Latino male)

Theme of Caring and Nurturing

The second source of a gender effect was the fundamental difference between girls and boys in their attitude to matters of caring and nurturing. The responses that the girls gave fitted the traditional profile of women as care giving and nurturing while the boys' responses tended generally to be harsher. For example, Story #1: "The Woman and the Tree Children", Question 10 asked: "How would you treat the tree children if you were the woman in the story? Write about what you would say to them or do with them after they broke your special dish?" Following are typical student response samples:

Sample Answers to Question 10, Story #1: The Woman and the Tree Children, (R=Respondent)

Female Responses
A wouldn' whup 'em, a wouldn' whup 'em but am a would tell 'em not to do it anymore . . .I would. . . I would just tell them not to do it no more, but I wouldn' whup my kids, cause I don' want nobody to whup me. (R #11, African American female)

I would talk to the person, or maybe have a talk with all of my children. (R #8, Tongan female)

I would say don't do that again, unless [or else] you'll get in big trouble next time. If I'm in a bad mood, I'll ground them next time. (R #16, African American female)

Male Responses
I would lock their room from outside the room; lock all the doors, and put the TV away where they can not find it. (R #19, Samoan male)

I'd put them in jail and lock them up in the bathroom; put chains on the window and the door. (R #22, Samoan male)

I'd make them slide for a little bit--<u>once</u>. . .just give them a chance, just give them a chance. (R #23, African American male)

In the preceding examples, differential amounts of sympathy and understanding show up in the answers that the girls and boys gave to this question. The female responses are softer and kinder than the male responses which tend to be harsher and more unforgiving, although the last example above (R #23) demonstrates that the boys are also capable of warmheartedness, but are perhaps less willing to reveal this side of them in the company of girls as they work together in groups.

The reason why the boys generally recommend harsher punishments than the girls do for the offending narrative characters is complex and its validity is certainly open to debate. The explanation seems to be related to home, community and society. In a recent discussion of this phenomenon with an African American male who heads the summer "Bridge" program for recent high school graduates at an elite California university, he suggested that the students in my study were simply giving answers that represented their own personal experiences and views of reality. He explained further that in his view, ethnic males (in particular Black and Latino) are dealt with more harshly than ethnic females at the hands of their own parents, and eventually at the hands of societal institutions like the police (for different reasons). As a spin-off of such conditions, parents come to believe that their sons need to be tough in order to survive the hardships of prejudice and discrimination that society offers as a result of complex historical and contemporary conditions. This explanation is certainly reasonable, but what it lacks is an acknowledgment that the boys might also be partially joking, or "grandstanding" in order to impress the mixed-gender group.

Another instance of the caring role of females in the study occurs in Story #2: "The Runaway Cow". In this narrative, Question 10 read: "What would you say to Pete after he got thrown from the cow, 'went sailing over Annette's head, over the barbed wire, and landed on his back in the meadow beyond.' " Again the girls take a different tack from the boys in their approach to this question. The girls take the moral high ground and scold Pete for riding an animal that didn't belong to him, and for skipping school. Again a nurturing concerned approach typical of the traditional female prototype, emerges from the sample of students quoted below:

Sample Answers to Question 10, Story #2: The Runaway Cow, (R=Respondent)

Female Responses
I would say what's your problem? You should not have been on that cow boy, what's up? What[ever] it is it is, the important thing is, are you okay?
I would um, make him go to school. (R #4, African American female)
I would say that's what you get and you shouldn't have never been on that cow.
I would am, help him up, and probably, am, see how he was doing. I would make him go to school and when he came home talk to him. (R #5, African American female)

I would say, "Are you OK? what were you doing? Are you hurt? And I would help him up and probably see how he was doing. (R #2, Tongan-Samoan female)

On the other hand, the boys also show concern for Pete's well-being, but feel that his action though defiant, was attractive and even admirable. Their reactions again conform to the social stereotype of boys as more adventuresome and intrepid than girls:

Male Responses
I'd ask him did you have fun? I'd ask him was you scared? I'd ask 'im would he try it again? you know, and I'd ask him if he got hurt.
I'd try it for myself, then I would go tell his mama on 'im an' I'd see if the cow was aright. That's all I'd do. (R #1, Latino male)

I would say are you alright? I would say you shouldn't try it again cause you might get hurt, knowing I'm gonna try it for myself.
And I would help him up and I would say, you ever try it again? And I'd say, naw, you shouldn't do it. (R #3, African American male)

I would say, are you alright and why did you do this?
I would punish him and I would laugh at him. (R #6, Fijian male)

Theme of Realism versus Fiction

The third source of the gender difference was the difference in students' perception of the world of reality and of its intersection with the world of fiction. Question 11 of Story #3 revealed this dichotomy: "What do you think happened after Brer Rabbit and the girl got married? Write a sentence that describes their new life together." Following are a sample of answers to this question:

Sample Answers to Question 11, Story #3: Brer Rabbit Falls in Love, (R=Respondent)

Female Responses
They were happy but they had some problems, and they got through them. (R #2, Tongan-Samoan female)

After they got married, they went on their honeymoon and got more close and into each other. (R #5, African American female)

They probably lived happily ever after or maby [maybe] they kept arguing and got devorced [divorced], I don't know. (R #8, Tongan female)

I think Brer Rabbit wold have tried all he could to keep his wife happy. I think they would have a good life together because Brer Rabbit got to marry the girl, since the girl got the sign she wanted. (R #14, Fijian female)

Male Responses
They might have half-human and half-rabbit children. (R #10, African American male)

They had some babies that came out half rabbit and half human. (R #18, African American male)

People started teasing the girl for marrieng [marrying] the rabbit. (R #20, Samoan male).

They probably stad [stayed] merry for the rest of their life. (R #22, Samoan male)

These answers reveal a discernible gender difference in students' approach to this question. The female responses transpose the animal-human marriage into a real-life human union and comment on it in that realm. Students mention the couple going through rough times but making it through, growing closer to each other, divorcing, and so on. But the male responses are limited to a text-bound level of interpretation and analysis--they tend to focus on the prosaic specifics of the narrative situation, and are constrained by thoughts centering on the physical outcome of the rabbit-girl union.

Theme of Superstition

The fourth source of the gender effect was the differential between boys and girls in their belief in superstition. Girls tended to be more superstitious than boys. For example Question 6 of Story #3: Brer Rabbit falls in Love asked: "Do you think it was smart or stupid for Miz Meadows' daughter to insist on a 'sign' before agreeing to marry someone? Give a reason for your answer." Many more girls than boys believed it was smart to wait for a sign before getting married. Further, the tenor of their responses showed that their thinking on this question was socially conditioned and differentiated. The girls had a belief system that tolerated superstition, while the boys did not. Their approach was more practical. The girls felt that a sign was akin to divine intervention, and that a good sign would bestow a blessing on the marriage while the boys largely found superstitious practices worthless. Following are some of the answers the two groups gave:

Answers to Question 6, Story #3: Brer Rabbit falls in Love, (R=Respondent)

Female Responses
I think it was smart of Miz Meadows daughter to insist on a sign because she would really know if her husband would like her or not, she would also know if she would have a nice life or not. (R #14, Fijian female)

It was smart because mabey [maybe] she'll find out how he loves her and if he loves her enough to give her a sign. (R #17, African American female)

It was smart because you have to see the person and know how he is, and think about getting with him or does she like her future husband. (R #9, African American female)

Male Responses
It was stupid because I don't believe in that kind of stuff. I think that everyone has there [their] own reasons why they don't want to do things or eather [either] why they do want to do things. That's ther=[their] choice. (R #13, African American male)

It was a stupid idea because some people don't need a sign just to get married. (#10, African-American male).

It is stupid because if Brer Rabbit had never know[n] about her sign, she would never of [have] gotten married. (R #1, Latino male).

Rapping and Rhyming Ability: A Group Effort

Finally, boys and girls showed different abilities with respect to rhyming and rapping. Question 10 of Story #3: Brer Rabbit Falls in Love best demonstrates this point. It read: "There are several rhymes in this story. Towards the end of the story (p.4), Brer Rabbit sings the following rhyming song to Miz Meadows' daughter to try to win her:

'I want the girl that's after a sign, / I want the girl and she must be mine, / She'll see her lover down by the big pine.' Compose a short song or rhyme to tell someone how much you care about him or her." Like the other Creative Reading Questions 10, this question asked students to create a message that conveyed caring.

This particular Question 10 motivated the most genuine cooperative group effort, perhaps because students were so excited by the question itself. They discussed alternative verses among themselves before arriving at final consensus. Students brought their knowledge and expertise from their own pre-teen (and teen) experiences with the popular rap genre and hip-hop music to bear on the question. But whereas the girls were usually the dominant force in the other questions (especially the more nurturing question 10, "What would you say or do to help. . .", and in their general question-answering abilities), the boys seemed to hold forth on this question because they had honed more skills in this area.

The students took turns composing individual lines for their rhymes and helped each other with the rules of poetry as they composed. For instance, one student paraphrased the assignment to "compose a song" for his group buddies thus: "You gotta say a rap or a rhyme or something. Go." Students were also overheard explaining details of the principles of rhyming to each other. One boy explained to his group that rhyming verses did not necessarily have to follow the AA BB rhyme scheme; it would be just as acceptable, he said, if their group (Group 5) came up with a rhyme that was organized around the ABAB rhyme scheme. He did not use those words, of course--rather, he blurted out a few quick examples by way of demonstration. Although his counsel evidently did not prevail (in fact it was Group 2 that came closest to the ABAB pattern of rhyming), his group did make an attempt at this latter scheme. In the Vygotskyan sense, students clearly reached their zone of proximal development in working with their peers at creating verse. Truly, in the words of Forman & Cazden, (1995; p. 161), their effort was "a mutual task in which the partners work[ed] together to produce something that neither could have produced alone." Their teacher thanked me for including a question that tapped into a different "modality," because in his own words "children learn according to many different modalities and this modality is very important for my children."

In general, their verses ranged from the trite lines of love to a tribute of admiration and respect for their teacher (Group 4). But they all succeeded in creating verse as the assignment required. Many of their creations did conform to the standard AA BB CC rhyme scheme common to the culture of pop poetry. Following are some of the verses that students composed:

Sample Group Answers to Question 10, Story #3: Brer Rabbit Falls in Love

Now my days are sad and blue
All because I will lose you.
Roses are red, violets are blue
Life is hairy and so are you. (Group #1)

Roses are red
Some socks are black
Would you be
My Daddy Mack?

Roses are red
Jasmine here is black
I love you
And that's a fact. (Group #2)

If you see a monkey up a tree
Pull his tail and think of me
When you see a monkey up a tree
Pull his tongue--think of Sharon! (Group #3)

Mr. Peters is nice, he teaches us things
He don't gang-bang and he don't wear rings
Mr. Peters is educated
And his teaching highly rated. (Group #4)

Roses are red, violets are blue
I'm so much in love with you
On my bike I got some pegs
Baby, look at them big old legs
Do you love me or do you not
You told me once but I forgot. (Group #5)

I really like you so very much
Especially when you give me a very soft touch. (Group #5, extra)

In sum, students appreciated the opportunity that the creative reading questions gave them to let their creative juices pour, and they attacked these questions with a verve and sense of purpose that teachers yearn for in their students. Although the intrusion of street-type slang (as in Group 4's use of the word "gang-bang") occasionally mars what would otherwise be a commendable attempt at verse, students' involvement with this activity cannot go unnoticed. Such engagement comes from exposing below average students to activities and tasks that tap into their areas of strength, and that give them a sense of empowerment in regular classroom routines such as comprehension questions. This is an idea that carries great potential, and one that is reflected in a variety of ways in innovative classroom practice, including, more recently, Isabel Beck's concept of questioning the author (Beck et al., 1994). It is important to centralize students' ideas as they react to texts that they are asked to read. Strategic and careful comprehension question planning can achieve this.

Effect of Gender and Ethnicity: Ethnicity

Evidence of the lack of an ethnicity effect in the data is embedded in the individual and group responses cited in the preceding analyses. As would be expected, the cosmopolitan nature of each group generated this effect intrinsically in the two questions that required collaborative efforts. But the effect pervaded the entire data set, and was not limited to this circumstance. At the inception of the study, I felt that maybe the African American students in the study might relate to the Black texts in ways that were different from and more positive than students in the other ethnic groups represented in the classroom. Earlier also, I discussed my initial desire to use text materials in the study that reflected the wide range of cultures and ethnicities that were represented in the classroom. But as previously explained, I decided to be more focused in this study, while planning to revisit the issues of other ethnic tales some time later. Already there was a significant number of variables involved, and adding more would have diluted the results. As it turns out, however, the African American students did not perform better on the comprehension questions relating to the study narratives than the other ethnic students who participated in the study. Students across all ethnicities did well generally, an outcome that contributed to the negative effect of ethnicity, or to the lack of correlation between achievement scores and specific ethnic group membership in this study.

Indeed, students seemed to perform as a unified and coherent group, all responding to the comprehension questions generally at higher or lower levels of achievement depending on other factors such as story and question characteristics. Where distinctions did exist, comprehension question answers clustered according to more traditional subject factors--such as gender as pointed out above.

At least two explanations might be offered for this phenomenon. Firstly, there was a significant amount of cross-ethnic identity in this multi-ethnic classroom. In this diverse ethnic community, the youth seemed to coalesce under the identity of one people of color. Though the circumstances of their being in poor mixed ethnic communities may vary--through generations of socio-historical experiences, immigration experiences, or life adaptation situations-- they are affiliated in that they are all collectively identified as "ethnic" or "of color", and are all growing up in a marginalized ethnic community ignored, neglected, or critiqued by mainstream society. Under these circumstances, young people especially tend to adopt similar ways of thinking, acting and valuing. Compounding this unified identity is the lure of youth peer-group culture as middle-schoolers congregate together, and experience common ties in the type of clothing and shoes they wear, in the concepts they express in their language and idioms, and in their attraction to rap music, hip-hop, and other forms of popular street culture. These commonalities push them closer to one another as they distance themselves from the rest of society, especially the older segments that look upon youth as "the other", and erode lines of ethnic demarcation as they negotiate the difficult teenage years.

Secondly, the class teacher practiced an each-one-help-one philosophy in his classroom that helped break down vestiges of exclusionary behavior. He also demonstrated an intense appreciation of multiculturalism that under girded his language arts teaching program and his philosophy of teaching (for details on Mr. Peters' teaching philosophy see Chapter 4). The teacher therefore modeled behavior that was inclusive of all ethnicities present in the classroom, and this practice was emulated by the students in his class.

As already suggested, the demographics of the group members that the teacher identified for the creative reading and group activities, clinch the argument I make for a classroom situation in which ethnic group membership was subsumed beneath the mantle of class unity and multicultural integration. The groups were heterogeneous in terms of gender and ethnicity, and were devolved thus:

Group 1:
    African American Female
    Samoan Male
    African American Male
    Fijian Female
    African American Female

Group 2:
    African American Male
    African American Male
    African American Female
    Fijian Female
    Samoan Male

Group 3:
    African American Female
    Samoan Male
    Tongan Female
    African American Female
    African American Female

Group 4:
    African American Male
    Latino Male
    African American Male
    African American Female
    Tongan-Samoan Female

Group 5:
    African American Female
    Fijian Female
    African American Female
    Samoan Male
    African American Male

Finally, the fact that their classroom teacher and this researcher are both ethnic individuals (African American), may have had a positive effect on the students' reaction to the Afro-based narratives, and may have contributed in some way to the lack of an effect of ethnicity in the data. But if so, only minimally I would argue, because there were bigger forces at work. As already mentioned, students all seemed to admire and respect their teacher, not because of his race, but because he himself embraced high values by treating each of them with the utmost dignity and compassion *regardless* of race. With the strength of this background, I believe that the students would have warmed to the stories as long as they were good, regardless of their specific brand of ethnic focus.

Chapter Summary

In this chapter I discussed the sources and outcomes of the effect of the creative reading question category, the effect of gender and the absence of an effect of ethnicity in the comprehension study. I used qualitative excerpts from the students' work to support the themes that emerged in the data analyses, and to reinforce the arguments that I made.

PART IV
IMPLICATIONS OF STUDY

CHAPTER 12

SUMMARY, IMPLICATIONS, AND CONCLUSIONS

I believe I can fly
I believe I can touch the sky
Think about it every night and day
Spread my wings and fly away.

                R. Kelly, Songwriter

Why teach them to march, when they can learn to fly?

              Robert Calfee, Educator and Psychologist

Summary of the Study

    This study grew out of my conviction that schools must become more responsive to the cultural dimensions of learning in order to meet the needs of all children, especially those of historically marginalized ethnic minority student populations. I asked the basic but critically important question: If we wanted to make inner-city students more highly motivated and challenged, what *could* we do? The results of this study indicate that we could do several things.

One thing we could do is shape our teaching materials to suit the needs of the children. That is, teachers could incorporate ethnic literature into their language arts curriculum, not in token ways, but integrally and significantly. The study examined the efficacy of using African American literature texts from two genres--folk tales and contemporary narratives--and demonstrated that these narrative selections motivated middle school students from ethnically diverse backgrounds to become engaged in reading and narrative comprehension.

A second thing we could do is choose good stories for narrative reading and comprehension. Since the structural base of the selected texts played a crucial role in the analysis of the stories, in the technique used for constructing strategic comprehension questions, and in critiquing the students' responses to these questions, selecting structurally sound stories is vital, and is something else that we could do to help children learn. Indeed the dimension of narrative structure was foundational to the study.

A third, and perhaps the single most important thing we could do is to raise the standard of teaching that these students receive, by improving pedagogy and practice. For example, teachers can ask comprehension questions that induce high levels of critical thinking, analysis, and problem-solving. Students who test low on reading, or who are experiencing reading difficulties need not be subjected to dull, humdrum reading materials, and vapid, unimaginative comprehension questions, as many educators seem to assume. These children are capable of more, and when we expect and demand more of them, they will achieve more.

The study participants consisted of a cross section of students who are at risk for academic failure in a community of low socioeconomic status in East Tall Tree, northern California. The students were primarily African American, but they included also Latinos and Pacific Islanders (Tongans, Samoans, and Fijians). I investigated multiple facets of their narrative comprehension skills in the analysis and appreciation of six selected stories. In analyzing the data, I combined both quantitative and qualitative methods, and used students' comprehension responses as an indicator of their cognitive engagement with the stories.

What I found was that despite their varied and multicultural backgrounds, all the students were able to appreciate reading and exploring literature drawn from the cultural roots of the African

American experience, even though the African Americans represented only one of the ethnic groups in the class. This result leads us to rethink the inter-ethnic and cross-cultural dynamic of students in our schools. Building on and fostering this kind of genuine multicultural exchange in our inner city school children and beyond, is therefore another thing that we could do.

In what follows, I further discuss the conclusions and implications of the study, building on my previous remarks, and drawing on the five main effects that emerged from my research. They are restated here:

*An effect of question-type: Students did better on the higher-order (interpretive and creative reading) questions than on the lower-order (literal recall) questions.

*An effect of length: Students were more challenged by the longer, more complex stories with high readability levels than they were by the shorter, simpler stories with low readability levels.

*An effect of gender: Female students consistently gained higher scores than male students (as is generally the norm in literacy studies).

*No effect of narrative genre: Students showed the same preference for folk tale as for non-folk tale narrative selections.

*No effect of ethnicity: Students who represented the same ethnicity portrayed in the texts--the African American students, did not perform better in the comprehension tasks than did the students from other ethnic minority backgrounds, nor did they show greater liking for the stories. In general, students demonstrated appreciation of one another's cultures and all the students showed appreciation for the specific African American ethnic orientation that pervaded the narrative texts.

Conclusions and Implications of the Study

The outcomes of the comprehension-cognition study may be construed in terms of several issues important to the field of education:
1) *The efficacy of ethnic-based literature materials;*
2) *The significance of culture-based teaching pedagogy;*
3) *The efficacy of challenging reading selections;*
4) *The need for strategic narrative comprehension questioning techniques;*
5) *The advantages of building a strong classroom environment, in which healthy teacher-student and student-student relationships are facilitated; and*
6) *The cross-ethnic identity of multi-ethnic youth.*

I will now elaborate on each of these issues.

1) The efficacy of ethnic-based literature materials

The research suggests that narrative texts that include dimensions of an ethnically diverse culture in a natural and authentic way can inspire and motivate middle school ethnic youth who are indifferent to education. These materials can act as stimuli for effective engagement with literary works and for heightened cognitive activity in students who are generally turned off to mainstream texts that marginalize and alienate them. Such ethno-cultural texts serve to represent and validate students' diverse backgrounds, and can have an empowering effect on them.

This conclusion is part of a more general outcome of the study. My work reiterates recommendations regarding ideal conditions for learning that earlier educators have noted. For example, as early as 1977, Bruner articulated a process of education that explored ways of bringing all students to the full utilization of their intellectual powers, and this country to "a better chance of surviving as a democracy in an age of enormous technological and social complexity" (p. 10). Given the fact that the social complexity has increased since Bruner authored this statement, both in terms of the diversity of ethnic groups coming to America, and the challenges of poverty, congestion, drugs and violence in communities in which they live, the tenets that he outlined are now particularly germane. One of his recommendations pertained precisely to the selection of curricular materials designed to motivate student learning discussed here.

Bruner's sentiment that "interest in the material to be learned is the best stimulus to learning" (p. 14), is a spin-off of this important idea, and one that this study also validates. Although the psychology of interest is a factor that psychologists "know little about" (Claude Steele, Stanford University psychologist, personal communication) my study adds to the evidence of other researchers (see, for instance, Hornburger 1985 and Andersen, 1985 among others) and to the experience of many teachers who support this fundamental concept: the kind of teaching materials that the teacher chooses does matter and does make a difference to learning. More specifically, this study demonstrates that using curricular materials that portray persons of color in leading roles, and that incorporate (at least some of the time) their corresponding style and language was perceived positively by this

Summary, Implications, and Conclusions 213

entire diverse group of students, and promoted interest in the material to be learned. (On this point, compare Grant 1973; Gregory & Woollard 1985; Harris 1995; Meier 1997, Van Keulen, Weddington, & De Bose 1998, among others.) Gregory and Woollard's work is particularly relevant to this issue. These teacher-researchers, based in England, believe that language diversity in the classroom, can lead naturally to inquiry into language and language differences, and thus to a wider awareness of the diverse nature of society. In their collection of case studies, articles, and reviews, they showcase classrooms where teachers use as literature, stories that incorporate the languages of students in their classrooms--Afro-Caribbean Creole, Hindi, Pakistani, Punjabi, Greek, Bengali, Arabic, French, German, Italian, Dutch, and so on, to capture the interest and imagination of their children. The philosophy behind the research is that we can gain new and important insights into curriculum change, and the need for reappraisal of the underlying values and ethos of our schools. They contend that:

> our acknowledgment of language diversity must not be a study of 'otherness' and 'exotica', nor a fringe of light relief to the exam syllabus. It should, with all its assertions and hesitations, be part of our search for social reality, and our enquiry into learning. It should lead to a true valuing of the multilingual and multicultural society in which we live. (Gregory & Woollard, 1985; Introduction, p. vii).

As the students in my study themselves noted, the ethnic literature offered them something positive and uplifting in the way of self identity. It served to reflect and affirm a measure of esteem in the fact of ethnicity and fostered interest in the stories. Based on this outcome, I would recommend that teachers try to incorporate ethnically diverse texts for the study, enjoyment, and edification of students from all backgrounds. Teachers should pull away from dependence on heavy doses of the dominant mainstream literature that has had a stronghold in the classroom for scores of years, and incorporate instead these kinds of innovative teaching materials.

Despite the recent controversies surrounding African American Vernacular English or Ebonics (and the issues are complex, greatly misrepresented by the media and misconceived by the public, as noted by Rickford 1997), it is simply true that as children approach pre-adolescence and the teen years, they become increasingly aware of the significance of group membership in their lives, and at that time their language becomes an outward demonstration of their inner sense of self-worth, and of their participation in the group (see Delpit 1995). Also, as Dorian (1986) argues, children's use of their native languages or vernaculars usually helps to transmit the ethnic history and traditional lifeways belonging to those languages. Furthermore, these traditions, which are very important and often forcefully proclaimed by their owner groups, typically become threatened when the languages do. As Dorian aptly proposes, "the self-awareness and self-confidence which can be gained through the recovery of such information have value in themselves" (p. 64).

Teachers must therefore learn to respect the language of students, whether it is Ebonics or Spanish or Vietnamese, and build on it to prepare them for success in school, in the job market, and in their lives more generally. It is not at all necessary to strip them of their language and culture to achieve these ends. When aspects of students' language and culture are valued and honored, cognitive and socio-psychological growth ensues.

Furthermore, in some cases where no substantive written literature exists in a particular culture (e.g. the Hmong), teachers should create alternative ways of incorporating manifestations of the specific culture as a source of inspiration and motivation to students. To do this, teachers will need to confront the potential web of complexities that attention to the efficacy of ethnic literature might open up. For example, decision details such as which cultures should be featured (especially if several are represented in a classroom as was the case in this study), and in what order in diverse classrooms, earlier or later in the year, and other specifics, will have to be determined by the intuition and expertise of local teachers and the contingencies of their classroom situations. It is surrounding such issues that teacher action research groups (such as the teacher trainees from Hofstra University, New York, the University of Pennsylvania, Philadelphia, San Jose State University, California and elsewhere around the country who teach in local inner-city ethnic communities and return to the academy to discuss their problems and findings) can be an essential repository for informing the educational community about the viability and potential of these issues for practice. There is much more work to be done in this area.

2) The significance of culture-based pedagogy

Related to the approach of innovative curriculum materials, are investigations into the effect of culture-based teaching pedagogy in teaching and learning. The fact that Mr. Peters incorporated certain aspects of the Black Church culture into his classroom organization, discipline, and control techniques, and that they seemed to work, is an area of teaching pedagogy that also needs further exploration, investigation, and understanding.

Previous studies reporting positive outcomes have helped spotlight this somewhat fuzzy but significant area of culture-based pedagogy (Au & Mason, 1981; Hoover 1991; Ball 1991; Lee 1995; Foster, 1995; Ladson-Billings, 1995). For instance Au and Mason found success in applying dimensions of the Hawaiian culture-base of social organization in teaching Hawaiian children to read. Ball found that African American adolescents showed preference for certain organizational structures in their oral and written expositions. Lee drew on the vernacular strategies that African American students use in creating the text of their ritual verbal exchanges in teaching them strategies for comprehension. She did this by using the cultural word-play game of signifying as a scaffold for literary interpretation. And as mentioned earlier in the book, Foster showed how a teacher successfully used the Black culture-based language of control and critique to communicate curriculum. These studies are all evidence of the potential viability of culture-based pedagogy that need to be analyzed, examined, and built on.

Ladson-Billings has moved towards the formulation of a theoretical base for the concept of culturally relevant pedagogy. In the meantime, the opportunity for including in all classrooms a more deep-seated concept of multiculturalism that approaches such as these would engender, ought to be recognized and acknowledged. The potential for the resulting openness to and appreciation of cultural, ethnic and racial differences would transcend the ephemeral diet of multiculturalism often found in schools, such as the superficial recognition of Martin Luther King's birthday, or the Cinco de Mayo festivities.

3) The efficacy of challenging reading selections

The third implication of the study is one that complements the discussion of culture-based texts and culture-based pedagogy. As educators, we should try to give our students the best quality education, and challenging them academically through the use of stimulating reading materials, is one way to do this. Ever since the landmark study of the effect of teacher's expectations on pupils' intellectual development (Rosenthal & Jacobson, 1968), we've known that as teachers, we control the heights of children's achievements. Yet there continues to be grave concern for the generally poor quality of education given children from families of low income. Furthermore, studies continue to show that academic challenge in high-poverty classrooms is the way to go--that enriching the learning diet for these children with high-powered instruction, yields results superior to those of conventional practice (Knapp, Shields, & Turnbull, 1995). The fact that in the present study, participants earned higher scores on the longer, more complex stories than they did on the shorter, simpler texts leads us to a recommendation that resonates with the tenor of this discussion. Students who experience difficulty in reading should be given a chance to enjoy more complex, sophisticated reading material than they presently do. There is no need to confine them to literature pitched at low estimated or instructional grade levels as is often the practice, thereby depriving them of a richer literary diet.

Poor readers are not de facto poor listeners or poor understanders, and even though it might be reasonable to assume that they need manageable materials for reading on their own, it does not follow that they should be deprived of the challenges and cognitive journeys that more sophisticated texts afford whenever reading is required. The tendency in some schools in California (and undoubtedly elsewhere also), particularly among populations of students experiencing difficulty in reading, is to confine these children to low quality texts. This practice compounds the problem, especially given the fact that many ethnic minority students who already face some of the challenges discussed above, are the ones that swell the ranks of poor readers.

Some researchers have studied the practice of this remedial approach and found it to be severely wanting. Greene and Olsen (1985) examined second graders' preference for and comprehension of original and readability-adapted materials. They concluded that children prefer to read literature as written in the original form more than texts that were adapted from such material by formulae designed to meet the criteria of readability levels deemed appropriate for them. This was especially true of poor and average readers who were much more excited by the genuine article than the diluted one. They found further that readability-adapted materials are not easier to understand than the originals pitched at one or two grade levels higher, from which they were adapted. As they noted:

> The differences in word length, word frequency, and sentence length that are the stock in trade of the readability industry and the sacred cows of ignorant legislatures and adoption committees are irrelevant both to comprehensibility of texts...and children's preferences (Greene & Olson, 1985; p. 139).

Although the second grade population on which the Greene and Olson study was based represents a younger group of students than my middle-schoolers, the thrust of the study outcomes is the same--that more challenging reading texts produce more engagement and better comprehension. In the present study, the preferred narratives (namely Stories #5 and #6, the texts that were the longest and that gained the highest comprehension scores), contained the highest levels of complexity. This was reflected not only in external elements such as word and sentence length, but also in critical dramatic features such as the increase in character involvement per episode, and the concentrated increase in the levels of affective intensity and interaction that the characters displayed (see story graphics in Chapter 5 on narrative analysis). These are vital thematic features that reflect the dramatic flavor of the narratives and convey the angst of stories. If they were to be expunged from the structural frame in the interest of reduced readability levels, the vital human element appeal of the narratives would be reduced and the story's meaning and message would be compromised. There is no empirical evidence that the practice of attenuated literary texts for poor readers produces salutary results; in fact the present study provides additional evidence to the contrary.

The technique of tracking that obtains in many schools, often beginning as early as elementary school reading groups, is analogous to the practice of watered-down reading materials and can also have deleterious effects on readers. According to this system, poor performers are channeled into separate classes from the high achievers and are fed large doses of a remedy that fails to prepare them to play catch-up with their peers ahead of them. Not only are reading materials in these classrooms merely a shadow of the advanced and exciting program of the upper-level reading groups, but they are also used in classes sometimes staffed with the weakest and least experienced teachers, when what is needed instead are skillful and committed practitioners. As Oakes (1985) and others have observed, tracking of students has little to do with inherent intelligence or actual potential and more to do with maintaining the status quo in our nation's schools. This does not have to be so.

If we are to remain educationally and economically competitive as a nation, we need to revise some of our current approaches to remedial reading instruction in our schools. We should not be content to shunt off large segments of our population into remedial reading programs that support regression and limit improvement, when theory informed by empirical research points us in different directions. The short term result has the effect of maintaining a feeling of security in the systems of hierarchy that exist in our schools and society; the long term effect is much less sanguine on the personal, community and national levels. This is not to ignore the fact that inclusion in classrooms is often complex and difficult to achieve. But if special day and other low-track teachers and remedial personnel work in close consort with regular education and other mainstream faculty, much more could be achieved for weaker students.

4) The need for strategic narrative comprehension questioning techniques

Fourthly, because of its importance, the use of questioning techniques in teaching narrative comprehension to ethnic minority and at risk students warrants revision. The way in which students remember a story, the lessons they learn from it about life, how engaged they become with its characters and themes, and how they interpret a story, can constrain and limit students' responses, thoughts, ideas and imaginings. Since the technique of questioning is generally key to narrative appreciation and comprehension thus depicted. It is instructive that students in this study earned higher scores on the interpretive and critical-evaluative and creative type questions than they did in answering the literal recall questions.

Furthermore, since success in school ought to be encouraged, and success in a known area of academic endeavor can be used to build successful experiences in other areas, the implication to be drawn from this outcome is that ethnic minority students should be given more opportunities to engage with contextualized questioning strategies than with the decontextualized techniques of traditional memory or recall type questions.

Heath (1983) made a similar observation in her work with Black ethnic minority students in the Piedmont Carolinas. She found that, largely as a result of the kinds of talk to which they had been exposed, the White children of Roadville came to school with strong skills in the literal and factual recall areas which are emphasized in the early grades, but with little preparation for the contextualizing and imaginative conceptualizing skills which were needed in the higher grades. By contrast, but again because of the kinds of talk to which they had been exposed, the Black children of Trackton came to school with stronger higher order skills of contextualization and creative imagination, but weaker skills in the cognitive processes of identification and decontextualization which the schools emphasize at the lower levels. As a result, the Trackton kids "fail in the initial sequences of the school-defined hierarchy of skills, and when they reach the upper grades, the social demands and habits of failing are too strong to allow them to renew for school use the habits they brought to their first-grade classroom" (pp. 353-4). On the other hand, the Roadville children engage in social activities which "are constructed to make them focus for the most part on labels and features, and are given few occasions for extended narratives, imaginative flights of establishing new contexts, or manipulating features of an event or item" (p. 352).

Although one must beware of broad generalizations and sweeping statements, and although school failure is almost always compounded with multiple causes, the thrust of this research warrants close examination and attention. Researchers continue to call upon teachers to revamp their narrative comprehension questioning techniques to include more of the "higher-order" kinds of questions that the ethnic minority students are capable of exploring. I hereby add my voice to that call.

A contrast can be drawn between "poorly fitting questions e.g. detail questions dealing with trivial information" (Tierney and Pearson 1981, p. 866), and questions that are formulated as a result of matching an author's intentions with a reader's purposes. Tierney and Pearson argue that students' interactive processing patterns with texts might be either text-based or reader-based, and that each of these processes has its right time and text. For example, there are some situations when a loose, open-ended, reader-based interpretation of text is desirable, and readers should be encouraged to relate their understanding of the text to their own background of experience and to value the importance of their own ideas and voice. By the same token, there are situations when it might be reasonable and appropriate to expect a reader's understanding to remain close to the text, as in following a set of directions. However, the authors caution that current assessment procedures, "with their emphasis on correct answers and preferred interpretations" (Tierney and Pearson 1981; p. 862) seem to operate without due attention to the significance of individual (and group) differences and background knowledge. They recommend that teachers develop questions that encourage readers to engage their own background of experience prior to, during and after reading when necessary, and then to use these strengths as a bridge to developing skill in grappling with other, more specific and "text-based" kinds of questions.

These are noteworthy recommendations, instantiated and supported by the results of my study. The innovative process of assessing students' answers to the higher-order comprehension questions using the rubric system that this study upheld, in conjunction with the richly triangulated multiple-choice questioning system for the lower-order questions, acknowledges some of these issues. But an historical backdrop to these apparently dichotomous approaches to questioning helps clarify them.

Historically, in the age when the factory-model of teaching was predominant and schooling existed primarily for white Protestant male students who hailed from wealthy families, the exalted mode of teaching was by recitation. Teachers taught children to read so that they might learn facts and grammar, know to spell correctly, imbibe the correct morals and values to prepare them for a good Christian life, and to respect and obey authority. With the advent of the Mc Guffey Readers about the mid-nineteenth century, the textbook became the curriculum, the gospel of school as it were, and insofar as students read narratives, they did so to reinforce the general mission of schooling. The teacher's main purpose was to shape intellect as well as character, but within very tightly prescribed boundaries. Questions existed largely to reinforce factual knowledge and not to encourage the exploration of a broad range of ideas or interpretations of text.

On this model, the basal reader series and other reading primers were built, as the idea of American education extended to include a broader base of students, coupled with the desire to make a standard education available to all students in elementary school. These texts persisted through the early and mid decades of the twentieth century, when the basal reader and its accompanying teacher's manual became the conduit for teaching language arts skills, including narrative reading and comprehension. Their orientation reflected the highly routinized, rigid system of learning that the period of industrialization and behaviorism supported. Questions were comparable to the who, when, what and where type that could be answered directly, precisely and unambiguously in a single word or phrase (Heath, 1982).

Eventually, these readers came to represent the patina of teacher expertise. The reading of narrative text was followed by prescribed exercises in decoding, vocabulary development and concept formation, reading, comprehension and correlated writing. As for narrative comprehension, the questions based on stories were generally of a scope and sequence that corroborated the factory model approach to education. They asked students to remember and reproduce facts, describe characters and events, and complete worksheets.

During the early decades of the twentieth century, however, educators began to look beyond the confinement and predictability that education formerly embraced, to a more "applied" conception of learning. The prefabricated prescription worked for some students, but not for others, and while some thrived, others floundered. About the middle of the twentieth century, Bloom's Taxonomy of Educational Objectives (1956) came to symbolize the emerging unease. Designed by a committee of college and university examiners, the document was originally created with the intellectual advancement of an elitist student population in mind. Its objective was the classification of educational goals for college entrants.

On the matter of questioning, it established distinctive categories and steps for ordering different kinds of questions, on a classification paradigm that placed Recall and Recognition at the lower end of the knowledge continuum, and extended through more cognitive dimensions such as Application, Analysis, Synthesis, and Evaluation at the higher end. It was an apparently clean system to use in order to ensure a comprehensive approach to the technique of questioning. It therefore became the bible that teachers used to help them construct questions when they wanted to "test" students' understanding of narrative and expository passages. It was an accessible model to use, and in the hands of competent and well-trained teachers, it served well. They learned techniques for combining the prepared textual questions that accompanied many basal reader narratives with the open-ended approach to contextual questioning that tapped into synthesizing, analytical, deductive, inferential and evaluative thinking skills. It also had the potential to serve as a useful antidote to the compelling style of standardized tests that depended on the predictability of recall, recognition and stiff grammar questions.

In an informal interview with three elementary school teachers (including Mr. Peters, the teacher of the students involved in my study) undertaken in an effort to identify resources teachers currently use in constructing story questions, I was struck by the fact that they all mentioned Bloom's Taxonomy of Educational Objectives (1956) as the resource they use to compose comprehension questions based on narrative readings. One fifth grade teacher, a thirteen-year veteran with a Masters degree, who teaches at a prestigious elementary school in northern California, remarked that

> I use a lot of sources--teacher intuition questions, what kids like to do. . . When I first started teaching, I would sit with Bloom's taxonomy in front of me, and I would pull one from here and one from there. I like to use the higher-order questions. But the simple questions and the worksheets-- that's how we were taught, and that's what a lot of teachers use, especially the older ones, because it's easy. (M.H.)

Another teacher of second grade, and also a thirteen-year veteran, explained her perception of the use of questioning as it occurs in elementary and middle school:

> I was introduced to Bloom's Taxonomy in either my teacher education or Human Development class. Lots of teachers' manuals have those (interpretive) questions as a component, and some workbooks have questions, but you've got to be open to the value of the higher-order questions. They are harder to correct. In some of the poorer school districts, teachers have been there for a long time, and that's how they were taught (with the literal recall questions), and so that's how they teach. (S. C.)

Mr. Peters, the teacher in this study classroom, also mentioned Bloom's Taxonomy as the guide that he uses in composing questions:

> We try to get our kids to think on a higher order, so therefore using Bloom's taxonomy, we try to get kids to use higher-order thinking skills where they can be creative, resourceful, and they can create new applications. (M. D.)

It is a little ironic that there is apparently such heavy dependence on a document that was created neither in consideration of the great diversity of ethnic groups to be found in our schools today, nor with any attention to the kinds of problems that such groups encounter in today's language arts classrooms. Nonetheless, teachers who use Bloom's Taxonomy to good ends in designing questions are to be commended in that the system of classification seems to help point teachers in the direction of variety in questions, balancing so-called lower order against so-called higher order questions. In fact, Williams (1985) provides an excellent example of how Bloom's taxonomy might be used to develop a rich array of questions to accompany multi-ethnic literature.

It is possible for teachers to combine the strengths of the higher ends of Bloom's taxonomy with the additional techniques of comprehension questioning considered in this book, in deciding what elements of each story to focus on in developing questions. The two approaches can be complementary. Although in a very real sense, it is difficult to teach a skill that is best gleaned through experience and by trial and error (see M. H.'s quotation above), and although in attempting to "teach" questioning, one runs the risk of becoming locked in to yet another rigid routine, exposure to alternatives that facilitate the right kind of orientation to questioning techniques is a good thing. It may at least be possible to engage potential teachers in discussion about this topic, and in the requisite training and techniques, so that they become aware and knowledgeable of the limitations and potential of questioning strategies.

The procedure used in this study for constructing narrative comprehension questions rooted in the structure of stories, is potentially powerful, and can be adapted for use in elementary and upper level classrooms. When the author presented the results of her research to an audience of approximately fifty Bay Area elementary teachers in San Jose, a few of them asked if they needed to create detailed structural analysis graphics for their stories similar to the ones in Chapter 5 of this study, in order to construct the kinds of structure- and experience-based questions used in the Literal Meaning, Interpretive Reading with Critical Evaluation, and Creative Reading segments. The answer is a qualified no. No, because empirical research that is highly formalized and quantitative, an operation that is carried out under certain conditions to test or establish a hypothesis, is different from daily classroom teaching, although the two enterprises can be interrelated. It is impractical and certainly daunting to ask teachers, already inundated with all the stuff they must attend to in order to keep their classrooms functioning, to do that. But they could be taught ad hoc techniques for constructing these kinds of questions from the stories that their students read. And they must have a fundamental understanding of the importance of narrative structure in order to do so. Hence the "qualified" no. For example, simply by recognizing the emotional low and high points in the structure of a narrative they could formulate critical questions about characters' feelings. And the action filled episodes in stories lend themselves readily to questions about plot development and dramatic tension among the narrative personalities and in the real world. This is the real grist of the narrative encounter, and teachers should be taught thus in their teacher-training programs so that children can be guided in its discovery. Furthermore, folk tales from all cultures encourage discussion about the morals issuing from the theme of the story.

In addition, already existing texts that offer a practical guide of strategies and activities for narrative comprehension question construction (for example Rouch and Birr, 1984; Chuska, 1995) could be combined with the conceptual approach outlined in this study. Both Rouch and Birr and Chuska provide excellent clues and guidelines for teachers in helping them create and design questions that lead their students to become more actively involved in lessons, that facilitate deeper interactions with each other and with their teacher, and that transport students to the highest levels of learning and cognition.

Students should therefore be exposed to all kinds of questions-- including the "experience-opinion-what if" kinds that require the use of context and specifics of the narrative as a point of departure for the discussion of issues and situations that they can relate to their own real or imagined experiences. But students should also be taught to recognize the importance of traditional questions that require practice in decontextualization, and given the opportunity to excel at these kinds of questions also. Not only are these steps vital to dealing with material written in the expository genre, but these kinds of questions are typically the ones that are important in negotiating one's way in the world of business and in present-day information age situations.

Finally, teachers should remember that ideally, questions should serve to enhance students' engagement with text, build connections between the written word and the reader's world, open the mind to new ideas, learnings, and understandings, build character, make students better thinkers, and help equip them for success outside of the classroom. If we are to achieve this, students need to be taught to respond both to higher level questions of interpretation and analysis, and to lower level questions of memory and recall. But the latter should never be granted pride of place in the curriculum because, as a university professor (Sternberg, 1997; p.23) said recently,

> Never once in my career have I had to memorize a book or lecture. But I have continually needed to think analytically, creatively, and practically in my teaching, writing, and research.

Summary, Implications, and Conclusions 225

Ultimately, we should want all our students to respond like the high-track English student in Jeannie Oakes' research did when asked what was the most important thing he learned in his classes:

> I have learned to form my own opinion on situations. I have also learned to not be swayed so much by another person's opinion but to look at both opinions with an open mind. I know now that to have a good solid opinion on a subject, I must have facts to support my opinion. Decisions in later life will probably be made easier because of this (Oakes, 1985; p.35).

What we must avoid, is the kind of teaching and learning that give rise to the comment made by a low-track English junior high student in the same investigation:

> I have learned about many things like having good manners...and not talking when the teacher is talking (Oakes, 1985; p. 35).

There is nothing in the world wrong with having good manners, but as teachers and shapers of children's future, our charge ought to be loftier. Classrooms that relegate children to little more than the superficial and cosmetic aspects of learning do them a distinct disservice. The need for strategic questions, discussions, and interactions in the public school classroom cannot be underestimated.

(5) The advantages of building a strong classroom environment, in which healthy teacher-student and student-student relationships are facilitated

Beyond the pedagogical measures discussed above, there were other more elusive but equally important factors--including discipline and motivation--that combined to produce the positive outcomes of this study. These are the fuzzy areas, the teacher-effects if you will, that are undoubtedly embedded in my results, but are difficult to measure statistically. Mr. Peters was a strong and powerful presence in the classroom. Because of his personal beliefs in the potential of all his students regardless of color or creed, the high expectations for them which he reiterated almost daily, the fairness with which he resolved student-on-student disputes, and his outspoken love and respect for his students, he managed to create a sense of "family" and unity in his classroom that was unique and inspiring.

Mr. Peters used a dynamic "tough love" technique that won the students over, and eroded the barriers of poor discipline that seriously compromise many inner-city teachers' attempts to teach. Ultimately, he helped create the sense of a homogeneous though diverse ethnic group community in his classroom. Students worked together, not entirely without conflict, but always with effort and a positive attitude. The classroom relationships that he established, both teacher-student and student-student, were based on specific guidelines for interpersonal interactions. Mr. Peters worked at making the classroom a place where students felt safe, nurtured, and supported. They were not allowed to laugh at each other, or put each other down. By his example, he showed them another way--the way of helping and appreciating each other. He essentially taught them to think and act differently than they had become accustomed to. These techniques were effective both in creating an academic atmosphere in the classroom, and a socializing environment on the playground.

The implication here is that special teacher characteristics, knowledge and abilities are essential for success in teaching low-income ethnic minority elementary and middle-school students. This is an area that requires further investigation in light of the changing demographics in our schools, and some researchers (for example Willis, 1995), have already embarked on this endeavor. By "special", I am referring to the seemingly serendipitous combination of a variety of factors in the teacher's behavior and orientation that make for a classroom environment conducive to effort, achievement, friendliness, a sense of safety and mutual respect. Delpit's investigation (1995) into the factors that help teachers succeed in teaching other people's children has identified some of these factors that she considers important And as mentioned before, Ladson-Billings' (1994), in her portrayal of the dreamkeepers and Cochran-Smith (1995) and others, have also begun serious explorations into the components of a potential paradigm for successful orientations and pedagogical stances in teaching children of diversity. This brand of research calls out for continued development, analysis, and investigation.

Mr. Peters built a sturdy base of caring and nurturing mixed in with discipline and unwavering classroom control. Ultimately he made things work in his classroom because of who he was, what he did, how he did it, and because he worked very hard at it.

Among other things, Mr. Peters learned to use the church background that he had in common with many of his students to promote a pattern of routines and to inspire order. He was then able to build on this dimension to achieve his ultimate aim of motivating them to achieve in school. He transferred and translated some of the routines of the church to the classroom for them, and used these, along with the common experiences that they shared, as the glue that held his class together. It was clear that the relationship between him and his students was strong, and although all the students did not share the common Black church experience, enough of them did to influence and set the tone of order and respect for the entire class in a manner that was unthreatening, friendly, welcoming, and encouraging. They seemed to cooperate with him willingly and not coercively. As a result he was able to get them to engage in work-related activities even when they did not feel up to it. He communicated a sense of magic in the daily life of his classroom that was discernible to anyone who visited. It was not surprising that his children were rarely absent during the year that I spent visiting the classroom.

6) The cross-ethnic identity of multi-ethnic youth

The final implication of the study is that we need to review our perceptions of youth and ethnic boundaries. We need to change our conceptualization of individuals and groups solely in terms of racial and ethnic membership, and strive to teach students to value one another's cultures and ethnicities. If we dared to cash in on the cross-ethnic identities, friendships, and possibilities that can be established and nurtured in peer group cultures and settings of ethnic minority youth, we could make significant strides in improving relationships, tolerance, and understanding across ethnic boundaries. Ethnicity could be something that matters, and matters positively. Concern with ethnicity and race need not be, as one observer notes, "an American habit difficult to dislodge" (Heath, 1995, p.45).

This conclusion can be drawn from the behavior of the ethnicity variable in the study. Since all the ethnic narratives featured African and African American characters, and there were five different ethnic groups represented in the class, one might reasonably have expected that the African American students would have related to the texts in more positive ways than the students in the other ethnic groups. This turned out not to be the case. The study showed that using ethnic-dominant literature could be perceived as inclusive of all students and could have the effect of unifying the group aggregate response in favor of the narratives. This outcome reinforces a trend sometimes observed in diverse ethnic communities, and also in smaller groups, for members of different ethnic groups to come together as the result of a common background of experience. This is especially true when the circumstances and situations that support inter-ethnic mixing are positive and felicitous. For example, youth are sometimes drawn together by elements of popular culture which are strong and powerful in the early adolescent years. They are known to project a disregard for differences among them that is sometimes difficult for adult and older members of the community to embrace, and that can be exercised to build unity. Students can be taught to reach "beyond identity" (Heath & McLaughlin, 1993) in their dealings with each other both in literary encounters and in reality. I am in no way proposing a melting-pot or assimilationist syndrome, but merely an avowed recognition and appreciation of difference and diversity. Recently, a striking example of inter-ethnic power occurred in the form of a call for the recognition, appreciation and inclusion of diversity. Different ethnic groups in the San Francisco metropolitan area came together and urged the Board of Education to modify the English Literature reading list to include works by authors representative of their children's heritage.

Having summarized the principal findings and implications of this study, I can now bring it to a close. But let me add a final thought. People sometimes talk about inner-city students and similar groups of children as if they were individuals to be pitied, as if they were birds whose wings have been clipped. I argue in this book that this does not have to be the case. These are students who with the right kind of expectations and practices in our nation's schools, can be taught to soar. These are students who could be given wings. And these are students who could learn to fly.

APPENDIX A

STORIES AND COMPREHENSION QUESTIONS USED IN THE STUDY

STORY #1: THE WOMAN AND THE TREE CHILDREN
(From "How Many Spots Does A Leopard Have? by Julius Lester.
Text Copyright (c) 1989 by Julius Lester. Reprinted by permission of
Scholastic Inc.)

Once there was a woman who had grown old and whose days had been filled with trouble. "Why have I had so many problems and troubles in my life?" she said to herself.

She thought and thought. "Perhaps it is because I did not have a husband and did not have children."

She decided to go to the medicine man and ask him to give her a husband and children. [End Episode 1]

The medicine man lived deep in the forest beneath a giant tree and it took the woman many hours to reach him.

"I have had a very unhappy life," she explained to the medicine man. "I think it is because I did not have a husband and children. So I have come to ask you to give me a husband and some children."

"I cannot give you both," he answered. "You must choose one or the other."

The woman thought for a long time. Finally she said, "Children."
"This is what you must do. Take some of your cooking pots into the forest until you find a fruit-bearing sycamore tree. Fill the pots with the fruit, leave the fruit-filled pots in your house and go for a walk."
"That is all?" the woman wanted to know.
"That is all," the medicine man said. [End Episode 2]

The woman did exactly as the medicine man had told her. She cleaned her pots until they shone like stars. Then she carried as many as her arms could hold into the woods until she came to a fruit-bearing sycamore tree. She climbed the tree and picked the fruit and filled her pots. The pots were very heavy but she carried them to her house and set them inside. Then she went for a walk until the sun began to set.

She returned to her house. As she came close, she heard voices, children's voices. She hurried along the path and there, the yard of her house was filled with happy children playing with one another.

When she walked into her house, she saw that the children had swept and cleaned the floor, washed and dried all the dishes, made the bed and brought the cattle in from the field. The woman was very happy. [End Episode 3]

Many months passed and the woman and the children lived peacefully together. Then, one day, something happened. It does not matter what. It was nothing important. Perhaps the woman had not slept well the night before, and was feeling tired and irritable that day. Perhaps something she had eaten was hurting her stomach.

In any event, one of the children did something—laughed too loudly for the woman's ears, dropped a dish or a glass and broke it, or something else. The woman yelled at the child.

"It is no wonder you did that. You are nothing but a child of the tree. You are all nothing but children of the tree! One can't expect any better from children born out of a tree."

The children became very quiet and still and did not say a word to the woman. Later that day the woman went to visit a friend. That evening when she came home, the children were not there. The house felt empty and lonely, and the woman cried and cried and cried.

The next day the woman went to the medicine man and asked him what she should do. He said he did not know.

"Should I go back to the fruit-bearing sycamore tree?" she wanted to know.

The medicine man shrugged and said he did not know what she could do.

The woman returned to her home and washed all the pots and carried them to the fruit-bearing sycamore tree. She climbed the tree and reached to pick the fruit.

But the skin of the fruit parted and revealed eyes, the eyes of the children. They stared at the woman and their eyes were filled with tears. They stared and stared until the woman climbed down from the tree and returned to her home.

And she lived in sadness for the rest of her life. [End Episode 4]

COMPREHENSION QUESTIONS FOR STORY #1: THE WOMAN AND THE TREE CHILDREN

NAME: AGE:

GENERAL QUESTIONS

1. On a scale of 1 to 6, rate how much you like this story. Circle the answer that most shows the way you feel:
1   2   3   4   5   6
Not at all Very little More or less Much Very much Very very much

2. People sometimes like stories because they like what the story is about (its theme), or they like one or more of the people in the story (its characters), or they like the way the story unfolds (its plot), or they like the place in which the story was set (its setting) or they like the way it was written (the wording). People also dislike stories for some of these same reasons. Explain why you like or do not like this story.

_____ LIKE   _____ DO NOT LIKE
_____ THEME   _____ THEME
_____ CHARACTERS   _____ CHARACTERS
_____ PLOT   _____ PLOT
_____ SETTING   _____ SETTING
_____ WORDING   _____ WORDING
_____ OTHER (Explain)   _____ OTHER (Explain)

LITERAL MEANING

3. Why did the old woman think she had lived an unhappy life?
                                         BEST   WORST   POSSIBLE
   a) Because she had grown old   ------- ------- --------
   b) Because she had no husband
      and children   ------- ------- --------
   c) Because she had no friends   ------- ------- --------
   d) Because she had a husband but no
      children   ------- ------- --------
   e) Because she was a wicked old
      woman   ------- ------- --------

4. What happened one day that made the woman yell at the children?
                                         BEST   WORST   POSSIBLE
   a) One of the children laughed
      too loudly   ------- ------- --------
   b) One of the children dropped
      a glass   ------- ------- --------
   c) Nothing at all happened   ------- ------- --------
   d) The woman was tired
      and irritable   ------- ------- --------
   e) Something happened,
      but we are not told   ------- ------- --------

5. Where do you think the children went to when the woman returned home the second time and found the house empty and lonely?
                                         BEST   WORST   POSSIBLE
   a) Back to the sycamore tree   ------- ------- --------
   b) Out to buy groceries   ------- ------- --------
   c) Up to heaven   ------- ------- --------
   d) Back to the medicine man   ------- ------- --------
   e) To visit their mother's friend   ------- ------- --------

INTERPRETIVE READING AND CRITICAL EVALUATION

6. Was it right or wrong for the woman to lose her temper and scream at the children?
                    RIGHT _____   WRONG _____
   Give a reason for your answer. It was right, OR It was wrong, because
   . . .

_____
_____
_____
_____
_____

7. Who is your favorite character in the whole story? (Circle one.)
a) The medicine man
b) The old woman
c) The tree children

Explain why you like this character best. I like this character best, because . . .

_____
_____
_____
_____
_____

8. How do you think the children felt after the old woman got angry and told them she could not expect any better from them because they were nothing but "children of the tree"? Circle 3 qualities that best describe how they felt:

SAD	WANTED	HUNGRY
BETRAYED	ANGRY	HAPPY
DIRTY	ALONE	COMFORTABLE
LOVED	CLEAN	UNWANTED

Why did the children feel this way? Give reasons for your answer. They felt this way because . . .

_____
_____
_____
_____
_____

9. Early in the story, the medicine man made the woman choose between a husband and children. Later, after the children went away and she went back to him, he said he could not help her. Why do you think he said so? He said he could not help her because . . .

CREATIVE READING

10. How would you treat your tree children if you were the old woman in the story? Write about what you would say to them or do with them after they broke your special dish.

Things I Would Say	Things I Would Do

11. The end of the story goes: "And she lived in sadness for the rest of her life" (p.3). How would you end the story if you were the author and had a chance to write a different ending? Write 1 or 2 sentences to replace this one.

STORY #2: THE RUNAWAY COW
(From "The Runaway Cow" by Eleanor Frances Lattimore, adapted from *Bayou Boy* , 1946 by William Morrow & Co. Inc. Reprinted by permission of William Morrow & Co. Inc.)

Annette, the cow, led a peaceful life. She was Julie Brown's special care. Ever since Julie's father had gone to work in New Orleans it had been she who opened the shed door in the morning and drove the cow out to the pasture to graze. And it was Julie who on wet days carried moss to the shed for Annette to chew. Annette especially liked the moss that hung down from the live oak trees. It did not look good to eat, but it seemed to taste good to her.

Annette must have known how much Julie thought of her. Her large brown eyes looked at Julie very gently, and she never stamped her hoofs or swished her tail around if Julie were nearby.

"Julie has a charm over that cow," said her mother and Granny agreed.

Julie could even ride Annette, just as though the cow were a horse or a mule. When Annette was lying down in the meadow, chewing, Julie could sit on her back and say, "Get up, Annette, and take me for a ride. And they would go clear across the meadow to where there was a barbed-wire fence. Julie's brother, Louis, wished that Annette would take him for a ride some time. But Annette would not let Louis ride on her back. She would not let anyone get on her back except Julie. [End Episode 1]

One morning in school, Louis was having a hard time keeping his mind on his work. It was a beautiful day for playing outdoors. Suddenly a shout came from the yard outside, where the older pupils were having their recess. "A runaway horse! A runaway horse!"

Mr. Lovelace, the teacher, frowned and tapped with his ruler on his desk. There was some sort of foolish game going on, he thought. But Louis's head turned toward the open window. His pencil did not want to make words any more. His hand did not want to hold the pencil.

"That's not a horse. It's a cow running away!" shouted another voice. "There's somebody on its back too!" There was a rustle of excitement through the classroom. The children could not pretend to pay attention to their work. A runaway horse was something to see—but a runaway cow! They all jiggled up and down in their chairs.

Mr. Lovelace went over to the window and looked out. No, it was not a game. "You may all rise from your seats," he said turning to the children. "Class is dismissed until the cow is caught." The children all scrambled for the door.

Louis looked towards the meadow, and clapped his hands together in excitement. There was Annette charging towards the barbed-wire fence as though she meant to knock it down. Her head was lowered, and her hoofs were flying. And on Annette's back there was a rider, but it was not Julie. It was a boy, and he was managing to hold on in spite of the speed of the angry cow. The children in the schoolyard were jumping up and down. People were hurrying out of the houses along the street.

"Pete!" cried Louis. For surely the boy on Annette's back must be Pete.

"That's Pete, all right," said Alfred, beside him. "And he's going to get a bad fall. Oh!" For just then Annette reached the fence and pulled up with a jerk. Pete went sailing over her head, over the barbed wire, and landed on his back in the meadow beyond. [End Episode 2]

Two men, cutting across the field from the road, had nearly caught up with the runaway cow. "Catch the cow! Catch her!" everyone was crying. But there was no need to catch Annette now. As soon as she had got rid of her rider, she turned around and pointed her head toward home. Quietly she walked along, as though nothing at all had happened.

Pete was standing up when the two men reached him. He was feeling himself all over to see if he was hurt, and he looked quite surprised to find he wasn't.

"But what were you doing anyway, trying to ride a cow? said the men. "Don't you know that a cow is not a mule?" [End Episode 3]

"It all comes of not going to school," said Granny to Louis, when he came home for dinner. "Pete was just fooling around with nothing to do. And he'd seen Julie ride that cow, so he thought he could too."

"How did he ever get on her back?" asked Louis. "Annette never lets me get on her back. She starts to roll over."

"Annette forgot to look around," explained Julie. "She thought it was me.

Granny chuckled. "That's a smart cow, though," she said. "As soon as she got up and started to go, she knew she'd made a mistake. Pete is heavier than Julie."

"So she just ran and ran," said Julie. And Louis nodded. [End Episode 4]

Pete must have known that he, as well as Annette, had made a mistake. He never tried to ride a cow again. When he came to school, he bent over his books like a real scholar. If Louis or Alfred or anyone else started to ask him about the runaway cow, he just went on with his work, and he would not answer. [End Episode 5]

COMPREHENSION QUESTIONS FOR STORY #2: THE RUNAWAY COW

NAME: AGE:

GENERAL QUESTIONS

1. On a scale of 1 to 6, rate how much you like this story. Circle the answer that most shows the way you feel:

1   2   3   4   5   6
Not at all Very little More or less Much Very much Very very much

2. People sometimes like stories because they like what the story is about (its theme), or they like one or more of the people in the story (its characters), or they like the way the story unfolds (its plot), or they like the place in which the story was set (its setting) or they like the way it was written (the wording). People also dislike stories for some of these same reasons. Explain why you like or do not like this story.

_____ LIKE   _____ DO NOT LIKE
_____ THEME   _____ THEME
_____ CHARACTERS   _____ CHARACTERS
_____ PLOT   _____ PLOT
_____ SETTING   _____ SETTING
_____ WORDING   _____ WORDING
_____ OTHER (Explain)   _____ OTHER (Explain)

LITERAL MEANING

3. Why did Julie's mother and Granny think Julie had a charm over Annette?

	BEST	WORST	POSSIBLE
a) Because Annette led a peaceful life	--------	--------	--------
b) Because Annette's large eyes looked at Julie gently	--------	--------	--------
c) Because Julie fed her on wet days	--------	--------	--------
d) Because Julie could do magic	--------	--------	--------
e) Because Julie's father had gone to New Orleans	--------	--------	--------

Stories and Comprehension Questions 239

4. What did Annette do after Pete was thrown?

                                                                        BEST   WORST   POSSIBLE

a) She ran away and never came back   -------- -------- --------

b) She glared at him angrily   -------- -------- --------

c) She found a new meadow to graze in   -------- -------- --------

d) She looked for moss from live oak trees   -------- -------- --------

e) She turned and walked home quietly   -------- -------- --------

5. Why did Mr. Lovelace dismiss the class after he saw the runaway cow?

                                                                         BEST   WORST   POSSIBLE

a) Because he wanted the children to help catch the cow   -------- -------- --------

b) Because there was some sort of foolish game going on   -------- -------- --------

c) Because it was time for recess   -------- -------- --------

d) Because the children were being distracted by the cow   -------- -------- --------

e) Because he forgot something at home   -------- -------- --------

INTERPRETIVE READING AND CRITICAL EVALUATION

6. Do you think it was a good or bad idea for Pete to try to ride the cow?
GOOD _____   BAD _____
Give a reason for your answer. It was a good idea, OR It was a bad idea, because . . .

_____
_____
_____
_____
_____

7. Who is your favorite character in the whole story? (Circle one.)
a) Annette, the cow

b) Julie Brown
c) Louis, the brother
d) Pete
e) Mr. Lovelace

Explain why you like this character best. I like this character best, because . . .

_____
_____
_____
_____
_____

8. The two men who came to help Pete after he was thrown said to him, "But what were you doing anyway, trying to ride a cow? Don't you know that a cow is not a mule?" How do you think Pete felt after they said this to him? Circle 3 qualities that best describe the way he felt:

PUT DOWN	ASHAMED	GOOD
UPSET	CONTENT	ANGRY
COOL	SORRY	UNCOMFORTABLE
STRONG	GLAD	EMBARRASSED

Why did he feel this way? Give reasons for your answer. He felt this way because . . .

_____
_____
_____
_____
_____

9. At the end of the story, we are told that Pete changes very much: "When he came to school, he bent over his books like a real scholar." Do you believe that he really changed this much?

YES _____   NO _____

Explain your answer. I do believe he really changed this much, because . . . OR I do not believe he really changed this much, because . . .

_____
_____
_____

CREATIVE READING

10. What would you say to or do to / for Pete after he got thrown from the cow, "went sailing over [Annette's] head, over the barbed wire, and landed on his back in the meadow beyond"?

Things I Would Say	Things I Would Do
------------------------------	------------------------------
------------------------------	------------------------------
------------------------------	------------------------------
------------------------------	------------------------------
------------------------------	------------------------------
------------------------------	------------------------------

11. Why do you think the author included Louis in the story? Could she have written the story just as well without him? Give a reason for your answer. You may write: The author included Louis because . . . OR The author could have written the story just as well without Louis because . . .

STORY # 3: BRER RABBIT FALLS IN LOVE
(From "More Tales Of Uncle Remus" by Julius Lester. Copyright (c) 1988 by Julius Lester. Used by permission of Dial Books for Young Readers, a division of Penguin Putnam Inc.)

One spring it was so pretty that folks who had never heard of love, didn't want to be in love, or had given up on it fell in love like it was a hole in the ground. Them kind of springs are dangerous. I reckon you too young to know what I'm talking about, but you will one day, and the Lord help you then.

It was one of them kind of springs when the breezes were so soft you wanted to grab one and put it on your bed to use for a sheet. It was one of them springs when the little leaves coming out on the trees looked better than money. Tell me that wasn't a dangerous spring! It was one of them springs when Brer Rabbit couldn't even think about causing no devilment. There ought to be a law against a spring like that! (End Episode 1)

Yes, Brer Rabbit had fallen in love, and it was with one of Miz Meadows' girls. Don't nobody know why, 'cause he'd been knowing the girl longer than us folks have known hard times, but that's the way love is. One day you fine and the next day you in love.

Brer Rabbit would go over to Miz Meadows and the girls in the morning, but instead of being full of stories and jokes like always he'd just sit there and sigh. Miz Meadows thought he had some dread disease like the rutabago or the Winnebago, especially when he started to lose weight.

Finally she asked, "Brer Rabbit? What's the matter with you? You sick?"

He hemmed and hawed and finally admitted that he was in love with one of the girls. He couldn't sleep, couldn't eat, couldn't steal, couldn't scheme, and was even beginning to feel sorry about some of the tricks he'd played on Brer Wolf.

"You sho' 'nuf in bad shape," Miz Meadows told him. "Have you told the girl you in love with her?"

Brer Rabbit shook his head.

"I'm ashamed to say it, Miz Meadows, because I'm afraid the girl won't have me."

"Just hush up your mouth and get on away from here. You ain't Brer Rabbit. You somebody look like him what's parading around low-rating his name. The Brer Rabbit I know wouldn't be carrying on like this." (End Episode 2)

Brer Rabbit couldn't help himself, and he went on off down the road until he came to a shade tree by the creek. He hadn't been sitting there long before the girl he was in love with came up from the creek with a pail of water on her head, singing:

>   *Oh, says the woodpecker, pecking on the tree,*
>   *Once I courted Miz Kitty Killdee,*
>   *But she proved fickle and from me fled,*
>   *And since that time my head's been red.*

Brer Rabbit's heart started going pitty-pat, his ears jumped straight up in the air like antennae on a TV set, and he slicked down his hair real flat. When she finished singing, he sang back to her:

> *Katy, Katy! Won't you marry?*
> *Katy, Katy! Choose me then!*
> *Mamma says if you will marry,*
> *She will kill the turkey hen;*
> *Then we'll have a new convention,*
> *Then we'll know the rights of men.*

Now, don't be asking me what the last part of the song is about, 'cause I don't know. It was in the story when I got it, so I keep it. You can chunk it out for all I care.

By the time Brer Rabbit finished singing his song, the girl was standing there in front of him. She was very pretty and she put down her pail and giggled at Brer Rabbit's song.

"How you this morning?" Brer Rabbit asked.

"I'm fine. How you?"

"Weak as water," Brer Rabbit said. "I ain't been feeling too well."

"So's I noticed. You got all the signs of somebody what come down with love. That's worse than the double pneumonia, TB, and terminal ugliness put together. The only cure is for you to go off somewhere and get a wife."

It was clear from the way she talked that she hadn't been eyeballing him like he'd been eyeballing her, and that made him feel worse. He scrapped at the dirt with his foot, drawing little pictures in it. Folks do the foolishest things when they fall in love. Drawing dirt pictures with your foot! Finally he asked, "How come you don't get married?" (End Episode 3)

The girl bust out laughing. "I got too much sense than to do something like that without no sign or no dream."

"What kind of sign you want?" Brer Rabbit asked eagerly.

"Any kind! Don't make no difference to me. But I done tried all the spells, and I ain't seen no sign yet."

"What kind of spells have you tried?"

"So many I can't remember them all," the girl admitted. "I flung a ball of yarn out the window at midnight, and nobody came and wound it up. I took a looking glass and looked down the well. That was supposed to show me my future husband's face, but all I seen was water. I took a hard-boiled egg, scooped all the yellow out, and filled it up with salt and ate it without drinking any water. Then I went to bed, but I didn't dream about a blessed soul. I went out between sunset and dark and flung hempseed over my left shoulder, but my future husband didn't appear. Looks to me like I ain't gon' get no sign, and if I don't get a sign, I ain't gon' marry."

"If you'd told me about it, I bet you anything you would've seen your future husband."

The girl giggled. "Hush up, Brer Rabbit! If you don't get away from here, I'm gon' hit you! You too funny for words! Just who do you think I would've seen?"

Brer Rabbit drew another picture in the dirt with his foot, blushed, and finally said in a low voice, "You would've seen me."

The girl was shocked and hurt. "You ought to be ashamed of yourself, making fun of me like that. I got better things to do than stand here and let you hurt my feelings." And she flounced on up the path. (End Episode 4)

Brer Rabbit sat down and thought that if that's how things were, maybe love wasn't all it was cracked up to be. But he was too far in love to know what good sense he was thinking.

He sat there for a long time, scratching his fleas, pulling on his mustache, and sighing. Suddenly he jumped up, cracked his heels together, and laughed so hard that he started choking.

"You want a sign, huh? Well, I'm going to give you one, girl! I'll give you a hundred!"

He went down to the canebrake and cut a long reed like the kind folks used to use for fishing poles. He hollowed it out and, when dark came, went up to Miz Meadows and the girls' house. He could hear them sitting around the table, laughing and talking.

"I saw Brer Rabbit down at the creek today," he heard the girl say.

"What was he doing there?" the other girl asked.

"I don't know, but his hair was slicked down and shining like glass."

Miz Meadows sighed. "I don't care nothin' about Brer Rabbit. I wish somebody would come and wash all these dishes."

The girls didn't want to hear nothing about no dishes. "Brer Rabbit said he wanted to be my husband. But I told him I wasn't marrying nobody until I got a sign. That's the only way I can be sure."

When Brer Rabbit heard that, he took one end of the hollow reed and stuck it in a crack on the outside of the chimney and then ran to the other end, which was laying in the weeds. He held it to his ear, and he could hear almost as good as if he was in the room.

Miz Meadows was saying, "Well, what kind of sign do you want?"

"I don't care," the girl answered. "Just so it's a sign."

Brer Rabbit put his mouth to the end of the reed and sang in a hoarse voice:

> Some like cake and some like pie,
> Some love to laugh and some love to cry,
> But the girl that stays single will die, die, die.

"Who's that out there?" said Miz Meadows.

She and the girls jumped up and hunted all over the house, all around the house, and all under the house but didn't see a soul. They went back in, and just as they sat down again, Brer Rabbit sang out:

> The drought ain't wet and the rain ain't dry
> Where you sow your wheat you can't cut rye,
> But the girl that stays single will die, die, die.

Miz Meadows and the girls didn't know what to do this time, so they just sat there. Brer Rabbit sang out again:

> I want the girl that's after a sign,
> I want the girl and she must be mine—
> She'll see her lover down by the big pine.

(End Episode 5)

Next morning, bright and early, the girl went down to the big pine. There was Brer Rabbit looking as lifelike as he did in his pictures. The girl tried to pretend like she was out taking a walk and happened to come that way. Brer Rabbit knowed better, and she did too. Pretty soon they was arguing and disputing with one another like they was already married. I suspect that was the real sign the girl had been looking for. (End Episode 6)

COMPREHENSION QUESTIONS FOR STORY #3: BRER RABBIT FALLS IN LOVE

NAME: AGE:

GENERAL QUESTIONS

1. On a scale of 1 to 6, rate how much you like this story. Circle the answer that most shows the way you feel:

1   2   3   4   5   6
Not at all Very little More or less Much Very much Very very much

2. People sometimes like stories because they like what the story is about (its theme), or they like one or more of the people in the story (its characters), or they like the way the story unfolds (its plot), or they like the place in which the story was set (its setting) or they like the way it was written (the wording). People also dislike stories for some of these same reasons. Explain why you like or do not like this story.

_____ LIKE	_____ DO NOT LIKE
_____ THEME	_____ THEME
_____ CHARACTERS	_____ CHARACTERS
_____ PLOT	_____ PLOT
_____ SETTING	_____ SETTING
_____ WORDING	_____ WORDING
_____ OTHER (Explain)	_____ OTHER (Explain)

LITERAL MEANING

3. Why did Miss Meadows think that Brer Rabbit had some dread disease?

	BEST	WORST	POSSIBLE
a) Because he looked like a Winnebago	--------	--------	--------
b) Because he was very happy	--------	--------	--------
c) Because he'd just sit there and sigh	--------	--------	--------
d) Because he was sneezing a lot	--------	--------	--------
e) Because there were bumps on his skin	--------	--------	--------

4. Why did Brer Rabbit "suddenly jump up, crack his heels together, and laugh so hard he started choking"?

	BEST	WORST	POSSIBLE
a) Because his fleas were itching him	--------	--------	--------
b) Because he realized that love wasn't all it was cracked up to be	--------	--------	--------
c) Because Brer Wolf passed away	--------	--------	--------
d) Because he came up with a clever scheme to give the girl he loved a sign	--------	--------	--------
e) Because he was madly in love	--------	--------	--------

Stories and Comprehension Questions   *247*

5. Why do you think the girl "tried to pretend like she was out taking a walk and happened to come that way" when she went down to the big pine the morning after she got the sign?

                                                       BEST   WORST   POSSIBLE

a) Because she thought the sign might be false   --------   --------   --------

b) Because she did not like Brer Rabbit   --------   --------   --------

c) Because she wasn't interested in marriage   --------   --------   --------

d) Because she didn't want Miss Meadows to find out   --------   --------   --------

e) Because she didn't want to seem too excited   --------   --------   --------

INTERPRETIVE READING AND CRITICAL EVALUATION

6. Do you think it was smart or stupid for Miss Meadow's daughter to insist on a sign before agreeing to marry someone? Put an X next to the answer you select.
         SMART _____   STUPID _____
Give a reason for your answer. It was smart OR It was stupid, because . . .

_____
_____
_____
_____

7. Who is your favorite character in the whole story? (Circle one.)
a) Brer Rabbit
b) Miz Meadows
c) The girl he marries

Explain why you like this character best. I like this character best, because . . .

_____
_____
_____
_____

8. While Brer Rabbit was sitting by the creek, the girl he was in love with came by singing. The story says, "Brer Rabbit's heart started going pitty-pat, his ears jumped straight up in the air like antennae on a TV set, and he slicked down his hair real flat." How do you think Brer Rabbit felt at this moment? Circle 3 of the emotions that best describe how he felt:

HOPEFUL	DEPRESSED	MISERABLE
SICK	EXCITED	NERVOUS
AWFUL	WORRIED	CHEERFUL
DELIGHTED	ENTHUSIASTIC	LUCKY

Why did Brer Rabbit feel this way? Give reasons for your answer. He felt this way because . . .

9. Why does the author say that springs that are pretty are "dangerous"? He mean that . . .

CREATIVE READING

10. There are several rhymes in this story. Towards the end of the story, Brer Rabbit sings the following song to Miz Meadows' daughter to try to win her:

> I want the girl that's after a sign,
> I want the girl and she must be mine,
> She'll see her lover down by the big pine.

Compose a short song or rhyme to tell someone how much you care about her or him:

_____
_____
_____
_____
_____
_____

11. What do you think happened <u>after</u> Brer Rabbit and the girl got married? Write a sentence that describes their new life together..

_____
_____
_____
_____
_____
_____

OPINION QUESTION

12. Some parts of the BRER RABBIT story are written in dialect. Do you enjoy reading stories written like this?
     YES _____   NO _____
Give a reason for your answer.

_____
_____
_____
_____
_____
_____

STORY #4: REMEMBERING LAST SUMMER
(Reprinted by permission of Cricket magazine, May 1977, Vol. 4, No. 9 (c) 1977 by Carus Publishing Company.)

    I used to have this terrific old dog named Pepper. He wasn't any particular kind of dog, but he was one of the best friends I ever had. My other really good friend was Bobby Nelson. He lived next door. We built a great fort in a tree that had been hit by lightning and had fallen over in his yard. Every afternoon we'd all sit on my back steps, eating peanut butter on cheese crackers, and Bobby and I would tell each other the dreams we'd had the night before. Sometimes our dreams were so exciting we'd have to jump up and act them out. Then Pepper would jump up, too, and run around and bark as if he'd had the very same dream.

My grandma liked to sit in her rocker on the back porch and listen to us while she worked on her knitting. Grandma lives at our house. She doesn't look like the grandmothers in books, but she's really a neat person. She spends most of her time reading, taking care of her plants, and knitting. I must have a jillion sweaters.

One time she asked me if she should make a sweater for Pepper. I told her no, he wasn't that kind of a dog. I realized afterwards that she was just kidding me. She understood Pepper, and she knew he'd be embarrassed to run around the neighborhood in a sweater. Instead she made him a rug out of scraps of material. We put it in front of the kitchen radiator, and that was where Pepper always slept.

"He is old like me," Grandma used to say. "I expect the heat feels good to his old bones on chilly mornings."

Anyway, one of my favorite remembering things is those lazy days of sitting on the back steps, sharing dreams and listening to the click-click-click of Grandma's knitting needles. One time Grandma even told us her dream. She dreamed our house didn't have any doors, and the only way she could get in it was to climb up this gigantic ladder and slide down a wiggly slide that went through the picture window. That's the neat kind of person my grandma is. (End Episode 1)

Then one day last summer, Bobby called me on the tin-can telephone we'd hooked up between our bedrooms. He yelled, "My father's got a new job. We're moving to Ohio."

That made me very mad at Bobby, even though I knew it wasn't his fault. I kept picturing him telling someone else his dreams or maybe even telling someone my dreams! I don't know why, but it really made me mad.

The day that Bobby moved was awful. First a big van came, and the movers packed up everything except the suitcases and boxes the Nelsons put in their station wagon. The only things left in the house were the little dents in the living-room carpet where the furniture had been. When it was time to say good-bye, I gave Bobby my book on insects, which he was always borrowing, and he gave me two of his Indian arrowheads.

Pepper and I watched the Nelsons drive off. Then we went and sat in the fort awhile and talked. Pepper was the best listener I ever met. I told him how upset I was and how I felt alone all of a sudden. He licked my nose a couple of times to let me know he understood, but I could tell he wanted to do something more interesting. He hated for me to be sad. The fort was starting to feel kind of creepy anyway, so we went home.

After Bobby left, Pepper and I were together all the time. The people who moved in next door just had two grown-up boys, so there was no one else in the neighborhood to play with. One day a man came out with a chain saw and cut our fort up into little pieces and hauled it away, so Pepper and I started spending a lot of time down by the river. Sometimes I'd take my fishing pole and a can of worms, and sometimes we'd just look for turtles and wild flowers. On other days we'd stay home and help Grandma in the garden. Pepper liked cucumbers, and Grandma always gave him a fat juicy one if he was good and didn't dig.

Pepper even stayed with me when I practiced the piano. He would sit at my feet and make little growly sounds. He never cared too much for the piano except when I played "The Happy Farmer." Then he'd raise his head high and sing his heart out. He really liked that one, maybe because I had practiced it enough to get rid of most of the mistakes. (End Episode 2)]

Then one terrible night, when we were catching lightning bugs, Pepper let out a cry and fell over. He just lay there shaking and trying to wag his tail a little. I ran and got Daddy, and right away he came back with me and carried Pepper into the house and laid him on his rug. I sat down next to Pepper and petted him and talked to him. He reached out and licked my hand, and then he just closed his eyes. Daddy reached down and felt Pepper's chest, and then he told me Pepper was dead. Daddy said his old heart had just stopped working.
"No, you're wrong!" I shouted. "You're wrong, wrong, wrong!"

I don't remember much more about that night, except that later Daddy wrapped Pepper up in his rug and carried him outside. I held the flashlight and knelt on the ground next to Pepper while Daddy dug a hole in the backyard. You know how your mouth feels after the dentist gives you a shot? Well, I felt like that all over, and I couldn't cry. I guess Mom put me to bed, because the next thing I knew, it was morning. (End Episode 3)

I lay in bed, pretending that the night before had just been the worst dream I'd ever had. Then I got up and tiptoed downstairs. No one else was awake yet. When I walked into the kitchen, Pepper's rug was gone. And when I went out to the backyard, there was the mound of lumpy dirt. I knew I couldn't pretend any more. I sat down on the back-porch steps and wished that Bobby still lived next door. I felt terrible.

Pretty soon I heard noises in the kitchen. Mom was up making coffee. I guess she knew how I felt, because for once she didn't make me eat breakfast. A little while later, Grandma came out and sat in her rocking chair. "Come and sit on my lap," she said to me.

"Oh, Grandma," I said. "I haven't sat on your lap in years. I'm way too big!"

"No, you're not," she said. "Come sit." I got on her lap, and she began rocking back and forth and humming a whispery tune. It was "The Happy Farmer." All of a sudden I started to cry, and Grandma kept humming and rocking while I cried and cried.

Finally I said, "Grandma, promise you'll never leave me."

"Oh, I can't promise that," she said. " Someday I'll have to leave you, just as Pepper did. Try not to be mad at me."

"I'd never be mad at you!" I told her.

"Oh, you just might," she said. "When Grandpa died, I got very angry at him."

"Why, Grandma? " I asked.

"For leaving me all alone. But I realized that Grandpa didn't want to leave me, and then I felt very sad."

"I'm so sad I don't think anything will be fun ever again," I said. "Did you ever stop feeling sad for Grandpa?"

"Yes, yes." She nodded. " I still miss Grandpa--I always will--but Grandpa didn't like me to be sad. He liked to see me laugh. 'Katherine,' he'd say, 'I love the way you crinkle up your nose when you laugh.' " And she laughed softly, remembering Grandpa.

"He was right," I said. "Your nose does get crinkly when you laugh. I never noticed before."

I was starting to feel a little better. We didn't say anything for a while. Grandma just rocked me and hummed some more, and I thought about what she had said and about how Pepper had hated for me to be sad. He would always try to cheer me up by licking me in the face or by bringing me some dumb toy to play with.

Later that morning, Grandma and I took a walk down by the river. I showed her all the river things Pepper and I loved—the yellow wild flowers buzzing with honeybees, the lovely plunky frogs, and even the wishing rock. Grandma and I each took a turn making a wish, and then we skipped stones on the river.

"Grandma," I said. "You never told me you knew how to skip stones!" I was really sort of surprised, and I suddenly realized there were a lot of things I didn't know about her.

On the way home, Grandma discovered a tiny tree growing among the flowers. She told me to run home and get her gardening shovel. When I got back, we dug up the tree, being careful not to cut off the roots. I carried it home, and we planted it right in the lumps that Pepper was buried under. Then we watered it with Grandma's sprinkling can. Grandma said that in the spring, when our tree bloomed, we'd always remember Pepper. In a way he'd become a part of the tree. The rest of that afternoon, Grandma and I sat on the back-porch steps and ate peanut butter on cheese crackers and talked. I bet she told me a hundred stories I'd never had time to listen to before. (End Episode 4)

That day I spent with Grandma after Pepper died was August twenty-first of last summer. And now it's spring already.

Today when I walked home from school, Grandma was watching for me at the picture window. "Come with me!" she said, as she came running out to meet me. "I could hardly wait for you to get here." I followed her out to the backyard, and she headed straight for our little tree. It had ten cottony white blossoms on it.

"Oh, the flowers are so pretty!" I said. "What kind of tree is it?"

"Why, it's a dogwood tree, of course!" she said. Then we laughed, and I gave her a big hug. Grandma is one of the most terrific friends I've ever had. (End Episode 5)

COMPREHENSION QUESTIONS FOR STORY #4: REMEMBERING LAST SUMMER

NAME: AGE:

GENERAL QUESTIONS

1. On a scale of 1 to 6, rate how much you like this story. Circle the answer that most shows the way you feel:

1   2   3   4   5   6
Not at all Very little More or less   Much Very much Very very much

2. People sometimes like stories because they like what the story is about (its theme), or they like one or more of the people in the story (its characters), or they like the way the story unfolds (its plot), or they like the place in which the story was set (its setting) or they like the way it was written (the wording). People also dislike stories for some of these same reasons. Explain why you like or do not like this story.

_____ LIKE	_____ DO NOT LIKE
_____ THEME	_____ THEME
_____ CHARACTERS	_____ CHARACTERS
_____ PLOT	_____ PLOT
_____ SETTING	_____ SETTING
_____ WORDING	_____ WORDING
_____ OTHER (Explain)	_____ OTHER (Explain)

LITERAL MEANING

3. What would the girl and her friend Bobby do sometimes when their dreams were very exciting?

	BEST	WORST	POSSIBLE
a) Build a fort in a tree	--------	--------	--------
b) Jump up and act out their dreams	--------	--------	--------
c) Sit on her back steps and chat	--------	--------	--------
d) Run back to bed and dream again	--------	--------	--------
e) Camp out under the dogwood tree	--------	--------	--------

4. Why did the girl start to feel better after she sat on her Grandma's lap?

	BEST	WORST	POSSIBLE
a) Because she remembered that Pepper would hate for her to be sad	--------	--------	--------
b) Because she went for a walk with Grandma	--------	--------	--------
c) Because Grandma let her cry	--------	--------	--------
d) Because she hated sitting on Grandma's lap	--------	--------	--------
e) Because Grandma explained that she would have to leave her someday	--------	--------	--------

5. Why do you think Pepper reached out and licked the girl's hand when he was dying?

	BEST	WORST	POSSIBLE
a) Because he was very thirsty	--------	--------	--------
b) Because he was very angry	--------	--------	--------
c) Because he wanted to say he loved her	--------	--------	--------
d) Because he was tired of lighting bugs	--------	--------	--------
e) Because the girl went to the dentist	--------	--------	--------

INTERPRETIVE READING AND CRITICAL EVALUATION

6. Was it right or wrong for the girl to be mad at her friend Bobby for moving to Ohio?
   RIGHT _____   WRONG _____
Give a reason for your answer. It was right OR It was wrong, because . . .

_____
_____
_____
_____
_____

7. Who is your favorite character in the whole story? (Circle one.)
a) The girl
b) Grandma
c) Pepper, the dog
d) Bobby
e) The girl's parents

Explain why you like this character best. I like this character best, because . . .

_____
_____
_____
_____
_____

8. After her dog Pepper died, the girl said she felt the way "your mouth feels after the dentist gives you a shot." What do you think she meant? Circle 3 of the qualities that best describe how she felt:

RELIEVED	ANNOYED	WEAK
NUMB	HUNGRY	GOOD
SAD	EMPTY	SATISFIED
NORMAL	FINE	TEARFUL

Why did she feel this way? Give reasons for your answer. She felt this way because . . .

_____
_____
_____
_____
_____
_____

9. When the girl's father told her that her dog Pepper was dead she shouted: "No, you're wrong! You're wrong, wrong, wrong!" Why do you think she said that? She said that because . . .

_____
_____
_____
_____
_____
_____

CREATIVE READING

10. The day that her good friend Bobby Nelson moved was an "awful" day for the girl. Write what you would say to her after he moved away and what you might do to help her?

Things I Would Say	Things I Would Do
------------------------------	------------------------------
------------------------------	------------------------------
------------------------------	------------------------------
------------------------------	------------------------------
------------------------------	------------------------------
------------------------------	------------------------------

11. At the end of the story, the girl and her Grandma have become very close friends ("Grandma is one of the most terrific friends I have ever

had."). How would *you* end the story if you were the author and had a chance to write a different ending? Write one or two sentences to show how you would end the story.

_____
_____
_____
_____
_____

STORY #5: WHY APES LOOK LIKE PEOPLE
(from "Black Folktales" by Julius Lester. Used by permission of the author.)

For a long time after the Lord created the world, the only creatures on it were animals. They swam rivers, climbed the mountains, flew through the air and lived their lives. They learned who to fear and who to greet as a friend, and they followed the fortunes and misfortunes of the seasons and the years, each day flowing from the one previous and toward the one to come.

One day, the Deer family was drinking at the lake. Suddenly, a loud noise caused the air to tremble, and the youngest Deer fell at the water's edge, a trickle of blood coming from its side. Frightened, the other Deer ran to the safety of the woods, except for the oldest child. He, too was frightened, but his curiosity was so strong that he returned to the edge of the forest, and there hid behind a tree to see if the loud noise was going to be repeated or if anything else were going to happen.

He had scarcely hidden himself when an animal he had never seen came down to the lakeside. It was a horrible-looking creature. It walked on two legs and had no hair except for a little on its small, round head. The Deer had never heard of such an animal. He couldn't even remember his cousin, the Moose, ever talking about such an animal and the Moose would surely have seen such a creature for he often went up into the high mountains and had seen many strange things.

The deer bolted through the forest to tell his father what he had seen but his father found it hard to believe what his oldest son told him. The next day, however, he repeated the story to every animal he met and none of them had heard of such an animal, either. Several weeks passed and the Deer family found a new lake to drink from. (End Episode 1)

They had almost put the incident out of their minds, when, late one afternoon, while resting in a grove of shady trees, the father overheard two birds talking.
"Did you hear what happened this morning?"
"You mean about the Robin family?" the second bird responded.
"Yes."
"Everybody's been talking about it. One of the Robins was flying home after spending the morning with a sick relative, I heard. Suddenly there was a loud noise, and he fell out of the sky like a dead limb dropping from a tree."
"That's exactly what I heard," the first bird said. "What do you think happened?"
"Well, it sounds to me like he had a sudden attack of some sort. You know, this time of year you have to be careful just what kind of worms you eat. He could've eaten some bad worms and that could've caused a sudden attack of some kind."
"Maybe so, but I've never heard of anything like that happening before."
"Well, that's true."
"And I heard that after the loud noise, he started bleeding."
"Bleeding!"
The father Deer could contain himself no longer, and he excitedly told the birds what had happened to his youngest child, describing in detail the strange animal his oldest son had seen. The birds agreed to spread the news and to ask everyone to keep a sharp eye out for the strange creature. (End Episode 2)

Hardly a day had passed when the Hawk happened to see just such an animal near the lake where the young deer had been killed. The Hawk--who knows no fear--got closer and observed the new animal carefully. He watched the animal most of the day and saw it take wood and create a fire. This creature could do what the lightning could do when it struck a tree during a storm. Immediately the Hawk spread its great wings and went to tell the other animals what he had seen.

For many days, the animals talked among themselves, wondering what kind of animal it was that talked to no other animal and considered all other animals its enemy. Finally, the Rabbit sent word through the forest that all the animals should send a representative to a meeting to discuss the situation. The other animals agreed that the Rabbit always did have good ideas, and the next evening, as the sun was setting, a group of them met in the deepest part of the forest. (End Episode 3)

"Well, I think everybody knows why we're here," the Rabbit began. "Anybody have any ideas?"

There was a long silence. Finally, the Frog spoke. "Well, Mr. Rabbit, we never had a problem like this."

"That's right," the Elephant added. "This new animal don't obey no rules. There doesn't seem to be anybody he likes."

The other animals all muttered in agreement, but no one had any feasible suggestions.

"So what do we do now?" the Deer asked.

"Kill him!" the Rabbit exclaimed. "Mr. Lion? You're always roaring like you're the baddest thing around. You go get him."

The Lion shook his head. "One of my cousins tried to fight him, and the creature has a stick that spits fire and kills. That's how my cousin was killed. Sorry. Can't help."

After several hours, they decided that part of their problem was that they didn't know what kind of animal it was. If they knew that, it might give them some idea what to do. So they decided that the next morning the Rabbit, the Deer, and the Frog would go up to Heaven to see God. If anybody knew, God had to know. (End Episode 4)

It was late morning when they got to Heaven, but God was just waking up and he saw them only after he had finished his coffee.

"Well, well, well," he said sitting down in his rocking chair. "It's been a long time since any of you have been up here. Must be something wrong." He chuckled. "I think the last time you brought a delegation up here, Mr. Rabbit, was when you got that petition together asking me to stop wintertime."

The Rabbit smiled sheepishly. "Well, I've gotten used to that Lord."

"Didn't I tell you you would? I hope everything's all right now."

"Well, Lord, to tell you the truth, everything's not all right."

"What's the matter? You got plenty of water, don't you?"

"Water's fine, Lord, but--"

"Plenty tree-leaves to munch on for snacks?"

"Plenty tree-leaves, Lord. The thing is--there's a new animal down there, that walks on two legs and ain't got no hair."

"Oh! You must mean Man!" the Lord interrupted. "And let me tell you, Mr. Rabbit, it was a hard job putting *him* together--

"Uh-huh, Lord. Well, while we're up here talking with you, that man-animal is down there killing everything he can get his hands on."

"What was that?"

"That's the truth, Lord. Now you know we got things worked out among ourselves, so that the deer know to stay away from the lions, and the ground hog looks out for the snake and the fish try to stay out of the bear's way. It's a pretty good arrangement. We don't have to walk around being afraid of everybody else. But this man-animal!" And the Rabbit, the Deer, and the Frog took turns telling God the entire story.

After they finished, the Lord didn't say anything for a long while. He stared off into space and looked very sad. "Well," he said finally, "I think everything will work out all right. Take my word for it, everything'll be O.K." (End Episode 5)

The Rabbit, the Deer, and the Frog expressed some doubts, but after God reassured them several times, they went back and reported to the other animals. Things didn't get better though. More and more of the man-animals began to appear in the forest, and one evening the birds came home to find that some trees had been cut down, including the one they lived in. Everywhere the animals lived, the man-animals came. They put airplanes in the air. They put boats on the water and submarines in the sea. They built roads through the middle of mountains and laid pipes deep in the ground and the ground hogs and all their relatives had to move. They built cities beside rivers and poured gallons of foul liquids into the rivers, and many fish died. The smoke from their cities filled the air, and no birds could live in the cities. They sprayed plants to eat.

Eventually, the Owl who was the wisest of the animals, said, "The only sensible thing we can do is to become man-animals ourselves. That is the only way we will ever be as powerful as they are." The other animals agreed, and they quickly formed a delegation to go tell God the news. (End Episode 6)

The Lord thought it over for a long while. He didn't want to do it, but things hadn't worked out with man-animal as well as he had hoped. In fact, things had turned out pretty bad. "O.K., animals. Tomorrow morning there'll be a big pot of oil in the middle of the forest. Every animal who washes himself in that oil will become a man-animal."

The animals cheered and rushed back to tell the others. And when they heard the news, they were delirious with joy.

"When I get to be a man-animal," said the Bear, "I'm gon' get me a car. A red convertible with white seats. Tell me I ain't gon' be tough!"

"Wait'll you see me in one of them continental suits!" the Rabbit exclaimed. "Won't be nobody as dap as me nowhere. All them women gon' look at me and say, 'Who is that fine young Daddy?"

All night long the animals stayed up talking about what they were going to do when they became people. They were making so much noise that the Lord couldn't help but hear them. He listened for a while and became very sad. He couldn't help but think that if they were acting this way now, he didn't want to imagine how that would act when they became people. He got very depressed thinking that the world was in bad enough shape as it was. (End Episode 7)

So God threw a thunderbolt down from Heaven and broke the pot of oil, and when the animals came upon it the next morning, there were just a few drops left in some of the cracked pieces, and while the other animals were looking at it in shock and amazement, the Ape, the Gorilla, the Chimpanzee, and the Monkey rushed over and washed their faces, hands, and feet in the few drops that remained. And that's why those animals look like people. (End Episode 8)

COMPREHENSION QUESTIONS FOR STORY #5: WHY APES LOOK LIKE PEOPLE

NAME: AGE:

GENERAL QUESTIONS

1. On a scale of 1 to 6, rate how much you like this story. Circle the answer that most shows the way you feel:

1	2	3	4	5	6
Not at all	Very little	More or less	Much	Very much	Very very much

2. People sometimes like stories because they like what the story is about (its theme), or they like one or more of the people in the story (its characters), or they like the way the story unfolds (its plot), or they like the place in which the story was set (its setting) or they like the

way it was written (the wording). People also dislike stories for some of these same reasons. Explain why you like or do not like this story.

_____ LIKE	_____ DO NOT LIKE
_____ THEME	_____ THEME
_____ CHARACTERS	_____ CHARACTERS
_____ PLOT	_____ PLOT
_____ SETTING	_____ SETTING
_____ WORDING	_____ WORDING
_____ OTHER (Explain)	_____ OTHER (Explain)

LITERAL MEANING

3. Why did the other deer run into the woods after the youngest deer fell at the water's edge?

	BEST	WORST	POSSIBLE
a) Because they were sick	--------	--------	--------
b) Because their cousin the Moose told them to do so	--------	--------	--------
c) Because they were frightened	--------	--------	--------
d) Because the air trembled	--------	--------	--------
e) Because they wanted to tell their father what happened	--------	--------	--------

4. When the forest animals went up to heaven to see God about the man-animal, he mentioned that they hadn't come up to see him in a long time. What did they go to see God about on their previous visit?

	BEST	WORST	POSSIBLE
a) They wanted him to stop wintertime	--------	--------	--------
b) They wanted more snow in the forest	--------	--------	--------
c) They wanted more food and water	--------	--------	--------
d) They wanted their living conditions improved	--------	--------	--------
e) They wanted more munchies for snacks	--------	--------	--------

5. Why do you think God "stared off into space and looked very sad" when the Rabbit, Deer, and Frog told him of the destructive things that the man-animals were doing?

	BEST	WORST	POSSIBLE
a) Because he thought the forest animals might be lying	--------	--------	--------
b) Because he thought everything would work out just fine	--------	--------	--------
c) Because he forgot what he was thinking about	--------	--------	--------
d) Because he was very disappointed in man's behavior	--------	--------	--------
e) Because it was so difficult to create man	--------	--------	--------

INTERPRETIVE READING AND CRITICAL EVALUATION

6. Do you think it was right or wrong that God changed his mind after agreeing to turn the forest animals into man animals?
RIGHT _____   WRONG _____
Give a reason for your answer. It was right OR It was wrong, because . . .

_____
_____
_____
_____
_____

7. Who is your favorite character or group of characters in the whole story? (Circle a, b, or c.) If you circle (a), mark three animals that you like best in the story.
a) The forest animals: 1. Deer   2. Birds   3. Hawk   4. Rabbit   5. Frog   6. Elephant   7. Lion   8. Owl   9. Bear   10. Ape, Gorilla, Chimpanzee, Monkey
b) Man animal
c) God
Explain why you like this character or these characters best. I like this character or these characters best, because . . .

_____
_____
_____

_____
_____
_____

8. How do you think the forest animals felt at the point when the Rabbit called a meeting of their representatives to discuss the terrible situation that the man-animals caused? Circle 3 qualities that best describe the way they felt:

CONTENTED	CONCERNED	SCARED
INSECURE	PEACEFUL	HAPPY
WORRIED	ALARMED	ANGRY
RELAXED	CALM	THREATENED

Why did the animals feel this way? Give a reason for your answer. They felt this way because . . .

_____
_____
_____
_____
_____
_____

9. Why do you think the forest animals were so happy ("delirious with joy") when they found out that they themselves might become man animals? They were happy because . . .

_____
_____
_____
_____
_____
_____

CREATIVE READING

10. At the end of the story, after God threw a thunderbolt from Heaven and broke the pot of oil, the forest animals were shocked and amazed that they could no longer become man animals. How would you help them at this difficult moment? What would you say or do?

Things I Would Say   Things I Would Do
_____   _____
_____   _____

11. The story ends with only a few animals (the Ape, the Gorilla, the Chimpanzee, and the Monkey) being able to wash their faces, hands and feet in the drops of oil that remained after the pot broke. How would you end the story if you were the author and could write a different ending? Write a few sentences that give the story a different ending.

STORY #6: RIDE THE RED CYCLE
(Abridged text from "Ride The Red Cycle" by Harriette Gillem Robinet. Copyright (c) 1980 by Harriette Gillem Robinet. Reprinted by permission of Houghton Mifflin Company. All rights reserved.)

"Jerome's got something to say, Mama, and you gotta listen!"
Jerome felt a warm blush rise up from his neck as Tilly, his fifteen-year-old sister, spoke for him. He wished she wouldn't do that. It made him feel he wasn't for real. Once he had liked the word *special,* special classes, special bus. Then he decided it meant "not like other boys."
The trouble was that people were always helping him. His speech was slow and slurred, and someone was always finishing what he wanted to say. When he played baseball, he would kneel to bat the ball and someone would run the bases for him. When he tried to roll his wheelchair at school, one of the kids would insist on pushing it. Everything happened to him, but he never got a chance to make things happen himself. Like a chick breaking out of an egg, he wanted to break free. (End Episode 1)

Sitting at the breakfast table on that sunny spring morning, he felt a little dizzy; his heart beat faster, the room looked fuzzy to him. It was now or never, he thought. Would they laugh at him? It didn't matter, this was something he had to do. He had to make a break, and this was how he was going to do it. There was a dream that haunted him, and he had to do something about that dream. He wished he spoke more clearly, but since he couldn't he asked very slowly.

"I wann tricycle to rr-ride!"

"How's Jerome gonna ride, when he can't walk yet, Papa?" Liza asked innocently. Jerome picked up his fork and stuck her on the arm; when she screamed, Jerome made a face at her. "Jerome, you stop that!" Mama said. She looked thin and nervous, her fingers tapped on the table.

Round-faced Liza was only five, but already she could ride Tilly's big two-wheeler. She didn't mean to hurt anyone when she reminded the family that eleven-year-old Jerome, who was in fifth grade, couldn't even walk. As a baby, he had walked at nine months. By his first birthday he was running strong. But when he was two years old, a virus infection had gone to his brain and left damage that affected his whole body. When he got better, he had to learn to support his head, turn over, and crawl all over again. And his legs remained crippled.

"That ungrateful boy," Mama grumbled, "never says thank you, but always demandin' somethin'. It's take him here, take him there. Clinics, doctors, physical therapy, speech therapy. Seems that's all I do, take Jerome Johnson somewheres. Now he want a tricycle at eleven years old. Lordy, what's comin' next?" Papa, a short stocky man with dark brown skin, cleared his throat. "What *they* say, Mary?" *They* were the physical therapists who exercised his legs, the speech therapists, the bone doctors, the nerve doctors, the eye doctors, and the social workers who got money for Mama to pay for his braces and his special shoes and his eyeglasses and his wheelchair. *They* were all the people he had to be grateful to. Jerome was tired of being grateful. He hated to say thank you, it got stuck in his throat.

The wheelchair was all right, but Jerome had a wonderful dream. In it he was speeding fast, with the wind in his face, eyes squinted tight, leaning forward like the leather-jacket guys on motorcycles. A teenager with cerebral palsy told him that a two-wheeler was out of the question; but three wheels. . . That was his dream, and in his dreams hundreds of thousands watched as he raced along a track. Cheers and clapping sounded like thunder in the sky. He was reckless and calm and cool, and millions knew his name. And as he stepped off the cycle, he walked with a casual swagger. Jerome Johnson, cycle rider!

Mama answered Papa softly. "John, physical therapist say it be good leg motion, good for his legs. But Dr. Ryan say that leg real stiff."

Then in a louder voice aimed at Jerome, she said "Sides, that boy's gotta learn to be grateful for what he got!" "Ha!" Papa jumped at the mention of Dr. Ryan. "Dr. Ryan didn't think he could learn to crawl neither, but he did. I think the boy oughta have a tricycle!" (End Episode 2)

"Hey now Papa!" Tilly said triumphantly. "Jerome and me'll be ready to go shopping when you come home." Saturdays Papa worked half-day at the post office. Jerome had to admit Tilly sometimes knew how he felt. She was the one who made sure the kids called him his full name. He hated being called Jerry, it sounded like a girl's name or a baby's name to him. And he hated his skinny legs and the braces he wore attached to high-top shoes. None of that would matter, though, when he got his cycle.

In the bicycle shop window, Jerome saw what he wanted. The seat was higher than those on small two wheelers, the wheels were really big, and the color was orange fire-red. It was redder than any fire engine would dare to be. "Papa, Uh wannn-n tha'un," he called out. His heart beat faster and he felt breathless. This was the cycle he wanted. Would it be too much? He was thrilled and happy and afraid too. Maybe Mama was right and he was being foolish. Just then he saw Tilly's foot. He turned his wheelchair quickly and ran over it. He didn't mean to exactly, but he was anxious and getting angry. Papa, who had left to talk to the salesman, hadn't come back yet.

Tilly yelled out and looked at him sharply. Why was her brother so mean? Here she was backing him up and he was mean to her. Why did she ever bother with Jerome? The hurt brought tears to her eyes, but Jerome didn't say he was sorry. Papa came back and lifted his son onto the seat of the big red cycle. It must be all right; he'll buy it for me, Jerome thought. Then he turned to the salesman and said, "We'll take this 'un." Papa paid at the cash register, and soon Jerome was riding home with his dream cycle tied down in the trunk of the car. (End Episode 3)

At the house Mama and Mrs. Mullarkey, our neighbor, were standing in the sunshine talking.

"Lord-a-mighty! What's that?" Mama said, shocked at the big, bright-red, shiny cycle. "Boy's gonna kill himself on that, Mary!" Mrs. Mullarkey whispered.

It took Papa almost a week of evenings after work to finish outfitting the cycle. He attached the wooden blocks to the pedals and put leather straps on the blocks to hold his son's shoes. Without the straps Jerome couldn't keep his feet on the pedals. Since his son kept sliding off the seat, Papa made a new one from a secondhand chair and put a seat belt around it.

On the first of June, Jerome sat on his cycle outdoors for the first time. He kneeled forward panting, trying to push from his knees to the pedal, but his legs wouldn't move. His legs wouldn't move! After a while the neighbors and kids who gathered, grew tired of watching him and they agreed it would be a long time before he learned to ride, if ever. Mama now added *contrary* or *ungrateful* when she fussed at him. Then one night he thought and thought and came up with a plan.

"Eh, Tilly," he called the next day. "Take muh up by alley where slants to da strrrr-eet." "Trucks come by in the alley by the factory, Jerome. You gotta stay on the sidewalk," Tilly told him.

"Butt Tilly, yuh be wid muh," he begged. "I cann-nn rr-ride dere."

Three weeks passed and school was out. Every morning Tilly and Jerome went on their 'secret' trip for a couple of hours. Soon Jerome could shake the cycle enough on the slope so that his right leg got down fast enough for the left leg to reach the top of its pedal. Then he could grunt the stiff leg down. He pedaled, but not always. He never could be sure. The dream of success was becoming a nightmare. By July he could ride down the slant, but he fought and struggled to ride up. Soon his legs moved one after the other, and he was riding. Some days Jerome nearly burst with triumph but other days there was only failure. Then gradually Jerome became more sure of being able to pedal; his legs worked more often than they didn't.

Besides Tilly, no one else knew how hard he was trying. At home, Mama was afraid to hope; it broke her heart to watch him sit still out front on that red cycle. Papa was afraid not to hope. The kids on the block had already decided that Jerome would never ride. He had been fun the way he as; if only he would be satisfied with himself. (End Episode 4)

By the end of August, he could hardly wait to show off. As he became sure of himself, the perfect occasion came up. The neighbors planned a block party for Labor Day weekend. That Saturday morning police closed the street at both ends, and the teenagers decorated trees with yellow crepe-paper banners. Neighbors held brightly colored balloons, and marching music filled the air. When the little girls' dance finished, Mrs. Mullarkey called out "And next on our program is Jerome Johnson who will, who will. . . Jerome Johnson, folks!"

Everyone clapped politely. Then there was an eerie quiet. What was he going to do? Jerome, frowning and gritting his teeth, struggled for what seemed like hours to get his legs moving. After two long minutes, slowly but firmly, he began pedaling--gripping the handles and leaning forward as though he were speeding along. There was no wind whipping in his face, but that didn't matter. He was riding his cycle himself; he was riding. That was all he could think. His progress down the street was slow, deliberate and strangely rhythmic. People could hardly wait to applaud and, as he neared the end, clapping burst forth and the kids cheered, but he remained calm and cool.

"O.K.," he muttered to himself, "wid Tilly's help Uh learnnnn tuh ride. But nnnnnn-now Uh really show um."

He stopped in the middle of the street, opened the seat belt, and bowed with a flourish to the people on his right and on his left. Then he heard himself saying, "Uh wannn-na tank evv-body help muh, 'specially muh sister Tilly, and muh Papa, and muh Mama." He nodded at Mama--he had said thank you and it didn't stick in his throat this time. (End Episode 5)

There was a mild sprinkling of applause. Then, while eighty people held their breath, he let go of the cycle. His arms wavered at his sides, balancing him. His head was high, his chin jutted forward.

He slid his stiff left leg forward, feet and knees twisted in; then he stepped jerkily off on his right foot. He dragged his left leg, stepped with his right. Jerome Johnson walked. It was stiff and clumsy walking, with twisted legs, but these were his first steps, practiced late at night. Clapping and cheering could be heard for five blocks. It was almost like thunder in the sky. His dream had come true.

Mama was thanking the Lord, Papa cried and didn't care who saw him. Liza was staring with mouth hanging open. Tilly rolled on the grass, laughing and crying and hugging herself for joy. Jerome was thinking maybe next summer he would be running--even running his own bases. Maybe he'd even. . .

Jerome was dreaming again. (End Episode 6)

COMPREHENSION QUESTIONS FOR STORY #6: RIDE THE RED CYCLE

NAME: _____ AGE: _____

GENERAL QUESTIONS

1. On a scale of 1 to 6, rate how much you like this story. Circle the answer that most shows the way you feel:

1	2	3	4	5	6
Not at all	Very little	More or less	Much	Very much	Very very much

2. People sometimes like stories because they like what the story is about (its theme), or they like one or more of the people in the story (its characters), or they like the way the story unfolds (its plot), or they like the place in which the story was set (its setting) or they like the way it was written (the wording). People also dislike stories for some of these same reasons. Explain why you like or do not like this story.

_____ LIKE		_____ DO NOT LIKE	
_____ THEME		_____ THEME	
_____ CHARACTERS		_____ CHARACTERS	
_____ PLOT		_____ PLOT	
_____ SETTING		_____ SETTING	
_____ WORDING		_____ WORDING	
_____ OTHER (Explain)		_____ OTHER (Explain)	

LITERAL MEANING

3. Why was Jerome upset that people were always helping him?

	BEST	WORST	POSSIBLE
a) Because his speech was slow and slurred	-------	-------	-------
b) Because he never got a chance to make things happen himself	-------	-------	-------
c) Because people really hated him	-------	-------	-------
d) Because someone ran the bases for him	-------	-------	-------
e) Because he wanted to break an egg	-------	-------	-------

Stories and Comprehension Questions *271*

4. Why was there an eerie quiet after Mrs. Mullarkey announced that Jerome Johnson was next on the program?

	BEST	WORST	POSSIBLE
a) Because he was frowning and gritting his teeth	--------	--------	--------
b) Because they thought he would be great	--------	--------	--------
c) Because everyone clapped politely	--------	--------	--------
d) Because Mrs. Mullarkey had great faith in Jerome	--------	--------	--------
e) Because nobody knew what he was going to do and they were afraid he'd mess up	--------	--------	--------

5. Why was Jerome's dad so hopeful that his son would be able to ride the new cycle?

	BEST	WORST	POSSIBLE
a) Because he had worked hard at outfitting it for Jerome and really wanted him to ride	--------	--------	--------
b) Because all dads are helpful and all moms are not	--------	--------	--------
c) Because the other kids on the block thought he would never be able to ride	--------	--------	--------
d) Because he wanted to get him several more new tricycles	--------	--------	--------
e) Because he thought there was more to Jerome than him being ungrateful	--------	--------	-------

INTERPRETIVE READING AND CRITICAL EVALUATION

6. Was it right or wrong for Jerome to run over his sister Tilly's foot with his wheelchair and not say he was sorry?
 RIGHT _____ WRONG _____
Give a reason for your answer. It was right OR It was wrong, because..
_____
_____
_____

7. Who was your favorite character in the whole story? (Circle one.)
a) Jerome
b) Tilly (big sister)
c) Liza (little sister)
d) Papa
e) Mama

Explain why you like this character best. I like this character best, because . . .

_____
_____
_____
_____
_____

8. How do you think Jerome felt when Mrs. Mullarkey introduced him at the block party in the following way: "And next on our program is Jerome Johnson who will . . . Jerome Johnson, folks!" Circle 3 qualities that best describe the way he felt:

WELCOME	INSECURE	WONDERFUL
UNDERVALUED	DETERMINED	SCARED
UNCOMFORTABLE	SUPPORTED	CALM
HAPPY	EXCITED	INSULTED

Why did he feel this way? Give reasons for your answer. He felt this way because . . .

_____
_____
_____
_____
_____

9. Why do you think Jerome's Mama called him "contrary" and "ungrateful" even though he had such a rough life? Give reasons for your answer. She called him those things because . . .

_____
_____

_____
_____
_____
_____

CREATIVE READING

10. While Jerome was struggling to master his new tricycle, the kids on the block had already decided that he would never be able to ride. The story says they thought "he had been fun the way he was; if only he would be satisfied with himself." How would you help him through this difficult time? What would you say or do?

Things I Would Say	Things I Would Do
--------------------------------	--------------------------------
--------------------------------	--------------------------------
--------------------------------	--------------------------------
--------------------------------	--------------------------------
--------------------------------	--------------------------------
--------------------------------	--------------------------------

11. The story ends with Jerome dreaming again--this time about maybe being able to run his own bases next summer. How would you end the story if you were the author and could write a different ending? Write a few sentences that give the story a different ending.

_____
_____
_____
_____
_____
_____

APPENDIX B

TEACHER INTERVIEW PROTOCOL

The interview was divided into the following sections: background information (questions 1-3), Mr. Peters' philosophy of teaching (questions 4 and 5), approaches to narrative comprehension (questions 6 and 7), questions pertaining to the specific study (questions 8 to 14), questions on possible effects of the study (questions 15 and 16), and a final question on his prognosis and teacher intuitions for the students in his class (question 17). The entire interview questionnaire is reproduced below.

General and Background Information

1. How many years have you been a teacher?
2. What schools did you teach at prior to coming to Lantana?
3. Please tell me about the effect of your transfer from your former school to Lantana? (For example I've heard that some students followed you here; also Ms. Phillips said you were one of the best teachers that had ever worked with her, and so on.)

Philosophy of Teaching

4. Tell me a little about your philosophy of teaching and of relating to your students. From my frequent visits to your classroom, I've noticed that you are a firm but kind presence in your classroom, that the kids seem to feel a sense of genuine caring and concern from you, and respond to this. Please shed some light on my perceptions.
5. There also seems to be much more classroom control, discipline and motivation on the part of the students this year than there was last year in their former class. In fact, during my interview session with the students last time, some of them were reminiscing about the "terrible" times in that class and comparing them with their present class situation which they said was much "better". How would you explain this drastic change in their attitude?

Approaches to Narrative Comprehension

6. Do you support my idea about using ethnic narratives to motivate and to teach reading and language arts to ethnic students, for example, using African-American folktales (and other ethnic narratives) to teach classes of diverse students etc.?
7. What are some of the strategies that you use for teaching Reading comprehension when teaching language arts in your class?

On The Research Study: Reflections on Study Narratives and Comprehension Questions

8. What did you think of the stories I selected to study with your class? Did you have any special favorites among the set of six? If so, what were they and why?
9. In general, the students rated the African-American folktales and other ethnic short stories quite high. Why do you think this was so?
10. The story they liked best of all was "Ride the Red Cycle". Why do you suppose they enjoyed this story so much? (It was actually the longest.)
11. The story they liked least of all was "The Runaway Cow" (incidentally one of the shortest). Can you suggest why?
12. What was your reaction to the dialect contained in some of the stories, for example "Brer Rabbit", "Why Apes look like People", and

"Ride the Red Cycle?" Do you think this feature helped the students' comprehension of the stories?

13. Of the four categories of questions on which my comprehension study was built, which do you like the best for your class? Why?

14. Do you think the use of ethnic illustrations was a good idea? Why?

On effects of the Cognition/Comprehension Study

15. Do you perceive any growth in the class as a whole or in the case of individuals in Reading comprehension and the Language Arts this year?

16. Have the recent CTBS or any other test scores shown any indication of improved interest and-or performance in Reading and Comprehension in the classroom?

Teacher Prognosis for the Future

17. What do you see as the future of these students? Please refer to the range of student ability in the class as you consider your answer.

NOTES

PREFACE

1. These words are taken from a popular song by R. Kelly which I saw a group of elementary school children in Oakland rise to sing one morning as a source of motivation and affirmation. The theme of flying is a powerful one in many cultures, but it is especially well-established as a motif in African American literature (e.g. in Toni Morrison's *Song of Solomon*) and folklore (e.g. in Virginia Hamilton's *The People Could Fly*). It grew out of the crushing situations of Black enslavement and subjugation in the South. For example, tales were often told of slaves escaping and flying back to Africa. The act of flying then became a symbol of freedom and of the boundless possibilities contained in the human spirit. It is this sense of the symbolic and liberating power of flying that I intend to recreate and reinforce by selecting this verse as the epigram for this work.

2. These and other data from the 1989-90 California Assessment Program are discussed in more detail in Rickford and Rickford (1995).

3. The data reported in this paragraph were presented by Michael Casserly, Executive Director of the Council of the Great City Schools, in testimony before the US Senate Appropriations Subcommittee on Labor, Health and Human Services and Education on January 23, 1997.

4. Kingston's remarks were quoted by San Francisco School Board member Steve Phillips in the *San Francisco Chronicle*, March 19, 1998, in the context of his proposal that more writers of color be included in the school

curriculum.

CHAPTER ONE

1· Despite the "controversy" about authenticity surrounding the tales of Joel Chandler Harris who recorded the Uncle Remus-Brer Rabbit tales, a true translation and interpretation of his tales eventually came from the Black experience.

CHAPTER THREE

1. It is unfortunate that the experimental CLAS test did not receive the kind of positive reception its creators intended, and that it was subsequently revoked. Ironically, it was intended to promote precisely the kind of critical or high-level thinking that I explore in this study, and that a forward thinking language arts framework ought to underwrite.
2. The teacher has since transferred to a kindergarten class and is doing very well there. The students also appear to be thriving under her direction and teaching.

CHAPTER FIVE

1. S#1, *The Woman and the Tree Children* was retained in its original version and length. All other stories were reduced in length in order to match the requirements of the study design. In this undertaking, I relied on the suggestions of the informants who read and analyzed the stories in terms of their episodes. I requested that they indicate by using a simple number system (1=least important, 2=more important, and 3=most important), how critical they considered each episode for the integrity of the story. With this information in hand, I was able to make reliable decisions about which story lines to cut in the process of reducing story length. S#2, *The Runaway Cow* was reduced from 1155 words; S#3, *Brer Rabbit Falls in Love* was reduced from 1674 words; S#4, *Remembering Last Summer* was reduced from 1788 words; S#5, *Why Apes Look Like People* was reduced from 4300 words; S#6, *Ride the Red Cycle* was reduced from 3700 words.

2. In order to determine the readability level using the Fry scale, I used the following procedure. I randomly selected three 100-word passages from each text. Then I counted the number of syllables contained in those words, determined the number of sentences for each 100 words and averaged the

findings. Next, using the Fry Readability Scale ruler, I positioned the movable block on the ruler under the syllable count on the horizontal scale as instructed. Again using the ruler provided, I located the closest sentence count in the column provided. The approximate grade level was then revealed in the window opposite the sentence count. I followed this procedure in establishing the readability level for each text, and then I corroborated the results using the Flesch-Kincaid Readability Statistics Method. This computer-based program scanned the texts, then spun out the average sentence, word and paragraph length. This was followed by the Reading Ease score, and finally the grade level at which the text would be easy for most readers. In each case, the two readability formulae that I used yielded the same reading level results indicating thereby that the procedures were reliable.

REFERENCES

Abrahams, R. D. (1995). *Afro-American folktales.* New York: Pantheon Books.

Adams, M. J., and Collins, A. A. (1979). Schema-theoretic view of reading. In H. Singer and R.B. Ruddell (eds.), *Theoretical models and processes of reading,* 2nd ed., 404-425. Newark, Delaware: International Reading Association.

Anderson E. (1985). Using folk literature in teaching composition. In C. K. Brooks (ed.), *Tapping potential: English and language arts for the black learner, 219-225.* Illinois: National Council of Teachers of English.

Anderson, R. C. (1985). Role of the reader's schema in comprehension, learning and memory. In H. Singer and R. B. Ruddell (eds.), *Theoretical models and processes of reading,* (3rd ed.). 372-384. Newark, Delaware: International Reading Association.

Anderson, V., Bereiter C. & Anderson, T. G. (1985). *Burning Bright: The headway program Level H.* La Salle, Illinois: Open Court.

Applebee, A. N. (1979). Children and stories: Learning the rules of the game. *Language Arts 56* (6).

Athey, I. (1985). Language models and reading. In H. Singer and R. B. Ruddell (eds.), *Theoretical models and processes of reading,* (3rd ed.). 35-62. Newark, Delaware: International Reading Association.

Au, K. H., & Mason, J. (1981). Social organization factors in learning to read: the balance of rights hypothesis. *Reading Research Quarterly 17,* 115-152.

Bakhtin, M. (1986). *Speech genres and other late essays.* Austin: University of Texas Press.
Ball, A. (1991). *Organizational patterns in the oral and written expository language of African American adolescents.* Unpublished doctoral dissertation, Stanford University, Stanford, California.
Ball, A. (1992). Cultural preference and the expository writing of African American adolescents. *Written Communication 9.*4: 501-32.
Banks, J. A. (1993). Multicultural education: Development, dimensions and challenges. *Kappan, 75,* 22-28.
Bartlett, F. C. (1932). *Remembering.* A study in experimental and social psychology. Cambridge, England: Cambridge University Press.
Baugh, J. (1983). *Black street speech.* Austin, Texas: University of Texas Press.
Beck, I. L., Mc Keown, R. Hamilton & Kucan, L. (1997). *Questioning the Author: An approach for enhancing student engagement with text.* Newark, Delaware: International Reading Association.
Bennett, W. J. (ed.), (1993). *The book of virtues: A treasury of great moral stories.* New York: Simon and Schuster.
Bloom, B. S. (1956). *Taxonomy of educational objectives: the classification of educational goals, by a committee of college and University examiners.* New York: Longmans, Green.
Bower, G. H., Black, J.B., & Turner, T. J. (1985). Scripts in memory for text. In H. Singer and R. B. Ruddell (eds.), *Theoretical models and processes of reading,* (3rd ed.). 434-476. Newark, Delaware: International Reading Association.
Bruner, G. S. (1977). *The process of education..* Cambridge: Harvard University Press.
Calfee, R. C. (1990). School-wide programs to improve literacy instruction for students at-risk. In B. Means & M. Knave (eds.), *Teaching advanced skills to educationally disadvantaged students.* SRI International.
Calfee, R. C. & Patrick, C. L. (1995). *Teach our children well.* Portable Stanford Book Series. California, Stanford University.
California English Language Arts Curriculum Framework. 1987. California State Board of Education. Sacramento, California.
Carawan, G. (1989). *Ain't you got a right to the tree of life.* Athens: University of Georgia Press.
Chomsky, N. (1957). *Syntactic Structures.* The Hague: Mouton.
Chuska, K. (1995). *Improving classroom questions: A teacher's guide to increasing student motivation, participation, and higher-level*

thinking. Indiana: Phi Delta Kappa Educational Foundation.
Clay, Marie M. (1981). *The early detection of reading difficulties: A diagnostic survey with recovery procedures.* Auckland, New Zealand: Heinemann.
Clark, M. L. (1972). *Hierarchical structure of comprehension skills.* Victoria: Australian Council for Educational Research.
Cochran-Smith, M. (1995). Color blindness and basket making are not the answers: Confronting the dilemmas of race, culture and language diversity in teacher education. *American Educational Research Journal, 32,* 493-522.
Comprehensive Tests of Basic Skills (1985). CTBS Complete Battery, Fourth Edition. Form A; Level 17-18. CTB/Mc Graw- Hill.
Cooper, Eric J. (1995). Curriculum reform and testing. In Vivian L. Gadsden and Daniel A. Wagner (eds.), *Literacy among African American youth.* 281-98, Cresskill, NJ: Hampton Press, Inc.
Courlander, H. & Eshugbayi, E. (1992). *In African American literature: Voices in a tradition.* Orlando, Florida: Holt, Rinehart and Winston, Inc.
Dance, D. C. (1978). *Shuckin' and jivin': folklore from contemporary Black Americans.* Bloomington and London: Indiana University Press.
Darling-Hammond, L. (1985). *Equality and excellence: The educational status of Black Americans.* New York: College Board.
Darling-Hammond, L. (1997). *The right to learn.* San Francisco: Jossey-Bass.
Delpit, L. D. (1991). The silenced dialogue: Power and pedagogy in educating other people's children. In Minami, M. & Kennedy, B. P. (eds.), *Language Issues in literacy and bilingual/multi-cultural education.* 483-502. Cambridge, Mass: Harvard Educational Review, Reprint Series #22.
Delpit, L. D. (1995). *Other people's children: Cultural conflict in the classroom.* New York: The New Press.
Dorian, N. C. (1987). The value of language-maintenance efforts which are unlikely to succeed. *International Journal of the Sociology of Language, 68:* 57-67.
Doyle, D. P. (1997). Education and character: A conservative view. In *Phi Delta Kappa 78,* #6: 440-443.
Erickson, F. (1988). School literacy, reasoning, and civility: An anthropologist's perspective. In Kintgen, E. R., Kroll, B. M. & Rose, M. (eds.), *Perspectives on literacy.* Southern Illinois University Press.

Forman, E. A. & Cazden, C. B. (1995). Exploring Vygotskian perspectives in education: the cognitive value of peer instruction. In R. B. Ruddell, M. R. Ruddell, & H. Singer, (eds.), *Theoretical models and processes of reading.* 4th ed. 155-178. Newark: Delaware: International Reading Association. .

Foster, M. (1992). Sociolinguistics and the African American community: Implications for Literacy. *Theory into Practice, 31,* 303-311.

Foster, M. (1995). Talking that talk: The language of control, curriculum, and critique. In *Linguistics and Education, 7,* 129-150.

Freire, P. & Macedo, D. (1987). *Literacy: Reading the word and the world.* New York: Bergin & Garvey.

Fry, E. (1977). Fry's readability graph: Clarification, validity, and extension to level 17. *Journal of Reading, 21:* 242-53.

Garbarino, J., Dubrow, N., Kostelny, K., Pardo, C. (1992). *Children in danger: coping with the consequences of community violence.* San Francisco, CA: Jossey-Bass.

Garcia, E. E. (1995). Educating Mexican-American students: Past treatment and recent developments in theory, research, policy, and practice. In Banks, J. A. & Mc Gee Banks, C. A. (eds.), *Handbook of research on multicultural education,* 372-87. USA: Macmillan Publishing.

Gee, J. P. (1996). *Social Linguistics and Literacies.* Pennsylvania: Taylor & Francis.

Grant, C. (1973). Black studies materials do make a difference. *The Journal of Educational Research, 66:* 400-4.

Greene, G. M. & Olsen, M. S. (1988). Preferences for and comprehension of original and readability-adapted materials. In A. Davison & G. M. Green (eds.), *Linguistic complexity and text comprehension.* 115-139. New Jersey: L. Erlbaum Associates.

Greene, S. & Ackerman, J. M. (1995). Expanding the constructivist metaphor: A rhetorical perspective on literacy research and practice. *Review of Educational Research, 65,* 383-420.

Gregory, A. & Woollard, N. (1985). *Looking into language diversity in the classroom.* Trentham, England: Trentham Books.

Guthrie, J. T. (1985). Story comprehension and fables. In H. Singer and R. B. Ruddell (eds.), *Theoretical models and processes of reading,* (3rd ed.), 434-476. Newark, Delaware: International Reading Association.

Hamilton, V. (1985). *The people could fly: American black folktales.* New York: Knopf Publishers.

Harris, V. J. (1995). Using African American literature in the classroom. In V. L. Gadsden and D. A. Wagner (eds.), *Literacy among African American youth*, 229-59. Cresskil, NJ: Hampton Press, Inc.

Heath, S. B. (1982b). Questioning at home and at school: A comparative study. In G. Spindler (ed.), *Doing the ethnography of schooling: Educational anthropology in action*. New York: Holt, Rinehart & Winston.

Heath, S. B. (1983). *Ways with words: Language, life and work in communities and classrooms*. Cambridge: Cambridge University Press.

Heath, S. B. & Mc Laughlin, M.W. (1993). Ethnicity and gender in theory and practice: The youth perspective. In S. B. Heath & M.W. McLaughlin (eds.), *Identity & inner-city youth: Beyond ethnicity and gender*, 13-35. New York and London: Teachers College, Columbia University.

Heath, S. B. (1995). Race, ethnicity, and the defiance of categories. In W. D. Hawley & A.W. Jackson (eds.), *Toward a common destiny: Improving race and ethnic relations in America*, 39-70. San Francisco: Jossey-Bass Publishers.

Heisinger C. & Wolf, S. (1989). *Literacy through literature: Designing thematic units*. Unpublished paper. Stanford University.

Hoover, M. (1991). Using the ethnography of African-American communications in teaching composition to bidialectal students. In M. E. McGroarty and C. J. Faltis (eds.), *Languages in schools and society: Policy and pedagogy*, 465-85. Berlin: Walter de Gruyter.

Hornburger, J. (1985). Literature and black children. In C. K. Brooks (ed.), *Tapping potential: English and language arts for the black learner, 280-85*. Illinois: National Council of Teachers of English.

Irvine, J. J. & York. D. E. (1995). Learning styles and culturally diverse students: A literature review. In Banks, J. A. & Mc Gee Banks, C. A. (eds.), *Handbook of research on multicultural education*, 484-497. USA: Macmillan Publishing.

Jackson, K. (1996). *Americas is we: 170 fresh questions and answers on Black American history*. New York: Harper Collins Publishers.

Jaquith, P. (1981). *Bo Rabbit smart for true: Folktales from the Gullah*. New York: Philomel Books.

Jones, C. D. (1979). Ebonics and reading. *Journal of Black Studies, 9:* 4, 423-448.

King, J. E. (1995). Culture-centered knowledge: Black studies, curriculum transformation, and social action. In Banks, J. A. & Mc

Gee Banks, C. A. (eds.) *Handbook of research on multicultural education*, 265-92. Macmillan Publishing, USA.

Kirby, P. (1996). Teacher questions during story-book readings: Who's building whose building? *Reading, 30: 1*, 8-14.

Knapp, M. S., Shields, P. M., & Turnbull, B. J. (1995). Academic challenge in high-poverty classrooms. *Phi Delta Kappan, 76*:10, 770-776.

Kohn, A. (1997). How not to teach values: A critical look at character education. In *Phi Delta Kappa 78,* #6: 429-439.

Labov, W. (1970). *The study of non standard English.* Champaign, Illinois: National Council of Teachers of English.

Ladson-Billings, G. (1995). Toward a theory of culturally relevant pedagogy. *American Educational Research Journal, 32*: 465-492.

Lee, C. (1993). *Signifying as a scaffold for literary interpretation.* Urbana, Illinois: National Journal of Teachers of English.

Lester, J. (1987). *The tales of Uncle Remus: The adventures of Brer Rabbit.* New York: Dial Books.

Lester, J. (1989). *How many spots does a leopard have and other tales.* New York: Scholastic.

Lionni, L. (1985). *Frederick's Fables. A Leo Lionni Treasury of Favorite Stories.* New York: Pantheon Books.

Lucas, T, Henze, R. & Donato, R. (1991). Promoting the success of Latino language minority students: An exploratory study of six high schools. In Minami, M & Kennedy, B. (eds.). *Language issues in literacy and bilingual-multicultural education,* 456-482: Cambridge, MA: Harvard Educational Review.

Lukens, R. J. (1976). *A critical handbook of children's literature.* Glenview, Illinois: Scott, Foresman and Company.

Marshall, K. (1996). The Kim Marshall reading series. In *Education Publishing Service, Inc.*, 1996 Catalog, K-12, p. 19.

Meier, T. (1997). Kitchen poets and classroom books: Literature from children's roots. In *Rethinking Schools, 12:1.* Special Issue on The Real Ebonics Debate, T. Perry & L. Delpit (eds.), 20-21.

Michaels, S. (1981). Sharing time: Children's narrative styles and differential access to literacy. *Language in Society, 10,* 423-442.

Minsky, M. (1975). A framework for representing knowledge. In P.H. Winston (ed.), *The psychology of computer vision.* New York: McGraw-Hill.

Noddings, N. (1995). Teaching themes of care. *Phi Delta Kappan, 76,* 675-679.

Oakes, J. (1985). *Keeping track: How schools structure inequality.*

New Haven: Yale University Press.

Ogbu, J. (1983). Literacy & schooling in subordinate cultures: The case of Black Americans. In E. R. Kintgen, B. M. Kroll & M. Rose (eds.), *Perspectives on literacy.* Carbondale, S. Illinois University Press.

Pang, V. O. (1995). Asian Pacific American Students. A diverse and complex population. In Banks, J. A. & Mc Gee Banks, C. A. (eds.), *Handbook of research on multicultural education,* 412-26. Macmillan Publishing, USA.

Pearson, P. D., & Camperell, K. (1985). Comprehension of text structures. In H. Singer and R. B. Ruddell (Eds.), *Theoretical models and processes of reading,* (3rd ed.), 323-342. Newark, Delaware: International Reading Association.

Perret-Clermont, A. N. (1980). *Social interaction and cognitive development in children.* London: Academic Press.

Propp, V. (1977). *Morphology of the folktale.* Austin & London: University of Texas Press.

Rickford, J. R. & Rickford, A. E. (1995). Dialect readers revisited. *Linguistics and Education, 7,* 107-128.

Rickford, J. R. (1997). Suite for ebony and phonics: *Discover 18*:12, 82-87.

Rogers-Zegarra, N., and Singer, H. (1981). Anglo and Chicano comprehension of ethnic stories. In H. Singer and R. B. Ruddell (eds.), Theoretical models and processes of reading, (3rd ed.), 611-617. Newark, Delaware: International Reading Association.

Rosenthal, R. & Jacobson, L. (1968). *Pygmalion in the classroom: Teacher expectations and pupils' intellectual development.* New York: Holt.

Rouch, R. L. & Birr. S. (1984). *Teaching reading: A practical guide of strategies and activities.* New York: Teachers College Press.

Ruddell, R. (1996). *Comprehension instruction and active meaning construction.* Paper presented at plenary session of IRA, Atlanta, Georgia.

Schank, R. C., and Abelson, R. (1977). *Plans, scripts, goals, and understanding.* Hillsdale, N. J.: Erlbaum Publishers.

Siddle-Walker, V. (1996). *Their highest potential.* Chapel Hill: University of North Carolina Press.

Silverstein, S. (1974). *Where the sidewalk ends.* New York: Harper & Row.

Sims, R. (1982). Children's books about blacks: A mid-eighties status report. *Literature Review, 8,* 9-13.

Singer, H., & Donlan, D. (1985). Problem-solving schema with question generation for comprehension of complex short stories. In H. Singer & R. B. Ruddell (Eds.), *Theoretical models and processes of reading.* Delaware: International Reading Association.

Smitherman, G. (1986). *Talkin and Testifyin: The language of Black America.* Detroit, Michigan: Wayne State University Press.

Snyder, S. K. (1967). *The Egypt game.* New York: Dell.

Sockett, Hugh. (1992). The moral aspects of the curriculum. In P. W. Jackson (ed.), *Handbook of research on curriculum,* 543-569. New York: Macmillan.

Standards for the English Language Arts. (1996). Newark, Delaware, Urbana, Illinois: IRA and NCTE

Steele, C. M. (1992). Race and the schooling of black Americans. *The Atlantic Monthly, 4,* 68-78.

Stein, N. L., and Glenn, C. G. (1978). An analysis of strong comprehension in elementary school children. In R. Freedle (ed.), *Discourse processing: Multidisciplinary perspectives.* Hillsdale, New Jersey: Erlbaum.

Steptoe, J. (1987). *Mufaro's beautiful daughters.* New York: Scholastic Inc.

Sternberg, R. J. (1997). What does it mean to be smart? *Educational Leadership 54: 6,* 20-24.

Tauber, R. T. (1997). *Self-Fulfilling prophecy: A Practical guide to its use in education.* Westport, CT: Praeger Publishers.

Thompson, S. (1984). Folklore. *The new Encyclopedia Britannica, Macropedia,* 15 th ed., vol. 7, 454-461. Chicago: Encyclopedia Britannica.

Tierney, R. J. and Pearson, P. D. (1985). Learning to learn from text: A framework for improving classroom practice. In H. Singer and R. B. Ruddell (eds.), *Theoretical models and processes of reading,* (3rd ed.), 860-878. Newark, Delaware: International Reading Association.

Tudge, J. R. H. (1990). Vygotsky, the zone of proximal development, and peer collaboration: Implications for classroom practice. In Luis C. Moll (ed.), *Vygotsky and education: Instructional implications and applications of sociohistorical psychology,* 155-72: Cambridge University Press.

Van Den Broek P., & Trabasso, T. (1986). Causal networks versus goal hierarchies in summarizing text. *Discourse Processes, 9,* 1-15.

Van Dijk, T., and Kintsch, W. (1985). Cognitive psychology and discourse: Recalling and summarizing stories. In H. Singer and R. B. Ruddell (eds.), *Theoretical models and processes of reading,* (3rd ed.), 794-812. Newark, Delaware: International Reading Association.

Van Keulen, J., Weddington, G. T. , & De Bose, C. E. (1998). *Speech, language, learning, and the African American child.* Boston: Allyn and Bacon.

Williams, S. W. (1985). Exploring multi-ethnic literature for children through a hierarchy of questioning skills. In C. K. Brooks (ed.). *Tapping potential: English and language arts for the black learner.* Urbana, Illinois: National Council of Teachers of English.

Willis, M. G. (1995). Creating success through family in an African American public elementary school. Paper based on unpublished doctoral dissertation, *We're family: Creating success in an African American public elementary school.* College of Education, Georgia State University.

Index

AAVE. See African American Vernacular English
ability ranges, 50
Abrahams, R. D., 16
absolutism, 71
achievement: context of, ix; motivation and, viii–ix
Ackerman, J. M., 25
adaptations, 216–17; of research question construction methods, 223
adolescents, viii, 213
advice, 111
affirmation, 45
African American literature, 9–10; appeal of, 16–18; contemporary narrative, 18; distinction between types of, 18–20. See also folk tales
African American students, xi–xii, 3–4. See also ethnic minority students
African American Vernacular English (AAVE), 17, 20, 213; use in stories, 115, 135–36 (see also dialect)
alcoholism, 5
alienation, 75, 212
Angelou, Maya, 18
Anglo students, xi; reading achievement scores, xi–xii, 3–4
archetypes, 71
argumentation skills, 153, 154, 169; in moral judgment questions,

159
Au, K. H., 215
authenticity, 26, 27; of folk tales, 67; in questions, 96, 140, 146, 153, 186

Bakhtin, Mikhail, 11
Baldwin, James, 18, 132
Ball, A., 215
Beck, Isabel, 203
behavior, xiv, 35, 46, 53–55; folk tale standards, 73; link to feelings, 159; management techniques, 35–36, 40–41. See also discipline
Bennett, William, 154
Birr, S., 26, 224
Bloom's Taxonomy of Educational Objectives, 221, 222–23
Bower, G. H., 94
Brer Rabbit, 16, 17, 162–63
Brer Rabbit Falls in Love, 68, 71–72; narrative map, 90; narrative summary, 81; question responses, 162–63, 166–67, 195, 199–201, 202–3; text, 240–44
Bruner, G. S., 212

Calfee, Robert C., 147
California Learning Assessment System (CLAS), 33–34
caring, 42, 49, 56–57, 226; gender differences in, 194, 196–98; messages re, 201; morality and, 154; for students, xiii
Casserly, Michael, 3
Cazden, C. B., 202
character, xii, 5, 15, 21; favorite, 105–6 (see also favorite character questions); identification with, 13, 105, 159, 162, 194–95, 198; interaction of, 86–87, 94, 176; mapping, 85–88, 94; prototypes, 70; questions re, 28; specific, 19; as structural component, 66, 96, 159, 192; unnecessary, 74, 192–93
character feelings and qualities questions, 106–7, 152, 223; responses, 165–68; students' ability in, 154
characters' qualities, 66, 159–64, 178–79
Chomsky, Noam, 21
churches, 52–53, 227
Chuska, K., 26, 224
clap and click routine, 55
CLAS. See California

Learning Assessment System
class, social, vii, 31
Class Monitor, 53, 54–55
classroom: attention-getting in, 55; description/environment, 34–35, 47, 225–27; organization, 47–48; seating procedure, 53–54. See also behavior; discipline; teaching
Cohen, Elizabeth, 110
Cole, Johnnetta B., 183
collaboration, 110–11, 185
Collins, Marva, 45
community: characteristics, 5; description/demographics, 32–33
compassion, xiii, 104, 155, 156. See also caring
comprehension. See narrative comprehension
comprehension questions: categories of, 26; formulation of, 10–11, 28–30, 66, 85, 94–95; higher-order, 4, 120; samples, 26–27, 231–71; student achievement re, 120–22; types of, 96–97; uses of, 147, 172, 210

comprehension skills, 26
Comprehensive Test of Basic Skills (CTBS), 100
conceptualizing skills, 219
contextualization, 153, 172, 219
cooperation, 48, 227
Council of the Great City Schools, 3
Courlander, Harold, 12
creative reading questions, 11, 12, 28, 29, 95; ethnicity influences, 203–6; gender influences, 193–203; results, 183–93; scoring, 110–12; story length and, 175, 180–82
crime, 32
critical analysis, 4
critical evaluation, 4
critical thinking questions. See interpretive reading-critical evaluation questions
CTBS. See Comprehensive Test of Basic Skills
cultural autonomy, 44
cultural congruence, xii, 41, 75
cultural diversity, 32, 38, 48
cultural hegemony, 44
cultural heritage, 9, 120

culture: appreciation of, 9–10, 137, 228; in education, 42–43, 130; including in teaching, 214; shared, 38, 204, 228
curriculum, xiii; multicultural, 10. See also multiculturalism

Darling-Hammond, L., 51
death, 167–68
decontextualization, 224
deduction, 27, 140
deductive reasoning questions, 107–8, 152, 176
Delpit, Lisa D., 44, 119, 226
demographics of researched community, 32–33
detail. See literal meaning questions
dialect, 17, 66; desirability of use, 115; student response to, 131, 135–36. See also language
didactism, 19
difference, 215, 220
dignity, xiii, 56, 137
disadvantage, overcoming, 72, 73
discipline, xiii, xiv, 115, 225; church-based, 52–54, 227; culture-based, 35–36, 40, 42; parental-style, 56–57, 226
discussion: open-ended, 27; skills, 153
diversity, 228; cultural, 32, 38, 48; language, 213
Dorian, N. C., 214
drugs, 5, 32

Ebonics, 17, 115, 132, 135; controversy re, 138, 213. See also African American Vernacular English
education, 174; challenge in, 215–16; culture in, 42–44; elementary, xiii, 26; family in, 56; goals, 150, 221; historical background, 220–23; morals in, 154; quality of, xiii, 215–18. See also learning
Egypt Game, The, 7
emotion, 22; of characters, 165–68; intensity, 77, 87, 106, 176
empathy, 104, 154, 155, 180, 186
empowerment, 44, 203, 212
English, vii
entitlement, 51
episodes, 5, 21, 76; analysis of, 94;

questions and, 223;
  segmentation, 76–77;
  signals of, 77–78
escape, 16, 19
Eshugbayi, Ezekiel, 12
ethnic identities, viii, ix, 227
ethnic minority students, 36–38, 209; "Americanization" of, 44; connection with texts, 20; cross-cultural identities, 204, 227; educational environment, 42–44, 226; groupings, 205–6; reading achievement scores, xi–xii, 3–4, 6–7; teaching and teachers, xi–xiii, 226–27
ethnicity, 227–28; effect on study results, 127, 128–29, 184, 194, 203–6, 211
ethno-cultural narrative, 7, 14, 212–14
evaluation tools, 11, 33–34, 100
events, 21
experiences: common, 12, 228; schemata and, 23, 144–45

failure, xii, xiii, 147, 219
fairy tales, 8
family conflict, 76
fantasy, 8, 9. See also magic; superstition

favorite character questions, 105–6, 152, 159–64, 176, 178; gender and, 194–96
feelings, 106–7, 159
Ferlatte, Diane, 67
Flesch-Kincaid Readability Statistics, 28
folk tales (ethnic), 9, 15, 16, 66–67; appeal of, 16–18, 130–32; characteristics and function, 19; features of, 70, 134; morals of, 224; selection criteria, 67–70; student appreciation of, 126–27, 203–4, 210
Forman, E. A., 202
Foster, M., 215
Freire, Paolo, vii, 42, 174
Freud, Sigmund, 15
Fry Readability scale, 28

gangs, 5
Garcia, E. E., 44
Gates, Jr., Henry Louis, 132
gender: achievement differences by, 120, 194, 211; effect on study results, 127–28, 184, 185, 194; relations, viii, ix; response differences, 194–203
general questions, 11, 28,

29; effect of genre, 130–32; scoring, 98–99; for study, 95
genres, 13, 28; differences between, 70, 134; results related to, 120, 126, 211; story length and, 123–24; as study variable, 130–32
grandparents, 74
graphics, 85. See also illustrations; narrative map
greed, 157
Greene, G. M., 216–17
Greene, S., 25
Gregory, A., 213
group membership, 205, 213–14
group work, 110–11, 185, 201–2; gender and, 197, 201; ethnic groupings, 205–6
Gullah, 67

happiness, 71
Harris, Wilson, 18
Heath, Shirley Brice, viii, 47, 147, 218
homicide, 32

identification, sociocultural, viii
identity: changing, 158; cross-cultural, 20, 136–37, 204, 227; ethnic, viii, ix, 227; gender-based, 194
illustrations, 69, 112, 115; ethnic, 131, 137–38
imagination, 219
inference, 27
information retrieval, 140
inquiry, 50–51
interaction: of characters, 86–87, 94, 176; cognitive, 110; with text, 176, 219
interactivity, 19
interest: psychology of, 131, 212; in educational materials, 6, 7, 212; in school, 47
inter-ethnic relations, 110
interpretation, 5, 27; schemata and, 144–45; variance in, 23
interpretive reading, 5
interpretive reading-critical evaluation questions, 11, 12, 28; construction of, 151–52, 168–69; purpose, 151–52; results, 121, 151, 153–72, 175; scoring, 103–9; story length and, 175–80; for study, 95
interviews, 113–16
Irvine, J. J., 43

Jackson, Kennell, 17, 67
Jacobson, L., 44, 216

Jones, C. D., 132
justice, 104, 155

King, J. E., 44
Kingston, Maxine Hong, xii
Kintsch, W., 24, 148
knowledge: background, 220; culture-centered, 44

Ladson-Billings, G., 43, 215, 226
language: comprehensibility, 67–68; culturally familiar, 45–46 (see also dialect); dialect (see dialect); diversity, 213; ethnic models, 132; ethnicity and, 213–14; exposure to, 218–19; non-standard, 20
Latino students, 3–4. See also ethnic minority students
leadership, 54
learning: applied, 221; conditions for, 212; cultural dimensions of, 209; improving, 110; interest in materials for, 212; modalities, 50, 136, 202; responsibility for, 50; sources of, 51. See also education
Lee, C., 215
Lester, Julius, 68
literacy, vii, xi. See also narrative comprehension; reading
literal meaning questions, xii, 11, 28, 29; construction of, 139; purpose, 151; results, 121, 138–48; scoring, 99–102, 138; for study, 95
literal skills, 99
literary modes, 18–19
literature: analysis of, 108; complexity of, 175, 217; culturally relevant, xii, 7, 14; elements of, 5 (see also narrative structure); ethnic, 9, 48, 98, 203–4, 210, 212–14; oral, 18–19; preferences, 114; range of appeal, 9–10, 228; student engagement/involvement with, xiv, 4, 6–8, 13, 15, 209, 212, 217. See also folk tales; narratives
location, 21
love, 56, 58–59, 226

magazines, 7
magic, 19. See also superstition

marginalization, 49
Mason, J., 215
meaning: construction of, 25; negotiation of, 103
Meier, T., 132
memory aids, 19
memory questions, 4, 220, 224
memory skills, 99, 121
moral judgment questions, 104–5, 152, 154–59, 176
morality, 104, 178, 224; perspectives re, 153, 154–59
mores, 16
motivation, xiv, 225; factors in, 131–32; through literature selections, 212; in questions, 142 (see also authenticity); techniques, 42, 227
Mufaro's Beautiful Daughters, 12
multiculturalism, 48, 205, 211, 215

NAEP. See National Assessment of Education Progress
Naipaul, V.S., 18
narrative composition, 5
narrative comprehension, 148; activities, 25; cognition and, 160; cultural interferences with, 23–24; ethnic narratives and, 131; improving, 4, 24–25; reader-based intrusions, 24–25; socio-cultural factors in, 31; story structure and, 15, 21–22 (see also narrative structure); strategies/techniques, 140; teaching, xiii, 218, 221
narrative construction, 5
narrative map, xiii, xiv, 4–5, 22, 76, 85–94
narrative structure, 14, 131, 132–34; analysis, 65–66; analysis phases, 66–85; comprehension and, 15, 21–22; importance of, 223; need for, 210; story structure, xiii, 68, 190, 210 (see also story elements); theme and, 141. See also narrative map
narratives: appeal of, 15–16, 217; components, 96; contemporary, 70; density, 193; ethnic, xiii, 114, 120, 210 (see also folk tales); ethno-cultural, 7, 14, 212–14; location of information, 141–42; reaction to, 98, 130–32; selection of,

66–70; shared features, 134; structural analysis of, 14, 66 (see also narrative map; narrative structure); summaries, 79–84. See also stories
National Assessment of Education Progress (NAEP), xii
negotiation, 24; of meaning, 103, 147
Noddings, Nel, 42, 154
nurturing. See caring

Oakes, Jeannie, 217, 225
Olode the Hunter, 12
Olson, M. S., 216–17
oral literature, 18–19
order, 47–48
origin tales, 73

Pang, V. O., 44
parents, 51–52
Paris, Scott, viii
Patrick, C. L., 147
Pearson, P. D., 24, 219
peer relations, viii
Perret-Clermont, A. N., 110
Piaget, Jean, 22
plot, 5, 15, 21; in folk tales, 70; questions re, 28; as structural component, 66, 70, 96
poverty, 31
praise, 57–58

problems, 17
problem-solving, 66, 103; gender differences in, 194
problem-solving questions, 110, 176, 184
promises, 157
punishment, 196–97

questioning, 50; improving, 26–28, 96; strategies, 10, 14; techniques, xiii, 218, 221, 223; unfamiliar mode of, 140
questions: appeal of, 11, 99, 176; authenticity of, 96, 140, 146, 153, 186; re characters, 28 (see also character feelings and qualities questions; favorite character questions); complexity of, 143, 145–46; comprehension (see comprehension questions); creative reading (see creative reading questions); deductive reasoning, 107–8, 152, 176; essay-type, 103, 152; experience-based, 29, 220; formulating, xiv, 221–24; gender perception of, 194;

general (see general questions); higher-order, 12, 153, 219, 224 (see also interpretive reading-critical evaluation questions); metacognitive, 98; moral judgment, 104–5, 152, 154–59, 176; motivation and, 142; multiple-choice format, 100, 220; open-ended, 103, 221; plot, 28; problem-solving, 110, 176, 184; purpose of, 26, 224; quality of, 172; recall (text-based), 4, 220, 224 (see also literal meaning questions); research, 97–98, 223; student-as-author, 110, 176, 181–82, 184, 189–93; student engagement with, 153; trivial, 11, 140; types of, xiv, 7–8, 11, 211, 221; variety in, 223, 224

race, viii. See also ethnic minority students
rap, 189–90, 194, 201–3
readability level, 28, 68–70, 124; challenge and, 211, 216–17; variance in, 174–75

reader-based intrusions, 24–25
reading, xi, 41; ability, 216; achievement statistics, 3, 33–34; components of, 113; comprehension assessment tools, xii–xiii, 100; for enjoyment, 27; higher-order skills, 139; interpretive, 5; models of, 25; remedial instruction for, xiii, 217–18; teaching of, xi, xii, xiv, 220–23; of world, 43
readings: basal, 26, 220–21; readability level, 28; required, ix, 228
reality: appeal of, 17; fiction and, 198–99
real-life issues, 13
real-world themes, 8, 9
reasoning, 111, 154, 169; moral, 159, 178
recall, xii, 224. See also literal meaning questions
Remembering Last Summer, 68, 74–75; narrative map, 91; narrative summary, 82; question responses, 163–64, 167–68, 169, 185–86, 190–91; text, 248–51

research, 223; advisors, 77, 101; background, 5–8; demographic variables, 127–29; design, 14, 28, 30, 96; interviews, 113–16; methods and procedures, 98–112; protocols, 113; quantitative results, 119–29; question administration, 112–13; raters, 103–4; on story structure and comprehension, 21; study materials, 66–70; variables, 18, 127–30
resolution, 21
respect, 48, 49, 54, 59, 226–27; for dialect, 136; for language, 214; for students, xiii; for teacher, 206
responsibility, 50, 156
rhyme, 189–90, 194, 201–3
Ride the Red Cycle, 68, 75–76; narrative map, 93; narrative summary, 84; question responses, 171–72, 176, 177–82, 188–89; text, 263–70
Rosenthal, R., 44, 216
Rouch, R. L., 26, 224
rubrics, 103, 104–8, 220
Ruddell, R., 25
Runaway Cow, The, 68, 73–74; narrative map, 89;

narrative summary, 80; question responses, 156–57, 162, 192–93, 195, 197–98; text, 234–36

schema: author's, 151; development of, 24; experiences and, 23, 144–45; narrative, 94; story's, 22–24
schema theory, 22–23, 24
school. See education; learning; teaching
school description/demographics, 33–34
school-family partnerships, 51
security, 47
self-centeredness, viii
self-concept, 9, 158
self-esteem, xiv, 18; enhancement by stories, 24, 137, 138; raising, 47–48, 50, 54
self-image, 158
self-validation, xiv, 18
setting, 5, 15, 21; as structural component, 66, 96
short stories, 13, 18, 19. See also literature; narratives; stories
Siddle-Walker, V., 42
signifying, 215
Snyder, Zilpha, 7
social class, vii, 31

social issues, gender-differentiated responses to, 128
society: classes in, vii, 31; distancing from, 204; dominant, 20, 38
special education, 6, 217
Spider, 16, 17
spoken word, 18
Sports Illustrated, 7
Steptoe, John, 12
stories: affective components, 85; elements of, 15, 21; grammar of, 21–22; importance of, 15–16; presentation order, 69; schemata of, 22–24; short, 13, 18, 19; structurally sound, 210; texts, 229–71. See also literature; narratives
story elements, 85; hierarchy, 21, 141; ordering of, 22; portrayal (see narrative map)
story grammar, 21–22, 94
story length, 21, 28, 68; results related to, 120, 123–25, 175–82, 211; variation in, 174–75
story schemata, 22–24
story structure. See narrative structure
storytelling, 15

structural analysis, xiii, 14, 66. See also narrative structure
student-as-author questions, 110, 176, 181–82, 184, 189–93
student interviews, 113–15
students: data on, 113–14; descriptions of, 36–38; intermixing, 48–49, 185, 205–6, 226; peer help, 48; potential of, 225; relations between, 110, 226; as study participants, 41–42. See also ethnic minority students
success, opportunities for, xiii, 218
supernatural, 19
superstition, 194, 200–201
sympathy, 104, 111, 155, 160, 185, 187; gender differences and, 196–98
synthesis, 27

teacher expectations, 44–46, 51, 54, 210, 216, 225
teacher interviews, 115–16; protocol, 272–74
teachers, 33, 206; involvement in research study, 112,

115–16; quality of, 217, 225–26; as role models, 205; training of, 5, 226
teaching, 62; conceptual framework, 14, 28–30; culturally relevant/congruent, 43, 215; culture-based, 48, 214–15; folk tales as means of, 16; historical background, 220–23; improving, 210; metacognitive approaches, 24–25; successful, xiii, 43; tools, 5 (see also questions); tradition-based, 48; whole person, 58
teaching philosophy, 41, 44, 115, 205
tests: assessment/evaluation tools, 11, 33–34; of reading comprehension, xii–xiii, 100; standardized, 141, 142, 146, 221
texts. See literature; narratives; readings; stories
theme, 5, 15, 21; of Black folk tales, 16, 66–67, 70; developmentally appropriate, 132; didactic, 70; relevance of, 68, 160; as

structural component, 66, 96, 141
thinking skills, xiv, 25–26; higher-order, 11, 103, 108, 121, 140; use in testing, 221
Thompson, S., 16
Tierney, R. J., 24, 219
tracking, 217
traditions, 13, 214
trickster stories, 16
trust, 49–50, 58–59

underdogs, 159
universality, 16

values, 16; personal, 104, 155
Van Dijk, T., 24, 148
vernacular, 67, 214. See also dialect
Vygotsky, 110, 185, 202

Walker, Alice, 18
Why Apes Look Like People, 68, 72–73; narrative map, 92; narrative summary, 83; question responses, 157–58, 170–71, 186–87, 191–92; text, 255–59
Williams, S. W., 223
Willis, M. G., 56
Woman and the Tree Children, The, 68, 71; narrative map, 88;

narrative summary, 79; question responses, 155–56, 160–62, 165–66, 189–90, 196–97; text, 229–31
Woollard, N., 213
writing, 41
written word, 18

York, D. E., 43
<u>Young Sisters and Brothers</u> (YSB), 7

ABOUT THE AUTHOR

Angela Eunice Rickford is an assistant professor in the College of Education at San Jose State University in San Jose, California. Rickford earned her Ph.D. degree (1996) in Language, Literacy, and Culture from Stanford University. While at Stanford, she participated in Project Read, a program directed by her mentor Professor Robert Calfee that provides training in "critical literacy" methods for teachers from various parts of the country. Before attending Stanford, she managed her own child care and pre-school program for pre-Kindergarten age children in Palo Alto, California for ten years, 1982-1992. The backbone of the program was reading, both for the children's enjoyment and pleasure, and also to teach them the rudiments of this difficult but vital skill before their formal schooling began.

Rickford's entire professional career has been marked by an ongoing interest and involvement in literature and literacy. Born in Georgetown, Guyana, located on the northeastern shoulder of the continent of South America, she left her homeland in 1968 for the University of the West Indies in Kingston, Jamaica, where she studied towards a B. A. degree in English Language and Literature, graduating with Special Honors in 1971. She then moved to the United States, where in 1973 she earned a Master of Science degree in Education with a specialty in Teaching English as a Second Language from the University of Pennsylvania. While in Philadelphia, she also taught for a while in an inner-city public elementary school.

Rickford then returned to her native Guyana, where she taught English Literature in the then all-boys Queen's College High School for one year before studying for her Diploma in Education (the equivalent of teaching credentials), which she earned from the University of Guyana in 1975, graduating with distinction. She also held the position of Lecturer in the Teacher Education Department of the University of Guyana from 1975 to 1980. During this period, Rickford studied at the Johns Hopkins University (1977-78), taking courses with a focus on teaching Reading to students with learning disabilities.

Rickford's area of expertise is teaching Reading in multicultural populations. She has conducted research in the ethnically diverse community of East Palo Alto in the San Francisco Bay Area, and in her capacity as a Reading consultant with the Consortium on Reading Excellence, she has conducted numerous workshops on the teaching of Reading to elementary, middle and high school teachers in various school districts in California. She has also conducted Reading workshops for Stanford University students who participate in the East Palo Alto Tutoring Program, and to teachers in the Teacher Preparation Program at the University of the West Indies in Barbados. Rickford was recently awarded a Fulbright Fellowship tenable at the University of the West Indies in Jamaica, where she hopes to teach for one semester and continue her research in the teaching of Reading to diverse student populations. In addition to her duties in the College of Education at San Jose State University, she has also taught in the Summer Bridge Program in Linguistics there. She is currently involved in training elementary school teachers in the Oakland Unified School District in techniques and strategies for teaching Reading effectively to students from ethnic minority backgrounds.

Rickford has published articles in Linguistics and Education, Urban Education, and the Journal of American Folklore. She lives with her husband John Rickford and their four children in Palo Alto, California. She has been a Resident Fellow at Stanford University for the past ten years.